HISTORIC PRESERVATION
& THE IMAGINED WEST

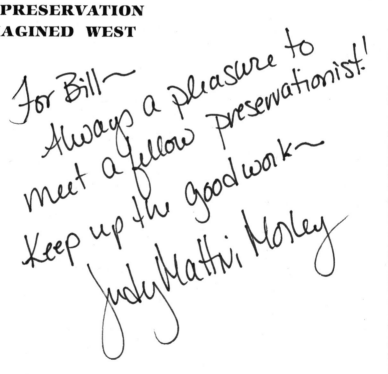

For Bill~
Always a pleasure to
meet a fellow preservationist!
Keep up the good work~
Judy Mattivi Morley

Judy Mattivi Morley

Historic Preservation & the Imagined West

ALBUQUERQUE, DENVER, & SEATTLE

University Press of Kansas

Photographs not otherwise credited are the author's.

Published by the University Press of Kansas (Lawrence, Kansas
66045), which was organized by the Kansas Board of Regents
and is operated and funded by Emporia State University,
Fort Hays State University, Kansas State University,
Pittsburg State University, the University of Kansas,
and Wichita State University

Library of Congress Cataloging-in-Publication Data

Morley, Judy Mattivi.
   Historic preservation & the imagined West : Albuquerque, Denver, &
Seattle / Judy Mattivi Morley.
      p. cm.
   Includes bibliographical references and index.
   ISBN 0-7006-1477-X (cloth : alk. paper)
   1. Historic preservation—West (U.S.)—Case studies.   2. Historic
buildings—Conservation and restoration—West (U.S.)—Case studies.
3. Historic preservation—Economic aspects—West (U.S.)—Case
studies.   4. City planning—West (U.S.)—Case studies.   5. Historic
buildings—Conservation and restoration—New Mexico—Albuquerque.
6. Historic buildings—Conservation and restoration—Colorado—
Denver.   7. Historic buildings—Conservation and restoration—
Washington (State)—Seattle.   8. Albuquerque (N.M.)—Buildings,
structures, etc.   9. Denver (Colo.)—Buildings, structures, etc.
10. Seattle (Wash.)—Buildings, structures, etc.   I. Title.   II. Title:
Historic preservation and the imagined West.
   F590.7.M67 2006   363.6'90978—dc22

British Library Cataloguing-in-Publication Data is available.

Printed in the United States of America

10 9 8 7 6 5 4 3 2 1

AS ALWAYS, FOR KINSEY.

And for Bill, who broadened my perspective of past and future.

Contents

Illustrations

Acknowledgments

There are so many people to thank in a project like this. I'll begin by thanking the staff of all the archives I used, especially Fran Tapia and Ed Boles at the Albuquerque City Planning Office; the staff of the Center for Southwest Research at the University of New Mexico; Mo Palmer at the Albuquerque Museum; Barbara Walton, Phil Panum, Kay Wisnia, Bruce Hansen, Colleen Nunn, and the entire staff of the Denver Public Library Western History and Genealogy Department; Lynn Sargent at the Denver City Planning Office; Keith Schrum at the Colorado Historical Society; the staff of the University of Washington Manuscripts, Special Collections, and University Archives (who did not let an earthquake stop them from helping me); the staff of the Puget Sound Regional Archives; Rebekah Harvey and Suzanne Sermon; and Eric Hammersmark.

I'd also like to thank the people who took the time to discuss the project, read sections of the manuscript, or give me general feedback, including Chris Wilson, David Key, the late Howard Rabinowitz, Jim Hoffsis, Robert Hooton, Robert Romero, Dana Crawford, William Saslow, Barbara Gibson, Lisa Purdy, Jennifer Moulton, Kathleen Brooker, Ed White, Barbara Norgren, Ralph Anderson, Jennifer Meisner, Tom Quakenbush, Peter Steinbrueck, John Chaney, Marlys Erickson, John Turnbull, John Findlay, Gail Dubrow, William Deverell, and Hal Rothman.

Finally, I thank my editors and mentors. I thank Tom Noel for instilling in me an interest in local history and public history, and for always being available to answer questions and make connections; David Farber for giving me the idea to link historic preservation and identity, and for sharing his expertise and honest reading of the text; and Paul Hutton for introducing me to the expanse of western history. I am grateful to Nancy Jackson at the University Press of Kansas for her perceptive insights, motivation, and hand-holding. Last, but certainly not least, I want to thank Virginia Scharff, not only for devoting hours to phone discussions of the text, multiple critical readings of each chapter, and thoughtful responses to all my questions but also for being a steadfast cheerleader. When I was unsure how to proceed, Virginia helped me hear my own voice, and for that I am truly grateful.

Introduction

> Dean was the son of a wino, one of the most tottering bums of Larimer Street, and Dean had in fact been brought up generally on Larimer Street and thereabouts . . . He used to beg in front of Larimer alleys and sneak the money back to his father, who waited among the broken bottles with an old buddy.[1]

Standing in Denver's Larimer Square today, a visitor would hardly recognize the world of Dean Moriarty, described by Jack Kerouac in the classic *On the Road.* Larimer Street, once one of Denver's seediest districts, now boasts fancy boutiques, upscale restaurants, and plazas with park benches and lighted trees. The bums and winos disappeared in the 1970s when historic preservationists transformed Larimer Street into Larimer Square. Historic preservation changed the look of cities nationwide during the 1960s and 1970s and created new urban landscapes out of old buildings.

Formally designated historic districts sprang up in cities as a result of multiple factors. Changes in urban planning paradigms, neighborhood activism, downtown real estate development strategies, and the federal government's National Historic Preservation Act and Tax Reform Act all came together after World War II to create an environment in which residents, planners, and developers could use historic preservation as a tool to shape and control urban space.[2] Although this phenomenon was national, western cities such as Santa Fe, San Francisco, and Denver had some of the earliest and most economically successful historic districts in the nation. The creation of historic districts in western cities exemplified changing patterns in twentieth-century urban planning, western urban growth and development, and the importance of tourism as a western industry.

With a few earlier exceptions, the historic preservation movement began after the Civil War, as Americans searched for ways to heal the rift between North and South. Preservationists sought something quintessentially American, and saving old buildings minimized sectional differences by establishing national affiliations with past events and places. Early activists preserved places of national significance, especially sites associated with great events like the

American Revolution or great men like George Washington.[3] The preservation of historic sites also gave Americans a feeling of permanence as the population migrated westward and immigrants flooded into the expanding nation. Historic sites became symbolic of the timeless stability of American ideals.[4]

Historic preservation began as a private philanthropic enterprise. The Victorian "cult of domesticity" gave women the moral authority to preserve the nation's heritage, and ladies' associations dominated the early preservation movement. As early as 1853, South Carolinian Ann Pamela Cunningham formed the Mount Vernon Ladies' Association (MVLA), the first private preservation organization, to purchase and restore George Washington's Virginia plantation. Over the next eighty years, other ladies' groups, such as the Daughters of the American Revolution, the Colonial Dames of America, the Daughters of the Republic of Texas, and the Daughters of the Confederacy, worked to preserve landmarks like Congress Hall in Philadelphia, Pennsylvania; the Alamo in San Antonio, Texas; the White House of the Confederacy in Richmond, Virginia; and the Powder Magazine at Williamsburg, Virginia (before the establishment of Colonial Williamsburg).[5]

In addition to ladies' groups, historic preservation had advocates among wealthy descendants of New England textile merchants, progeny of antebellum Southern planters, and civic-minded multimillionaires.[6] These philanthropists believed historic preservation would forge a national identity and reinforce their inherited positions in the American power structure.[7] Millionaire John D. Rockefeller Jr., for example, funded the large-scale rebuilding of Colonial Williamsburg in the 1920s and 1930s. Rockefeller wanted not only to preserve the charm of the old town but also to use its founders as examples of patriotism and citizenship.[8] Rather than showcasing a single site, Colonial Williamsburg enabled visitors to fully experience lifestyles and social patterns of the colonial era.[9] Colonial Williamsburg also exemplified the economic potential of historic preservation and marked a turning point in preservation ideology when tourism to Colonial Williamsburg became the main support for the real town of Williamsburg.[10]

In 1931 Charleston, South Carolina, became the first U.S. city to use a zoning ordinance to create a historic district. During the 1920s, new traffic signals and gas stations began to change the look of older sections of Charleston. Residents feared that these innovations threatened the character of their neighborhood and petitioned the city for zoning protection. In response, Charleston's city planners created the Old and Historic Charleston District, with permanent zoning protection. The district, which tried to recapture the look of the city in the eighteenth and nineteenth centuries, regulated architectural styles and dictated new construction design while still allowing modern businesses.[11] Few, if any, of the buildings were significant by themselves, but they were vital to the character and aesthetic of the entire area.[12] By establishing the Old and Historic Charleston District, city planners acknowledged that the district as a whole was greater than the sum of its parts. Charleston's ordinance set the stage for other cities to use zoning for historic preservation, notably New Orleans in 1936, San Antonio in 1939, and Santa Barbara, California, in 1947.[13]

The designation of Old and Historic Charleston highlighted local government's role in historic preservation. Although Congress passed the Antiquities Act in 1906 to save Indian ruins and artifacts and created the National Park Service (NPS) in 1916 to manage natural resources, the federal government did little to preserve the built environment until the New Deal. In 1935 Congress passed the Historic Sites Act, which preserved public-use historic sites and objects of national significance. The act authorized the Historic American Building Survey, a national architectural archive. The buildings on the list frequently needed restoration, and the Civilian Conservation Corps, best known for building campgrounds and wilderness roads, did most of the work. After World War II, Congress chartered the National Trust for Historic Preservation to receive and administer contributions of money and historic properties.[14]

During the 1960s the federal government dramatically expanded its role in historic preservation when NPS leaders, in an effort to increase their influence, explored conserving the built environment.[15] Robert M. Utley, director of the NPS Division of History Studies, defined the discourse of contemporary historic preservation by distinguishing between "old" preservation and "new" preservation. According to Utley, "old" preservation, mandated by the 1935 Historic Sites Act, saved "a few shrines of transcendent significance to the nation," whereas "new" preservation developed local landmarks important to communities.[16] "New" preservation did not make museums out of landmarks but rather fostered the conservation of historic districts through the adaptation of buildings for compatible modern uses.

As NPS staff took a role in historic preservation, city officials also discussed saving the built environment. In 1965 the United States Conference of Mayors met and published *With Heritage So Rich,* a treatise on U.S. city planning policy. The authors of *With Heritage So Rich* denounced the prevailing strategy of urban renewal and offered historic preservation as an aesthetically pleasing alternative. The mayors even cited the 1954 Supreme Court decision in *Berman v. Parker,* in which the Court ruled that cities had an obligation to be beautiful as well as safe and clean.[17] *With Heritage So Rich* concluded that mayors, city councils, and planning departments should consider old buildings as economic resources and establish historic districts to save their architectural heritage.[18]

The federal government's watershed moment in historic preservation came in 1966, when Congress passed the National Historic Preservation Act. Utley and NPS personnel played a significant role in writing the act, which incorporated the concept of "new" preservation.[19] Unlike earlier preservation efforts, the National Historic Preservation Act provided city governments with federal support to designate entire neighborhoods as national landmarks. Preservation got another boost in 1976, when Congress passed the Tax Reform Act. This act created tax incentives for businesses to use existing buildings, popularizing the concept of "adaptive reuse." By taking an old "shell" and allowing extensive renovations for modern uses, developers saved downtown buildings while benefiting from tax breaks.[20]

The National Historic Preservation Act and the Tax Reform Act reflected and reinforced the emergence of new actors on the historic preservation stage. No longer the domain of benevolent ladies' societies, historic preservation was increasingly controlled by men, especially male architects, developers, business leaders, and city planners. By the 1950s the ladies' associations and private philanthropists who dominated preservation during the first half of the century had become supporting organizations for larger governmental bureaucracies.[21] During the 1960s and 1970s, a "populist" coalition of working-class white ethnics, white-collar downtown residents, and local city politicians also gained influence over historic preservation projects. This sometimes-uneasy alliance advocated historic preservation ordinances to protect neighborhoods from bulldozer-happy developers and promote gentrification, keeping racial and ethnic "others" from moving in.[22]

While the "populist" coalitions preserved neighborhoods, alliances of business interests redeveloped historic commercial districts. The Tax Reform Act and the practice of adaptive reuse made historic preservation profitable, and real estate developers and business owners formed partnerships with city planning officials, architects, and members of the suburban white-collar middle class to promote the development of inner-city historic districts as shopping areas.[23] Unlike the "populist" coalition, the "development" coalition used historic preservation to revitalize central business districts in major U.S. cities, including Boston, San Antonio, San Francisco, Denver, and Seattle.

The emphasis on redevelopment of historic districts shifted the focus of historic preservation from saving the rare and exceptional, such as Mount Vernon and the Alamo, to preserving the representative and typical.[24] As neighborhood rehabilitation and economic stimulation became preservationists' chief goals, lobbyists deemphasized accurate reconstruction of a historical past and began developing old buildings to ensure an economically viable future.[25] Municipalities across the country passed local preservation ordinances that provided more control over development than the honorary National Historic Preservation Act. National Register designation did not prohibit demolition of a building, for instance, but local ordinances and design review boards could. As historic districts proved profitable, they spread throughout the country. In 1955 only twenty cities had historic district commissions. By 1982 historic district commissions existed in more than 900 cities from Boston to San Francisco.[26]

The incorporation of historic preservation into city planning strategy both facilitated and reflected a paradigm shift in urban policy. From the end of the Civil War until the middle of the twentieth century, cities grew around industrial centers that focused on productive output, transportation of goods to markets, and housing industrial workers. City planners grappled with the challenge of making factories, laborers, and modes of transportation work together. Historian David Harvey defined this planning model as "modern."[27] "Modern" city planners focused on the central business district, with transportation, housing, and retail radiating from the core to the periphery. New transportation technologies such as streetcars and highways fostered suburbanization and created a rational division of uses. White middle-class men lived in the suburbs and worked in the central business district, and "modern" city planners fought to facilitate movement between the two areas.[28] The emphasis on cohesion and function standardized the downtown environment and failed to account for ethnic, class, or gender differences, remaking urban space to reflect the visions of generally white, middle-class, male urban planners.[29]

Suburbanization solved the problem of downtown congestion but led to the deterioration of central business districts after 1950. Although downtown remained the financial center of the city, retail businesses, light industry, and entertainment migrated to malls in the suburbs. Computer technology allowed greater mobility of capital, meaning that businesses did not need to locate in the financial district. Office complexes and technological centers chose suburban headquarters over downtowns, and manufacturing plants relocated outside city limits as highways provided flexible transportation access. Suburbs evolved into "edge cities," competing with the old downtown districts for businesses, shoppers, and residents.[30] The white middle-class migration to the suburbs in the 1950s and 1960s left inner cities segregated, poverty-ridden, and filled with crime. Without tax revenue, city councils either could not provide basic services or chose to focus their expenditures on more profitable middle-class neighborhoods.[31]

Central business districts also lost their market for leisure activities to the suburbs. For most of U.S. history, downtown was the hub of leisure and culture.[32] People of all classes and ethnicities enjoyed entertainments in the city. From 1890 to 1950 vaudeville houses, cabarets, baseball fields, amusement parks, and department stores embodied a vibrant urban culture. The post–World War II rise of suburban shopping malls, theme parks, and sports stadiums led to the breakdown of urban leisure, however, giving suburban residents even fewer reasons to come downtown.[33]

Modernist planners sought to revitalize central business districts using urban renewal policies. Urban renewal projects used federal funds to redevelop inner cities and stimulate economic growth. Following modernist logic, urban renewal projects concentrated on efficient movement through the city and standardization of architecture, creating a functional, if frequently unattractive, environment. Urban renewal funds underwrote housing developments, downtown shopping malls, parking structures, and office complexes.[34] Because city planners especially wanted to bring middle-class women downtown to do the family shopping, urban renewal designs imposed suburban-style architecture on the central business district, hoping to dispel the belief that cities were unsafe.[35] Yet urban renewal developments often created sterile landscapes, sometimes losing funding after tearing down buildings and leaving the inner city barren. Ultimately, most of these projects failed to attract shoppers, investors, or residents.[36]

The failure of many modernist urban renewal projects facilitated a paradigm shift to postmodern city planning, both an outgrowth of modernism and a reaction against it. Economically, the term *postmodern* describes the shift from production-centered capitalism to multinational consumer-centered capitalism.[37] Postmodern capital accumulation depended on control over the means of consumption rather than the means of production.[38] Although "consumer culture" began as early as 1890, it became the prevailing economic model by 1945.[39] The biggest participants in consumer culture were those with disposable income, namely the vastly white suburban middle class.

Culturally, postmodernism influenced Americans' ideas about identity and heritage. Groups previously absent from historical narratives, such as women, laborers, and racial/ethnic minorities, reclaimed their histories and integrated themselves into the larger American story. The face of the nation's cultural elite changed as power shifted from traditional white Anglo-Saxon Protestant families to a new generation of multiethnic individuals who rose to prominence through the meritocracy of excellent educations and powerful professions. These new elite, called "Bourgeois Bohemians," or "Bobos," by *New York Times* writer David Brooks, frequently included descendants of religious, racial, and ethnic minorities. These previously invisible groups saved and celebrated neighborhoods important to their personal heritage. Historic preservation provided the perfect postmodern city planning tool for this Bobo hippie-chic zeitgeist.[40]

In city planning, postmodernism represented the breakdown of modernist grand-planning schemes and the emergence of market-driven planning.[41] Whereas modern urban planners worked to create comprehensive social projects and large-scale urban order, postmodern city planners sought to compete with other localities for capital. Postmodern city planners constructed space piecemeal, more concerned with an individual's experience of a specific site than how the space fit into the rest of the city. Modern city planners brought capital to the city by creating production centers, but postmodern planners understood the need to attract *consumers*, especially suburban shoppers, tourists, and the leisure market. Thus, planners worked with city councils and conventions and visitor's bureaus to create places that stimulated consumption.[42] Historic districts increasingly provided those types of places. Because of their architectural character and pedestrian-friendly environments, these areas, once revitalized, brought tourists and suburban residents back to the inner city.

Although the transition from modern to postmodern city planning was a national phenomenon, western cities faced additional challenges peculiar to the region. Western cities had a slightly different pattern of growth than eastern cities. Most western cities began as nineteenth-century boomtowns, springing up almost overnight.[43] Because speculation drove the founding of many western towns, they developed haphazardly, with no cohesive planning and very little public space.[44] After initial booms, western cities usually grew slowly during the first part of the twentieth century. They were also fewer and farther apart than cities in the Northeast and Midwest, which forced them to reach beyond their immediate hinterlands for resources, goods, and markets, thus developing into regional political and economic centers exerting influence over a vast geographic area.[45]

Like all cities, transportation influenced the layout of western urban areas. Unlike Boston, New York, and Philadelphia, however, which started as walking cities, Los Angeles, Denver, Albuquerque, San Francisco, Phoenix, Seattle, and other western metropolises began during the railroad era and were still relatively small when automobiles arrived on the scene. By the 1920s, members of western city councils and planning departments factored automobiles into their urban design decisions, and highways played a prominent role in growth. Western cities also had vast expanses of vacant or agricultural land surrounding them, which facilitated suburbanization. Rather than imposing highways on an already-built landscape, western cities grew along highways, frequently making them more decentralized than eastern cities and giving rise to sprawl.[46]

Decentralization and sprawl remained the standard for western cities during World War II, and both intensified with explosive postwar population growth. During the war years, the national population began moving south and west, creating a new region dubbed the "Sunbelt." World War II, the Korean War, and Vietnam brought federal military installations, technology, and population to Sunbelt cities. The influx of capital to the West transformed the region from a colonial economy, dependent on the East for capital and population, to an integral part of a modern, urban-based, globally connected economic network. Western cities boomed as they had during mineral rushes of the previous century. Between 1950 and 1980, the West contained more than half of the nation's fastest-growing cities.[47]

Growth in western cities did not merely imitate earlier growth in eastern cities. Federal installations and light industry dominated western urban expansion, so cities did not stick as rigidly to the modernist model mandated by the requirements of heavy industry and preautomotive transportation systems. The reduced influence of large-scale manufacturing, and the labor relations it entailed, enabled business-dominated politics with a general lack of organized labor power.[48] Prior to 1940 westerners, perhaps naively, viewed their cities as free from the problems plaguing eastern cities, especially decaying industrial cores, ethnic and racial tensions, labor unrest, and urban congestion.[49]

Despite the fame of New York's Levittown, western cities, specifically Los Angeles, pioneered the movement of people to the suburbs after World War II. Highways tore through farmland, tracts of subdivisions claimed orchards, and shopping malls and other commercial zones sprang up along routes in and out of the city. In the midst of the growth, however, the central business district continued to decay, creating the racial tensions that led to riots in Watts and other inner-city neighborhoods in the 1960s. Urban decay in the midst of rampant suburban growth made western residents fear their cities were out of control. According to historian John Findlay, western city planners sought to impose order on the perceived chaos. Findlay identified a western model for city planning that used zoning ordinances to control pockets within the city; it in turn influenced urban planning strategies nationally. Findlay claimed that the western planning model strengthened regional identity by controlling growth and strengthening community ties.[50] Although Findlay dealt with districts built from the ground up, I will show that his model also accurately describes the establishment and regulation of historic districts.

The rapid growth of western cities also influenced architectural patterns. Architects and developers used standardized plans and materials to put buildings up quickly. Cookie-cutter subdivisions, pioneered by William and Alfred Levitt, spread across the nation. Shopping malls, strip malls, and other retail complexes looked the same in Seattle as in Syracuse, in Denver as in Dayton. Downtown urban renewal programs also standardized architecture. Rampant growth and homogenization of architecture overpowered variations in regional styles or building materials, leading western citizens to fear that their cities would end up looking like industrial eastern cities, with their corresponding challenges.[51]

The economic shift to postmodernism also had a western version, manifesting as a decline in industries associated with the West. Mining and resource extraction, cattle ranching, logging, and agriculture lost their primacy, replaced by service industries, high technology, and tourism.[52] National retail chains took over niches once dominated by local businesses. In Denver, for example, Safeway replaced locally owned Sav-A-Nickel in the 1950s, and the national May company bought out the Daniels and Fisher store, which had been a local retail staple since the gold rush.[53]

One of the fastest-growing industries in the West was tourism. City councils and chambers of commerce promoted tourism as a sustainable industry, environmentally friendly and immune to the boom-and-bust cycles that afflicted the extractive economy.[54] Tourism was, moreover, an old business in the West. The region had attracted eastern tourists looking for adventure ever since the fur trappers arrived in the 1820s. After the Civil War, as the railroads spread into remote country, eastern visitors sought the adventure of going West and experiencing the breathtaking landscape and different cultural traditions. The railroads promoted tourism, advertising both exotic landscapes and diverse people to attract passengers.[55] Although nineteenth- and early twentieth-century tourists came looking for adventure, they brought with them the amenities and comforts of home.[56]

By the 1950s, however, tourists came seeking something distinctively western. The popular culture of the era celebrated western stories, from Disney's *Davy Crockett* on television to John Wayne's typical fare in movie theaters. Tourists to the West wanted to see the "Wild West" of popular culture, not urban skylines that looked like New York, Chicago, Detroit, or other cities. Western city councils, tourism bureaus, private developers, and businesspeople happily obliged, creating tourist destinations to cater to people seeking the "authentic" Wild West. Dude ranches, kitschy attractions, and gambling halls in old mining towns took advantage of the cultural and geographical landscape to "sell" the West.[57] Few tourists objected to the irony of places *created* to give the illusion of authenticity, and tourism became an important industry in almost every western state.[58]

In reaction to exponential urban growth, architectural homogenization, and economic dependence on tourism, historic preservation policies offered western urban residents, city planners, community activists, and developers a tool to revitalize urban cores and reinvigorate a sense of regional difference. Historic districts created a new environment of civic sociability and stimulated consumption by exerting control over the physical environment to give favorable associations to products and amenities. The districts also reestablished the Victorian tradition of urban leisure and brought consumers back downtown. The revitalized areas especially targeted women by providing clean, well-lit, and well-patrolled urban spaces, dispelling any fear of crime or urban unrest.

Designated historic districts quickly grew into tourist attractions. Nineteenth-century warehouses became bookstores, old blacksmiths' shops found new life as gift emporia, and mercantile buildings turned into brewpubs. Tourists frequented historic districts to absorb the city's heritage as well as to shop and dine, consuming the essence of place. Tourist dollars generated in historic districts convinced city planners of the value of historic preservation, especially in the West, where urban economies depended on out-of-town visitors.[59] During the 1960s, preservationists also turned to tourism as a way to ensure that historic preservation would remain a city priority. Developers could be fickle allies, so preservation activists promoted the tourist appeal of historic districts to gain support from city planning offices and tourism bureaus.[60] By the late 1980s, successful tourist districts stimulated private investment downtown, relieving the burden on the city's funds for restoration, and further enticing visitors with new art galleries, restaurants, and retail stores.[61]

A national trend toward "heritage tourism" reinforced the success of historic districts as tourist destinations. Cold War fears about security and the upheaval of protests during the 1960s spurred Americans to seek associations with a time when life seemed simpler.[62] The old buildings in historic districts provided reassuring symbols of the past and offered goods and services appealing to heritage tourists. Historians Roy Rosenzweig and David Thelen found that people who would never consider taking history as a subject in school enjoyed visiting museums and historical sites on vacations.[63] Indeed, by the 1980s historic sites attracted more visitors than did natural sites, even in states that promoted national parks and other natural attractions.[64]

Despite the benefits, urban historians, cultural observers, Marxist critics, and postmodern deconstructionists criticized historic districts. Many observers noted that historic districts created something that was not historically accurate. According to detractors, these simulations, or "cities as theme parks," tried to recreate a nostalgic urban life that never existed. Historic districts claimed authenticity yet were renovated to relieve contemporary urban pressures, not to accurately depict the past.[65] By creating historic districts, critics argued, city planners detached those districts from the rest of the city, cleaning them up and homogenizing them. This mythical landscape promoted unrealistic and nostalgic paradigms of class interaction, ethnic behavior, and gender roles.[66] According to detractors, this was made worse by the fact that the masses did not even realize they were being duped. Rosenzweig and Thelen's study found that over half of the people they surveyed ranked historic sites a nine or ten on a ten-point scale for historical trustworthiness.[67]

Observers also criticized historic districts for commodifying history, promoting consumerism, and hiding changes in the power dynamic that benefited the upper and middle classes while exploiting workers and people of color. According to this school of thought, because downtown commercial historic districts became shopping and entertainment centers, the developers of the districts exploited the old buildings to promote consumption. Although historic district designation required the buildings to be "intact" and representative of their time, place, and style, the ordinances generally allowed extensive interior changes and a variety of uses. Thus, developers packaged a mythical heritage in the old buildings as a marketing ploy to bring visitors and tourists to the district. The city then heavily policed the area, so that middle-class consumers, including women and children, felt safe shopping there, and undesirable people, namely people without disposable income, would not loiter.[68] Historic districts separated those who had money to spend from those who did not, and they frequently drove residents and property owners out of the district as property values and taxes rose.[69] According to opponents, historic districts appropriated customs from indigenous groups and marketed replicas of these customs for tourists, while sending the profits to corporate headquarters. For example, Native American craftspeople did not benefit from the pottery and jewelry sold in western historic districts.[70]

Depending on the point of view, then, historic districts were either economic saviors with noble missions, helping preserve history and revitalizing downtown, or rip-offs that sold visitors a bill of goods while stealing power from neighborhood residents and packaging it for middle-class tourists. About the only point advocates and critics agreed on was the fact that urban historic districts were landscapes consciously created to fit the needs of late twentieth-century city planners.

Much of the criticism leveled at historic districts was valid, if irrelevant. Historic districts established after 1955 did tend to fake authenticity, promote consumerism, and mask power relationships. This criticism overlooks the importance of historic districting as a city planning strategy, however. Rather than evaluate a historic district compared to its historical antecedent, it is important to evaluate the district based on the choices that city planners, developers, and local officials faced in the 1950s and 1960s. Saying that a revitalized district in 1980 was different than it had been in 1880 is a pointless observation—of course it is different. More meaningful is the existence of the district in the face of what else might have gone there. By choosing to designate historic districts rather than create urban renewal wastelands, urban planners and city officials attracted investors, drew customers downtown, and created civic identity by preserving places where history happened.

In the West, citizens and city government officials used historic districts to address the regional factors that they feared were diluting their civic identity. Historic preservation activists argued for creating historic districts as a response to the changing urban conditions brought to the West by population growth, economic standardization, and architectural homogenization. The rampant growth, economic flux, and standardization of the built environment that occurred in the West during and after World War II led many westerners to fear a breakdown in their sense of place and heritage. Regional identity is a tricky subject. Before the mass media, transportation revolution, global economy, and the standardizing influences of popular culture, regional identity grew in relative isolation, founded on family structures, community traditions, religious commitments, generational consistency, and geographic features.[71] As American culture grew more global, mobile, mass mediated, and homogeneous, regional identity became a social construct to relieve a perception of rootlessness. Once the economic, cultural, and architectural differences between regions diminished, residents of the West felt compelled to reinforce the *idea* of difference between regions by defining a regional identity.[72]

Regional identity is a multifaceted, conditional concept based on history, economy, landscape, and cultural traditions.[73] During the nineteenth century the western landscape played the most significant role in defining regional identity, and extractive industries defined regional economic traditions.[74] Popular culture portrayals of the West greatly influenced identity in the first part of the twentieth century, creating a regional tradition in history, fiction, and art. Novelists such as Owen Wister and Zane Grey, historians such as Frederick Jackson Turner, and artists such as Frederick Remington created the "West of the imagination." This new West, defined as both a place and an idea, sought to explain the interaction between landscape and inhabitants in terms of regional identity.[75]

Western cities also had unique cultural traditions. The ethnic makeup of the region included Hispanics, Native Americans, African Americans, Asian Americans, and descendants of Welsh, Scottish, Southern European, and Eastern European miners. Fairs, ethnic holidays such as Cinco de Mayo, Indian powwows, and religious celebrations created cultural identity for numerous western cities. These cities also had museums specializing in regional or native art, public art displays reflecting Native American influences, and unique architecture, especially in the Southwest.

During the 1950s and 1960s, however, the factors that determined regional identity were in flux. As the economy of the West changed, so did the built landscape. Waves of newcomers diluted cultural traditions by changing the ethnic composition of western cities and adding to sprawling urbanization. The rural and small-town West disappeared as cities dominated the landscape.[76]

Ironically, the residents trying to define a western regional identity after World War II were largely newcomers, migrants from places in the East and Midwest. Without family and community ties, recent arrivals to the postwar West could define regional identity as it resonated with their expectations. Newcomers' perceptions of the West, garnered from popular culture portrayals, dictated ideas about the past as well as expectations for the future. As newcomers experienced cultural traditions that had been the basis of identity in the region prior to their arrival, they adopted the identity of the old-timers, consequently transforming it to reinforce their own preconceived notions. Creating a regional identity was a way for western residents to be positioned by, and position themselves within, stories of the city's past while having criteria to define themselves in the present and future. For example, one did not need to be a Hispanic villager in order to enjoy green chili, nor did one need to be a cowboy to wear boots and bolo ties.[77]

In this milieu, residents of western cities sought to define regional identity by preserving their "heritage." Since the 1980s, cultural historians have argued for a distinction between "history" and "heritage." "Heritage," historian Michael Kammen suggests, differs from history in that it celebrates only those aspects of the past agreed upon and valued by a group, leaving out any problematic information. Thus, "heritage" recreates the past as a time of innocence and consensus. Heritage is mythic, using symbols rather than facts to convey historical meaning. Heritage reinforces regional identity in that it acknowledges that certain parts of an area's history continue to have relevance to contemporary inhabitants. Historian David Lowenthal likens heritage to religious faith; people have no real proof that the events occurred but accept them based on a feeling that they must be true. History purports to tell the way things really were, and heritage transmits myths of origin and common purpose. In the post–World War II era, heritage references helped Americans feel connected to one another in the face of rapid cultural, economic, and global transformation and fragmentation.[78]

Maintaining contact with *places* where history happened was a vital part of regional identity.[79] Historic preservation functioned as a heritage tool by attempting to fix identity in bricks and mortar. *Preservation,* the magazine of the National Trust for Historic Preservation, summed up preservation philosophy in this way: "If the preservation movement is about something greater than the aesthetic rewards of fine architecture and urban design, it is the notion that enduring values of community, faith, and even freedom can be expressed in stone and wood as well as words. When we make a community, we inevitably struggle toward some sense of our own ideals, and thus our identity."[80]

The western historic districts representing regional civic identities were parts of high-tech commercial cities, however, no longer resembling frontier boomtowns. City planners, architects, preservationists, and developers had to reinvent the districts to resonate with expectations about the historic city, choosing from multiple identities to preserve. Frequently, preservation groups emphasized heritage by inventing a tradition. Invented traditions occur when rapid transformations weaken or destroy existing social patterns. When old traditions no longer apply to conditions, society discards them and invents new ones.[81] The growth, standardization, and ethereal quality of postmodern life made western citizens feel removed from the past and caused them to seek new traditions to define civic identity.[82] Invented traditions take symbols from the past and graft them to the present to give the feeling of continuity. In historic districts, the buildings became symbols of the invented tradition. The fact that the buildings were indeed old masked the transformed quality of these districts and mitigated the sensation of a "faked authenticity." The city ordinances that controlled historic districts also regulated growth and change, which gave stability to the area and imparted a sense of community.[83]

Thus, commercial historic districts created regional civic identities by focusing on an idealized heritage, then packaging that heritage for tourists and suburban visitors. By commodifying the created identity, preservation groups reinforced that identity by repeating and disseminating it. Residents and visitors experienced the created identity as a sense of community, an acknowledged heritage, and an identifiable tradition. In the interplay of market forces between groups packaging history and those consuming products and services in historic districts, these historic districts became repositories of regional civic identity.[84] Yet as historic districts represented identity, they also transformed it. In the five historic districts detailed in this book, historic preservation advocates created civic identities reflective of the conceptions of heritage in the late twentieth century, not a timeless cultural definition.

In the following chapters I show how five historic districts created civic identities in three western cities: Albuquerque, New Mexico; Denver, Colorado; and Seattle, Washington. I chose these three cities for a number of reasons. First, each represents a subregion of the West: Albuquerque, the Desert Southwest; Denver, the Rocky Mountain West; and Seattle, the Pacific Northwest. Although subregions are socially constructed spaces, I used this distinction based on the ideas residents of these areas had about the environments in which they lived.[85] Second, the historic districts of each of these three cities arose from similar impulses yet developed different identities, providing interesting comparisons. Third, historic preservation boards in all three cities kept extensive records detailing the creation of historic districts, the ideas behind their establishment, and the people involved, making them rich in sources. Finally, the downtown commercial historic districts of these cities all became entertainment districts or tourist attractions, confirming the connection between historic preservation and consumer culture.

These five historic districts changed urban space in numerous ways. First, the designation of these historic districts changed the social and economic demography. Prior to designation, the older areas of the city housed predominantly male racial/ethnic minorities of low socioeconomic class. Most were "skid rows," populated by bums, bars, and missions. The designation of the historic district brought gentrification, which transformed the social dynamic. As investors, developers, historic preservation advocates, and city officials worked to increase the city's tax base, they created the historic districts to appeal to consumers, which in the 1960s meant white middle-class women. The nature of the retail stores, architectural refinements, and district restoration attracted women by "cleaning up" the space and making it safe and appealing. Thus, the designated historic districts became havens for white middle-class women and families.

Second, in each district, power relationships changed. The designation of historic districts purported to celebrate local traditions but actually removed control from neighborhood associations and property owners and concentrated it in the hands of private developers and city historic preservation boards. The most commercially successful districts in this study had a powerful central authority—whether a single owner or stringent local zoning ordinances. Districts with multiple property owners and no powerful city oversight board faltered as both economic development engines and repositories for civic identity.

Third, in an ironic twist, historic district designation ultimately functioned like the urban renewal programs historic preservation advocates purported to oppose. In four of the five case studies that follow, the official designation of each historic district was the culmination of a grass-roots effort to stop an urban renewal plan. Yet the preservation of the historic district *became* urban renewal, bringing private-sector investment, tourists, commercial businesses, and residents. In three of the districts, federal urban renewal funds helped pay for the renovation of the historic buildings. In one case, Pike Place Market, the dependence on urban renewal funding to restore the old buildings compromised the original vision of historic preservationists. In the cases that follow, the historic preservation efforts became a modified urban renewal strategy.

Above all, the discourse regarding the desirability of local historic district designation revolved around civic identity. Because the concept of civic identity is ethereal and hard to define, it is frequently overlooked in accounts of preservation, but it was a key deciding factor in what got preserved and what did not. The more a structure or area of historic buildings resonated with and reinforced the identity that city officials, residents, boosters, and preservationists wanted to portray, the more likely the district was to be preserved. This, in turn, reinforced that preconceived identity, downplayed or eliminated competing narratives, and created a mythic landscape that met expectations rather than presented the full complexity of identity. Each historic district in this study became a repository for the city's mythic identity.

In Chapter 1 I examine Albuquerque's Old Town. In the milieu of postwar growth, Anglo newcomers to Albuquerque feared losing the identity inherent in the ethnic composition of the city. As Anglos outnumbered native-born Hispanics, and the Anglo presence in politics, business, architecture, and culture diluted or replaced what seemed to be more traditional structures, Anglo politicians, planners, and property owners annexed Old Town and designated it as a historic zone in order to appropriate a Hispanic heritage. Becoming a historic district transformed Old Town, however, shifting political and economic power out of the neighborhood and weakening cultural ties that had bound the community together for generations. Old Town did, however, become a popular destination for tourists and residents of greater Albuquerque and became representative of the city in convention and tourism literature.

In Chapter 2 I show how one woman's vision of Denver's Larimer Square changed city planning policy, as well as Denverites' idea of themselves. Dana Crawford formed Larimer Square to bring development into downtown, and she fought city planners and the Denver Urban Renewal Authority to create a place where the people of Denver could celebrate their heritage. Although Larimer Street was a notorious skid row, Crawford used the media to recreate the block as the "most famous street in the West." Architecturally, Larimer Square relied on rural symbols to invent a landscape that appealed to suburbanites—predominantly women—as clean, safe, and consumer friendly. The preservation of Larimer Square changed power relationships within the city, however, as the once-public block became privately owned and heavily patrolled, keeping out traditional urban populations, especially poor ethnic males. Larimer Square did spark a revitalization of Denver's downtown, however, and led, almost twenty years later, to the preservation of the much larger Lower Downtown Historic District. It also succeeded as the community gathering place and the symbol of Denver's historic identity.

The historic districts in Seattle provide interesting counterpoints to Old Town and Larimer Square. Chapter 3 examines Pioneer Square, which was the heart of Seattle's commercial district in the late nineteenth century and the supply center for the Klondike Gold Rush. The main street in Pioneer Square, Yesler Way, was the original Skid Road, from whence comes the term "skid road," or "skid row," a designator of deteriorating urbanity. In the 1960s groups of cultural elites began renovating old commercial buildings for offices in opposition to the city's urban renewal plan. Preservationists succeeded in designating Pioneer Square a local historic district in 1970, but the multiple property owners, city agencies, and other stakeholders could not agree on a heritage to promote: the "Skid Road" heritage undermined the triumphant "Seattle Spirit," and local business owners struggled to attract patrons, who feared the omnipresent bums. Pioneer Square's failure to encapsulate a single civic identity stemmed from the multiple stakeholders' determination to promote competing identities. Without a symbolic heritage that resonated with nostalgic expectations, Pioneer Square fought to remain economically viable. Pioneer Square also had competition for Seattle's civic identity from another district to the north—Pike Place Market.

Pike Place Market, discussed in Chapter 4, offered an alternative identity to the people of Seattle. Owned entirely by the Pike Place Preservation and Development Authority (PDA), Pike Place Market is a microcosm of rural nostalgia. By the 1950s suburban Seattle residents had stopped patronizing the market as grocery stores made fresh produce available closer to home. The market neighborhood housed single older men, mostly unemployed. With such an undesirable population, the city council approved the demolition of most of the market, keeping one acre of historic buildings surrounded by a high-rise hotel and upper-income apartments similar to Larimer Square. Led by architect Victor Steinbrueck, preservationists opposed the plan and went straight to the public with an initiative to save the market, which overwhelmingly passed. The initiative dictated preserving all of the market's historic buildings and uses. The old farmers' market became a place determined to sell food cheaply to those in need and also provided low-income housing and services. The city implemented a substantial zoning code monitoring the uses of the market, and the bureaucracy needed to keep capitalist forces out of the market led one former PDA director to call Pike Place "an experiment in socialism." It succeeded in becoming an icon for the city, however, and the "Public Market" marquee rivals the Space Needle as Seattle's predominant symbol.

Chronologically, the last historic district designated in this study was Lower Downtown, Denver, or LoDo, which is detailed in Chapter 5. LoDo was once the warehouse district of Denver. Like Pioneer Square, the area in the 1960s contained seedy bars, homeless people, vacant buildings, and flophouses. With the success of adjacent Larimer Square, however, the city council proposed designating LoDo as a historic district to provide residential units and promote arts and entertainment in the area. Most of the property owners opposed the initiative, but the council and mayor advocated preservation as a way to revitalize the central business district. Although Lower Downtown had been a manufacturing district, the historic district recreated the area as a community, transforming warehouses into million-dollar lofts. Commercial development also proved vital, and the construction of Coors Field, home of the Colorado Rockies baseball team, on the edge of the district promoted LoDo as an entertainment area. A stringent zoning ordinance and powerful design review board focused LoDo's identity. Unlike the two districts in Seattle, which competed to become the primary repository for civic identity, LoDo did not compete with Larimer Square but was viewed as an extension of the successful identity already established there.

In each district the coalitions working to designate historic districts created and enhanced civic identities. In the postmodern economy, where cities had to compete for capital investments, consumers, and residents, a city's history gave it a unique marketing niche that no other locality could claim. Historic districts provided valuable marketing tools, and as each historic area became associated with the identity of the city, it attracted more tourists. Historic districts profited because they created civic identities that drew residents and visitors alike to feel connected to the city's heritage in a fun way. Although different coalitions precipitated preservation in Albuquerque, Denver, and Seattle, they all justified the preservation using the rhetoric of identity. In each of the five cases, the groups advocating designation of the historic district argued for saving the thing that made that city unique as defined by a particular time in history. The preservation of each district transformed it, however, failing to fix a timeless identity in bricks and mortar but succeeding in providing each city with a vibrant economic future.

ALBUQUERQUE, NEW MEXICO, OR

ANYWHERE, USA? OLD TOWN

In the iconography of the Southwest, New Mexico is a sun-drenched paradise, containing desert vistas, colorful natives, and exotic architecture. Yet during World War II, the landscape of the Southwest increasingly contained urban skylines, not majestic expanses. People from the Northeast and the Midwest flooded into New Mexico to take advantage of the economic growth of the Sunbelt. Tourism also increased after World War II, and travelers came to the Southwest to experience the unique cultural characteristics of the region. From 1940 to 1975 Albuquerque experienced the trends of population growth, economic transition, and architectural homogenization that most western cities faced. To cope with the rapid pace of change, Albuquerque's city commission, planning commission, Anglo property owners, and developers used historic preservation to define the city's identity.

Alburquerque, originally spelled with two *r*'s, began in 1706 as a Spanish settlement along the Rio Abajo, or "lower river," region of the Rio Grande Valley.

Named for the Duke of Alburquerque, Viceroy of New Spain, the *villa* grew as the garrison for all the settlements in the Rio Abajo.[1] The plaza stood where it does today, approximately 500 yards from the Rio Grande to minimize the risk of flooding. With the exception of San Felipe de Neri Church, the buildings on the plaza were predominantly homes of settlers who farmed the land between the town and the river. In the 1790 Spanish census, occupations of Old Town residents varied from sheepherder to sexton, but there was not a merchant in the bunch.[2]

The town did not grow until the 1820s, when the Santa Fe trade brought commerce to Alburquerque. Although commerce did not venture south along the Camino Real to Alburquerque until markets to the north were saturated in the late 1820s, the introduction of U.S. goods caused a spurt of growth on the plaza, and merchants and storefronts became common sights in Old Town. The U.S. presence in Albuquerque became official in 1846, after Stephen Watts Kearney marched into Santa Fe and peacefully claimed New Mexico for the United States. Sometime after the arrival of the Americans, the first *r* was dropped from Albuquerque's name.

The U.S. acquisition of New Mexico, formalized under the Treaty of Guadalupe Hidalgo, brought Albuquerque under the dominance not only of the U.S. government but also of American land speculators and merchants following the frontier. Although some settled around Old Town, many immigrants had bigger plans for Albuquerque. In 1880, speculators convinced representatives of the Atchison, Topeka, and Santa Fe Railroad to build the rail depot one and a half miles southeast of the plaza. Along with financially attractive deals offered by land speculators like Franz Huning, the railroad representatives shunned a location near Old Town for fear of flooding. Indeed, an 1872 flood had wiped out a number of buildings on the plaza. In 1881 the first train arrived at the new settlement, also called Albuquerque, and New Town was on its way to dominance over Old Town.[3] Although the arrival of the railroad brought Anglo-American settlers and supplies from the East, growth was slow enough that people coming to the region in the early twentieth century still had an awareness of the area's Indian and Spanish past.[4] After 1880, New Town became the political and economic center of the region, while Old Town reverted to a predominantly residential farming settlement.

New Town and Old Town had distinct ethnic identities as well. Cultural anthropologists and historians have shown that *ethnic identity* is a created concept that is constantly reinvented and reinterpreted. Groups create their

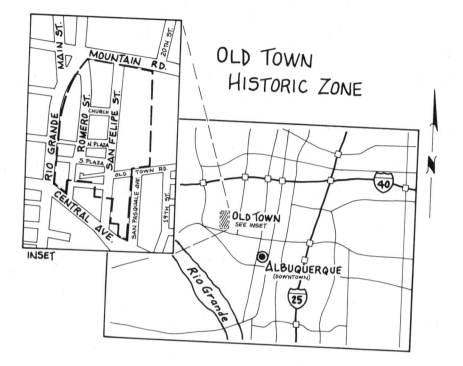

ethnic identity through a process of interreference between two or more cultural traditions, using one as a foil to define the other.[5] Ethnic identity in Old Town was based on Spanish or Mexican heritage, an association with the Catholic Church, and the use of the Spanish language. Old Town at the turn of the twentieth century had a distinct Hispanic identity, reinforced and redefined by the influx of Anglos moving to New Town.[6] Despite a strong Hispanic identity, Old Town was still ethnically diverse and representative of the mixed heritage of the region. Although most residents were native-born Hispanics, some Euro-American immigrants, including Herman Blueher, built houses there. By 1900 architecture around the plaza reflected Old Town's cultural diversity, consisting of a mixture of traditional low-slung adobe buildings with *portales* (porches covering sidewalks), Territorial-style brick buildings with flat roofs and dentated cornices, and Queen Anne brick houses, complete with gables and gingerbread trim.[7]

If Old Town's identity was predominantly Hispanic, New Town was overwhelmingly Anglo, with capital, goods, and settlers coming from the United

States. Settlers from the East, Midwest, and Europe settled in New Town because it was more "American" than Old Town. These new arrivals defined themselves as "Anglos," in opposition to the Hispanics in Old Town. "Anglo" came to mean non-Hispanic, and the distinction was evident in the population as well as the appearance of the town.[8] The architecture and layout of New Town looked like other western railroad boomtowns. The photos of early New Town show Victorian-style two-story buildings, false fronts, and a simple grid pattern to the streets.[9]

From the beginning of the twentieth century to World War II, New Town grew slowly but steadily, while Old Town's population remained flat. After World War II, Albuquerque experienced explosive growth, predominantly in New Town. Albuquerque led the nation in percentage population gain for the decade of the 1940s, with the population doubling between 1940 and 1950 and again between 1950 and 1960.[10] Albuquerque's position in the Sunbelt and the prevalence of Department of Defense installations attracted people wanting to take advantage of the sunny climate and booming economy in the 1950s.[11] Sandia National Laboratories and Kirtland Air Force Base emerged as major employers in Albuquerque. Because most of the growth came to New Town, Albuquerque sprawled to the north and east of the downtown rail depot. The city commission annexed land to accommodate the population increase, growing from 11.1 square miles in 1940 to 61.2 square miles in 1960.[12] Growth also changed the ethnic composition of the city, as arriving Anglo-Americans soon outnumbered native Hispanics and Indians.[13]

The city also experienced dramatic architectural changes. As Albuquerque grew, national builders used materials and architectural styles popular across the country. In 1954, Albuquerque's first International Style skyscraper, the Simms Building, rose downtown.[14] Residential developers in the Northeast Heights also departed from the regional building materials of stucco and adobe in favor of wood siding. With the exception of the Watson subdivision, just east of Old Town, residential subdivisions resembled Los Angeles, Phoenix, or Denver.[15] The city's first strip mall, Nob Hill along East Central Avenue, went up at the edge of town using a standardized art deco design popularized in Southern California decades earlier.[16]

Additionally, urban renewal projects in Albuquerque changed the character of the city. The Albuquerque City Commission initiated these projects in the 1950s, trying to give the aging city a face-lift to attract commerce to downtown. The commissioners approved the destruction of some of Albuquerque's most distinctive buildings, however, and further depopulated the central city. In 1955 developers bulldozed the historic Castle Huning on West Central Avenue. The stately mansion had been a symbol of Albuquerque's railroad era, but the city commission let potential development money influence its decision and allowed the landmark to be leveled.[17] Other landmarks, including the historic Hotel Alvarado, fell to bulldozers. The razing of these landmarks caused native-born New Mexicans and newcomers alike to reevaluate the policy of urban renewal.[18]

Albuquerque's commissioners also depended on tourism to bring commerce to the city after 1945. Clyde Tingley, who was chairman of the city commission during the 1920s, giving himself the ex-officio title "mayor of Albuquerque," was one of Albuquerque's most avid boosters. He served two two-year terms as governor of New Mexico, from 1935 to 1939, then returned to his position as chairman of the Albuquerque City Commission in the 1940s and 1950s. Tingley worked to bring New Deal money to the state and to improve Albuquerque so that it would be a place where people wanted to live and visit.[19] The city already had a viable tourist trade, channeled through the heart of downtown by Route 66 (Central Avenue). The loss of landmarks along the way threatened the character of the city, however, precisely at a time when heritage tourism was beginning nationwide.

Reacting to growth, homogenization, and tourism potential, the city commission began looking for ways to assert the uniqueness of Albuquerque. According to former Albuquerque planning director Jack Leaman, growth had to be controlled to preserve "the special sense of place and diversity of life styles which make Albuquerque different from other major growth cities." Leaman expressed his hope that Albuquerque would not become just another Phoenix, Dallas, Denver, or "Anywhere, USA."[20] In this capacity, planning professionals, city commission members, and historic preservation advocates used historic district designation to help Albuquerque manufacture a civic identity. The identity the city commission hoped to adopt did not reside around the rail depot in New Town, however. The city wanted to strengthen its association with Old Town, which in 1945 lay outside the city limits in unincorporated Bernalillo County.

Old Town in 1945 was still a place of a different era. Most streets were dirt or gravel, and many buildings did not have indoor plumbing, leading New Town residents to bemoan Old Town's poverty.[21] Old Town had strong community ties, and San Felipe de Neri Church served as the focal point of the neighborhood. The cohesion of Old Town began breaking down during the 1940s, however, as young Old Towners left the region to fight in World War II and Anglo newcomers began buying property around the plaza to take advantage of Old Town's rural atmosphere and small-town charm. Still, Old Town residents formed a community distinct and separate from New Town.[22]

Despite opposition from residents, the city commission sought jurisdiction over Old Town, purporting to provide the area with city services. Beginning in 1943, a combination of groups supported annexation of Old Town. The Chamber of Commerce, hoping to compete with other Sunbelt cities for corporate dollars, wanted increased population figures before the 1950 census.[23] Because of restrictions on incorporation, annexation was the primary way that the City of Albuquerque could grow.[24] Merchants in Old Town also supported annexation, hoping it would bring infrastructural improvements and publicity to the area. A small number of residents, mainly Anglos, advocated annexation to get city water and sewer services.[25]

Motives for annexing Old Town went beyond growth and services, however. Albuquerque's consolidation strategy converged with an ethos anthropologist Renato Rosaldo calls "imperialist nostalgia." In studies of cultures around the world, Rosaldo found that citizens of imperial powers have a longing for the traditional culture of a region, especially "a culture they had intentionally altered. People mourn the passing of what they have transformed."[26] Imperialist nostalgia describes the way Albuquerque's city government, and Anglo residents of New Town in general, felt about Old Town. As New Town grew at the end of the nineteenth century, there was very little interest in the old plaza area. If business or political leaders paid any attention to it at all, they viewed the plaza as competition to the growing railroad town.[27] By 1945, however, it was clear that Old Town posed no threat to New Town. Although Old Town had been able to influence politics in Bernalillo County prior to World War II, the village lost population during the war, weakening its political clout.[28] Anglo-dominated New Town had been the center of economic and political power for six decades, and the plaza was little more than a residential backwater compared to the central business district to the southeast. Once New Town's dominance was ensured, however, residents and politicians began to long for an association with that old Hispanic village. Indeed, Commissioner Clyde Tingley argued for support of annexation on the grounds that "the city of Albuquerque will get a historical background of great importance . . . we could advertise that the city was founded in 1706."[29]

Old Town residents actively opposed annexation, however. Albuquerque's city commission tried three times to bring Old Town under city jurisdiction before finally taking control. In its first attempt, the commission cited an ordinance allowing annexation of areas of less than five acres without a vote. Residents protested, however, since Old Town was over twenty acres.[30] In the second attempt, the commission claimed to have a petition signed by property owners advocating annexation. Supposedly, petition signers represented 54 percent of the land of Old Town, more than the simple majority needed for annexation. Old Town residents who had signed the petition came forward almost immediately, however, claiming that they did not fully understand what they were signing. They believed they were signing a petition for "improved city services," including water and sewer, street paving, and sanitation, not realizing that meant full annexation to New Town.[31] The city commission appointed a three-member board of arbitration, composed of two city commissioners and the Old Town residents' lawyer, G. W. Hannett, to review the validity of petition signatures.[32] After two weeks of review, the board asked for a one-week extension. The city commission denied the request, claiming that any delay would give opponents of annexation another week to convince petitioners to withdraw their signatures. Hannett resigned over the commission's refusal to allow the extension, but the now two-member board declared the petition valid anyway. The next day, the commission annexed Old Town, passing the resolution by the close vote of three to two. Old Town residents immediately filed a lawsuit against the city.[33]

Finally, to settle the dispute, the city commission held an election on annexing Old Town. Old Town voters elected three members to a new seven-member board of arbitration. The city commission also appointed three members, and a district judge chose the seventh member. Six candidates ran for the three positions from Old Town, half in favor of annexation, half opposed. When the election returns were tallied, Old Town residents voted two-to-one against annexation, with anti-annexation candidates receiving 395 votes to the pro-annexation candidates' 178 votes.[34] Despite electing three annexation opponents to the board of arbitration, Old Town became part of the city in 1949 when the board's other four members voted to uphold the city's annexation declaration.

Annexing Old Town was only the first step in creating a civic identity. Next, the city had to preserve the plaza's uniqueness and sense of isolation that annexation, ironically, threatened to destroy. The breakdown of the Hispanic community and an influx of development brought signs of growth to Old Town for the first time since the 1880 civic split. The Albuquerque Planning Commission, established in 1953, was overwhelmed with zoning and signage issues in Old Town by the second half of that decade.[35]

Growth in Old Town prompted a group of predominantly Anglo Old Town property owners to lobby the planning commission for zoning protection.[36] Nelda Sewell, who owned La Placita Restaurant in the historic Armijo House, and Mr. and Mrs. Richard Bennett, who ran shops out of the Springer House, had already been vital in establishing the Albuquerque Historical Society, with Richard Bennett serving as the society's first president in 1947.[37] In 1950 Robert Hooton and his wife, Peg, moved to Albuquerque and bought the Fred Stueckel House at 306 San Felipe. According to Hooton, they wanted the city to regulate building in Old Town to maintain the "small-town atmosphere" of the area.[38]

The Anglo property owners of Old Town, however, differed from the native Hispanic community centered in the congregation of San Felipe de Neri Church. Sewell, the Bennetts, and the Hootons belonged to a set of newcomers whose property fronted the plaza. They had a different perspective on the character of Old Town than did the native residents. The Anglo newcomers saw Old Town as a quaint vestige of an earlier era rather than a tight-knit ethnic community. These Anglo preservationists wanted to protect the area through city control, specifically through the regulation of architectural changes that might alter the look of the plaza and threaten property values. Although major architectural changes had to be approved by the city's board of adjustment, the Anglo residents feared that the board's ignorance of historic architecture would dramatically change the area.[39]

In 1956 Hooton and other local preservationists, with the sanction of the board of adjustment, proposed a change in the zoning laws to protect the historic architecture of Old Town. After studying the possibilities, the planning commission created a new zoning category for historic districts, "H" zones, in 1957. This was not an architectural overlay zone but rather a completely separate zoning category with its own use and design guidelines. Although not nearly as controversial as annexation, the establishment of an H-zone in Old Town did not pass without opposition. Nick Garcia, a native property owner on the plaza, opposed the historic district, mainly because of the restrictions it put on land usage. Garcia owned Nick's Wood Lot, next door to his residence, and feared that the H-zone ordinance would keep him from promoting his business effectively.[40]

Other opposition appeared during the public hearing on the zoning change. The minutes recorded statements from several "native residents" at the hearing, including this one: "Mr. Doloritas Lucero, 416 Romero Street, NW, rose to object to the establishment of a Historical Zone. He felt that Old Town is 'getting along all right as it is, so why not leave it alone.'"[41] Residents also protested the fact that there were no representatives from Old Town on the board of adjustment. At the end of the hearing, however, the opponents of the H-zone lost.[42] The law passed the city commission with ease, although it did not make much of a splash with the general public. The day after the commissioners adopted the law, the *Albuquerque Journal* ran a small two-paragraph article on page fifteen, announcing the creation of the Old Town historic zone along with another zoning change.[43]

After establishing the H-zone, the planning commission formed an advisory committee to consult on proposed architectural changes within the zone. Robert Hooton was instrumental in creating that group, called the Old Town Advisory Committee (OTAC). In conjunction with the planning commission, Hooton chose committee members who were "authorities on preservation."[44] The ethnic and socioeconomic composition of the OTAC, however, resembled New Town more than it did Old Town. The committee had only one resident of Old Town, Pete Duran, who was also its only member of Hispanic heritage. Otherwise, architects, an art history professor, and historic preservationists filled the committee. Initially the OTAC merely advised the board of adjustment on the propriety of structural alterations.[45] In 1967, however, it became an autonomous city board, renamed the Old Town Architectural Review Board (OTARB), with the power to make final decisions on architectural changes in Old Town.

With historic Old Town under city control, New Town had to create a heritage in Old Town that reinforced the identity that city planners, commissioners, and preservationists wanted to project. Thus, residents of greater Albuquerque co-opted Old Town's heritage.[46] Although none of the members of the planning commission lived in Old Town or had Hispanic surnames, they resolved that

> whereas the original site of the City now referred to as "Old Town" is the repository of history, the field of legend, a reverent spot—one to be preserved, to be seen, to be experienced by Americans as one of the matrices of their civilization, . . . BE IT RESOLVED THAT THE CITY COMMISSION [appoints the Advisory Committee to aid in] . . . Providing for public facilities and improvements to enhance

the availability, protect the historic monuments, preserve the character, and maintain the integrity of this ancient community for future generations to enjoy.[47]

Similarly, the city commission, in passing the Old Town Historic Zone ordinance, claimed that preservation was "to promote the cultural and economic general welfare."[48] Albuquerqueans were to adopt Old Town as part of their birthright.

Establishing heritage meant inventing a tradition. Invented traditions mask fundamental political and social changes.[49] Although Old Town was supposed to appear as it had in the nineteenth century, the power dynamics were different. Power in Old Town had shifted from Hispanic local control to Anglo city control. Economic power changed, also, as fewer native Hispanics owned property around the plaza by the late 1950s. According to the 1957 city directories, the Hispanic population was concentrated farther away from the plaza, north of Church Street, than it had been in 1940. Fewer people lived around the plaza in general, as Hispanic owners of historic homes sold or converted them to shops and restaurants.[50] The nature of businesses around the plaza changed as well. Whereas in 1940 there had been a locksmith, printer, interior decorator, and grocery store alongside the gift shops around the plaza, by 1969 the groceries and community-based businesses were north of the church, leaving the area around the plaza concentrated with curio shops, Indian trading posts, and Mexican food restaurants.[51]

Because Old Town was no longer a quaint Hispanic village, the people promoting it as the mainstay of Albuquerque's heritage had to reinvent it as one.[52] Old Town only worked as a basis for civic identity, for example, if it appeared, visually and culturally, like a nineteenth-century Spanish village, not part of a growing U.S. city. Thus, city commissioners, the OTARB, and the Old Town Association of merchants used architecture as their primary symbols by implementing strict design guidelines. By standardizing the style of buildings around the plaza, these groups invented a tradition in Old Town.[53]

Invented traditions, ironically, claim authenticity. Although visitors to an area seek authenticity, a facsimile will usually create the same favorable association with the past. According to New York Times architectural critic Ada Louise Huxtable, inventing traditions in historic districts set up a Catch–22. Once designated, a historic district began a process of "homogenization, an economic, cultural, and physical upgrading in which everything is made to resemble what it might have once been—only better."[54] The contradictory implications of this phenomenon appeared in the ordinance creating the Old Town historic zone. Although the law dictated acceptable architectural styles for Old Town, the ordinance was only concerned with the way a building *looked*. The law's wording addressed only the elevations of buildings, the use of external materials, and the overall facade. A building did not need to be made of adobe to be considered historic. A cement building with a stucco exterior qualified.[55]

The "faked authenticity" of Old Town perpetuated the fallacy that the area was an architectural snapshot of an earlier day. Although the historic zone portrayed a previous era, the buildings revealed more about the 1950s than the 1880s, the decade supposedly preserved in Old Town.[56] Building exteriors were substantially more homogeneous by the 1950s than they had been in the 1880s. From the turn of the century through World War II, Pueblo Revival architecture was the dominant style in New Mexico. Pueblo Revival was part of the picturesque tradition in American architecture, and it emphasized the use of local materials and vernacular styles. New Mexico's most famous architect, John Gaw Meem, added Territorial and art deco influences to Spanish and Pueblo styles, creating the Territorial Revival style, which quickly became the unofficial architecture of the state, especially in Santa Fe.[57] Property owners in Old Town followed the trend, renovating buildings to reflect the popularity of the Pueblo and Territorial Revival styles. Because Bernalillo County did not require building permits for most minor renovations, it is impossible to know when the buildings on the plaza were altered, but photographic evidence suggests that the bulk of the changes occurred between 1940 and the mid-1950s.[58]

The popularity of the Pueblo and Territorial Revival styles in Old Town also reflected merchants' attempts to create a favorable association with Santa Fe. Postwar Old Town business owners envied Santa Fe's tourist success and sought to emulate its architectural design.[59] Merchants stuccoed buildings or added Pueblo Revival flourishes to draw business to their "trading post" or restaurant.[60] Old Town never succeeded in implementing standardized stucco, however, and therefore remained more architecturally diverse than Santa Fe.[61] Some property owners appreciated the eclectic style of Old Town's buildings and restored Victorian styles.[62]

Although more diverse than Santa Fe, Old Town in 1957 was much more architecturally uniform than the village of the nineteenth century. Back then,

Old Town looked like part of a growing commercial city. Brick Queen Anne houses shared the plaza with Prairie Style homes, Italianate stores, and buildings with Greek Revival trim. The rectory of San Felipe de Neri Church began as a one-story adobe building but had a brick second story and a wooden verandah added in the 1880s. In the 1940s the church turned the wood into an adobe *portal* and stuccoed the brick.[63] The Manuel Springer House, on the corner of South Plaza and Romero, came into existence in 1913 as a brick Queen Anne house, complete with gabled roof and projecting bay windows. In 1943 Mr. and Mrs. Richard Bennett bought the house and changed the first story to a Pueblo Revival style, while keeping the second story truer to its Queen Anne look. The second story is now hidden, however, behind a wooden *portal* that obscures the Queen Anne section of the building from the street.[64]

Ironically, Cristobal Armijo built his house on South Plaza of adobe carved to look like brick. Begun in 1880, the home received a brick second story in 1886. Armijo, a successful merchant who settled in Old Town because of family ties, easily moved between Anglo and Hispanic worlds. He claimed he faked the brick construction of the first floor, and added brick to the second, in order to make the building look more pretentious.[65] Armijo's motivation shows how values in architecture changed and that the OTARB's guidelines were more congruent with contemporary ideas about the past than historical architectural preferences.

The most radical change in architecture on the plaza, however, came to the Herman Blueher House at 302 San Felipe. Originally a brick Queen Anne, this imposing structure would have been the pride of any Victorian U.S. city. Separated from the street by a spacious yard, the two-story building was further heightened by a gabled roof. The porch, laden with gingerbread trim, surrounded the home on both stories. During the Pueblo Revival period of the 1950s, however, new owners adapted the home for use as a restaurant and altered it radically. They flattened the gabled roof, creating a Territorial look. They removed the porches and all window trimming. Finally, the new owners built an extension on the first floor, bringing it right to the sidewalk and adding a low-slung, covered, wooden *portal*. This building would be completely unrecognizable to Herman Blueher.[66]

By preserving a homogenized exterior, the Old Town Architectural Review Board created the illusion that Albuquerque was now culturally homogeneous as well. Uniform architectural styles reduced any signs of cultural contestation—buildings of both Anglo and Hispanic architecture might

The rectory of San Felipe de Neri Church, c. 1920 (above) and in 1999 (below). Stucco replaced the brick and vines in the 1940s. (1920 photograph: Albuquerque Museum, neg. no. 1978.50.13)

The Manuel Springer House in 1999. The Queen Anne style is still barely visible on the second story.

imply the uncomfortable phenomenon of conquest. By assigning Hispanics in Albuquerque a place in the city's *past,* city institutions and Anglo Albuquerqueans could more easily ignore their existence in the *present.*[67] The strategy of historicizing an ethnic group denied the fact that Hispanics still lived, worked, and worshiped in Old Town. The buildings became symbols of larger cultural systems that ensured the hegemony of the dominant social powers.[68] Members of the OTARB, for example, were the only ones "qualified and sympathetic enough with the problems of Old Town" to regulate the architecture, failing to consult native residents before establishing building guidelines.[69]

The Hispanic community refused to be overlooked, however, and the OTARB members' decision to ignore the input of Old Town residents proved to be a mistake. Old Town's Hispanic community maintained its own identity, separate from the Anglo property owners allied with the various city boards. Although some of the residents were merchants who leased their plaza stores from absentee owners and advocated the commercial promotion of Old Town, most residents shunned Albuquerque's involvement in Old Town altogether.[70]

The Cristobal Armijo House, c. 1930 (above) and in 1999 (below). Notice the brick second story and the ornate, Victorian-style trim on the porch in the earlier photograph; the brick is now covered in stucco, and fake *vigas* adorn the porch. (1930 photograph: Albuquerque Museum, neg. no. 1980.018.001)

The Herman Blueher House, c. 1900 (above) and in 1999 (below). This imposing structure was originally an ornate example of the architecture popular in American cities around the turn of the century. Today's flattened roof, stuccoed exterior, and *portal* built to the street would make the house unrecognizable to the builder, but it projects the appropriate southwestern style. (1900 photograph: Albuquerque Museum, neg. no. 1978.50.737)

The Hispanic residents and merchants united in opposition to the architectural restrictions required by the OTARB.

The conflict between Hispanic residents in Old Town and the Anglo-dominated OTARB erupted in 1978 in an incident fraught with ethnic overtones. The disagreement pitted Father George Salazar and the congregation of San Felipe de Neri Church against the OTARB. When a water leak damaged the front of the church, the Hispanic maintenance supervisor of San Felipe recommended to Father Salazar that it be repaired using Permastone, a synthetic building material widely used in Hispanic vernacular architecture, but not a building material approved by the OTARB. Father Salazar agreed to the repair, and parishioners donated the material and their time to fix the church on a Saturday. Considering this a repair, Father Salazar did not seek approval from the OTARB before acting. When the chairperson of the OTARB, Betty Sabo, heard of the alteration, she sent a zoning representative to cite Father Salazar for failure to comply with the H-zone ordinance. The drama of the incident increased when the OTARB representative arrived to cite Father Salazar on Good Friday. When Salazar repeatedly refused to sign the citation, he was taken away in handcuffs after exchanging heated words with the OTARB representative. San Felipe de Neri won the long court battle that ensued. The state supreme court declared the review board unconstitutional because its guidelines were too vague, and the Permastone around the door of the church remained. The historic district ordinance stayed on the books, however, and the city commission reorganized the OTARB and renamed it the Landmarks and Urban Conservation Commission, with more specific guidelines and greater responsibilities.[71]

The so-called Permastone controversy illustrated the way OTARB members denied Hispanics a role in determining the look of the neighborhood. In an interview about the controversy a year after it happened, Sabo quoted another OTARB member, Joe McKinney, as saying that in the case of the church, the OTARB found itself "in a position that we are trying to protect the culture of these people from them."[72] Sabo claimed that San Felipe's congregation contained Anglos, as well as Hispanics, and that the church should belong to all of them, insinuating that historic preservation was for Anglos, not Hispanics. When the interviewer, historian Chris Wilson, pointed out that Permastone was widely used in private homes and vernacular architecture, Sabo countered by claiming she did not know of it being used in the historic preservation of any churches, and it therefore was not an acceptable material.[73]

The Permastone around the entrance of San Felipe de Neri Church in 1999.

Passions were no cooler on the other side of the issue. Father Salazar lambasted the "artists and architects" who wanted to keep everything old just for appearances. "I'm not going to heat the church with coal and wood, I'm going to heat it with gas . . . I'm not going to put little sheets of paper with lard on them in the windows and take out the windows, because that's the way they used to do them in the olden days."[74] Salazar pointed out that San Felipe was a living congregation and that its members should be able to repair the church however they saw fit. Finally, Salazar invoked the separation of church and state, claiming that the city government could not dictate the religious practices of people, including how they fixed their church.[75]

The increasing success of tourism on the plaza exacerbated the Permastone controversy. The OTARB had to maintain the illusion of authenticity to appeal to tourists, so it strictly prohibited any vernacular changes.[76] The architects and city appointees on the OTARB safeguarded the Anglo-invented tradition in Old Town against the vernacular tradition of the residents to create an area that resonated with tourists' expectations.[77]

Heritage tourism was an important way for Albuquerque to solidify the Spanish heritage portrayed in Old Town. By commodifying Albuquerque's image, the city's tourism bureau reinforced and broadcast that image for tourists and residents alike. To promote the city as a tourist destination, the tourism bureau exaggerated the area's Spanish flavor and portrayed the plaza as the center of the city's activity.[78] A typical excerpt from a tourist brochure of the 1970s read, "Old Town is the heart and soul of Albuquerque's heritage, where the first colonial families settled near the banks of the Rio Grande in 1706 . . . There remains a tranquility, a serenity about Old Town. We welcome you to our neighborhood."[79] Another brochure from 1980 suggested that visitors "take a walk through history around Albuquerque's Old Town Plaza, the serene village which has been the focal point of the community since 1706."[80]

As the tourism bureau marketed Albuquerque's image, it broadcast the image across the nation. An article in the 1961 tourism section of the *New York Times,* for example, romanticized Old Town in a headline that read, "Albuquerque's Old Town: Historic Site Recalls Era When Both City and West Were Young." The article continued:

About two miles west of downtown Albuquerque and but a few hundred yards from the banks of the Rio Grande is an image lost in the capsule of time. It is Old Town . . . Visiting Old Town by day or night, one is aware of the sudden slowing of time . . . Many unusual glimpses of the past are to be had on visits to the distinctive shops and restaurants that fringe the Plaza.[81]

Local merchants in Old Town joined the city's tourism bureau in their promotion of the area. The Old Town Association of merchants printed its own guide to the zone, highlighting the heritage of the plaza.[82] The merchants targeted tourists, but also residents of Albuquerque, marketing Old Town as a "getaway" that was still close to home.[83] The Hispanic merchants even co-opted a little heritage themselves, sponsoring a Wild West–style gunfight on the plaza every Sunday afternoon to bring locals and visitors alike into their stores.[84]

The merchants around the plaza also catered to tourists' expectations with the goods they carried. Old Town shops sold things that most Americans associated with the region. Indian jewelry, pottery, and rugs became mainstays in plaza shops, along with toy drums, beaded belts, and leather barrettes. It was not that merchants in New York could not market kachina dolls—the dolls came mostly from Japan and could be shipped anywhere. Kachinas would not sell in New York, however, because they did not fit the public perception of the region.[85]

The question of public perception in vending led to a controversy in 1990 over who could sell jewelry under the *portal* of La Placita Restaurant. The merchants around the plaza and the planning commission allowed Indians to sell jewelry off of blankets laid out along the sidewalk, similar to the practice in front of Santa Fe's Palace of the Governors. Non–Native American vendors were not allowed permits to sell their wares, however, because members of various city boards felt it would jeopardize the authenticity of Albuquerque's "top tourist attraction."[86] After native Mexican, but non-Indian, craftspeople protested, a compromise ordinance changed the wording to allow the sale of handmade goods regardless of the ethnicity of the craftsperson. The city hired a patrol officer, however, to regulate the vendors and "protect . . . the historic district's distinct flavor."[87]

Although tourism in Old Town commodified Albuquerque's regional identity, it also created something different from anything the founders of the historic zone ever imagined. According to historian Hal Rothman, tourism is a "devil's bargain . . . Success creates the seeds of its own destruction as more and more people seek the experience of an 'authentic' place transformed to seem more 'authentic' . . . These seekers of identity and amenity transform what they touch beyond recognition."[88] The use of historic preservation tools

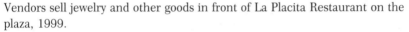

Vendors sell jewelry and other goods in front of La Placita Restaurant on the plaza, 1999.

such as historic district designation, zoning protection, and design review guidelines brought tourists, but it transformed Old Town by commercializing the plaza and co-opting the area's heritage for commerce and entertainment.[89] The creation of the H-zone boosted Old Town's economy but destroyed the "small-town atmosphere" the originators of the ordinance sought to save. As an inaugural member of the Old Town Advisory Committee, Bob Hooton felt that the success of Old Town was bittersweet. Instead of preserving the village atmosphere that attracted him and his wife to the area, he helped create a tourist attraction that divided what he perceived as a harmonious community.[90] Bette Castal, an Old Town resident who advocated annexation in the 1940s, later lamented the overdevelopment of the district and the lack of sensitivity to the character of the old village.[91]

Using historic preservation to create a civic identity for Albuquerque transformed Old Town. Just as anthropologists change the culture they study, so historic preservationists transform the identity they seek to preserve.[92] As more Anglos from New Town claimed Old Town as their own, the area lost local political and economic autonomy, and thus its uniqueness. It became instead a repository for an invented architectural and cultural tradition. Rather than protecting the residential Spanish village, historic preservationists created a homogenized district dependent on tourism.

Despite the transforming influences of historic preservation in Old Town, the historic zone did indeed create an identity for postwar Albuquerque. Instead of mass-produced, urban renewal–inspired buildings or parking lots and cheap motels, historic preservation in Old Town provided a way to update the city's frontier heritage and incorporate it into a civic identity that became a symbol of the city for residents and visitors alike.

"THE MOST FAMOUS STREET IN
THE WEST": DENVER'S
LARIMER SQUARE

In 1954 Dana Hudkins arrived in Denver. She had just com-
pleted a one-year Harvard/Radcliffe program in business administration and,
like most postwar transplants, came to Denver looking for a job. She chose
Denver because it was close to her home and family in Kansas, but far enough
away that she could be on her own. Hudkins relentlessly pursued a position
in public relations with Koska and Associates, hounding the firm's owner until
he hired her. She worked for Koska for one year and then, like most women
of her generation, left the workforce when she married. She and husband John
W. R. Crawford III had four sons, but Dana Crawford stayed involved outside
the home as a member of the Junior League and a volunteer for the Denver
Art Museum. Her entrepreneurial spirit would not rest, and in 1963 Crawford
began looking for something else to keep her busy. In the ensuing ten years,

Crawford purchased and restored a block of Denver's old buildings, created the Larimer Square Historic District, and in the process changed the trajectory of city planning in Denver.[1]

Ninety-six years before Crawford's arrival, another Kansas resident came to develop Denver. General William Larimer, a town promoter from Leavenworth, Kansas, traveled to the confluence of Cherry Creek and the South Platte River in the fall of 1858, following rumors of a gold strike. Larimer found three town sites staked along the rivers and jumped one of the claims to create the Denver City Town Company. He named his town after James Denver, governor of the Kansas Territory, but named the settlement's main street after himself.[2]

During the 1860s and 1870s Denver became the supply center for the entire Pikes Peak mining region, and Larimer Street grew into the commercial heart of the city. Merchants, saloons, and theaters lined the streets of the bustling boomtown. Con man "Soapy" Smith owned a tavern on Larimer Street, and madams Jennie Rogers and Mattie Silks established brothels. Silver magnate and lieutenant governor Horace A. W. Tabor built his office building, the Tabor Block, on Larimer Street, as did the owners of the luxurious Windsor Hotel. Larimer Street thrived until the 1890s, when Tabor and other promoters began buying property along 16th Street, and most of the commercial district relocated. After Union Station opened at the base of 17th Street in 1881, the financial district moved uptown as well.[3]

The silver crash of 1893, World War I, the Dust Bowl, and the Great Depression took a toll on Denver. The city fell from its position as third-largest town west of the Missouri River to fifth largest, following Los Angeles, San Francisco, Houston, and Seattle.[4] Larimer Street deteriorated into a skid row, with bars, liquor stores, and cheap hotels replacing the upscale businesses on the block.

Economic hardship changed the demographics of Larimer Street. Frontier Larimer Street catered mostly to men, but the theaters, restaurants, and clubs that arose on the thoroughfare in the late nineteenth century attracted both men and women. After the 1893 depression, however, women's leisure activities on Larimer Street decreased. The brothels housed "working women," but the legal whorehouses closed in 1914, and even the illicit bordellos moved during the 1930s. Larimer Street never attracted families, so no particular ethnic group formed community ties to the neighborhood. Consequently, the street became a multicultural melting pot of Hispanic, German, Asian, Irish, Jewish, and black men, all down on their luck.[5]

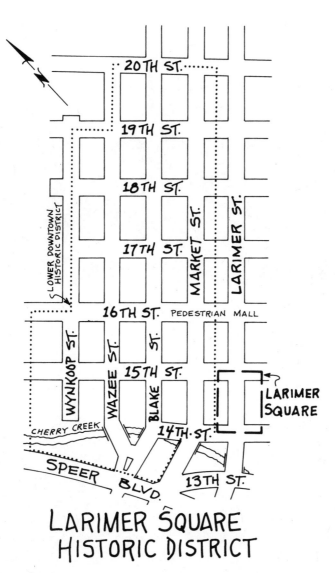

LARIMER SQUARE
HISTORIC DISTRICT

Larimer Street, 1900 (above); the 1400 block of Larimer Street in 1905 (below). (Denver Public Library Western History Department)

Denver's fortunes improved after World War II. The growing defense industry boosted the economy, and the Remington Arms Plant (later the Denver Federal Center), the Rocky Mountain Arsenal, and Lowry and Fitzsimons air bases brought high-technology workers to Denver. Denver grew much faster than anticipated, with the metropolitan area's population surpassing the one million mark in 1961, nine years earlier than demographers predicted.[6] The newcomers were relatively young, well educated, and inclined to spend money on leisure activities.[7]

Population growth reshaped the geography of the city. Small farming and mining communities near Denver, such as Littleton and Arvada, rapidly became suburbs of the metropolis. Commercial patterns changed as well, as highways transformed traditional shopping patterns. By 1970 the central business district had lost its position as the center for Denver's retail activity, challenged by outlying planned shopping areas like Cinderella City and Cherry Creek.[8] Larimer Street was by then a blighted area filled with crumbling buildings, flophouses, and bums. According to Dana Crawford, "nobody nice in Denver would ever come to Larimer Street."[9]

In the years between 1945 and 1960, economic power shifted from the conservative Denver elite to out-of-state investors and developers. New Yorker William Zeckendorf shook up Denver's business community with his aggressive investment and development strategies. In 1952 he purchased the former Arapahoe County Courthouse site in the middle of downtown and commissioned renowned architect I. M. Pei to build a Hilton Hotel and department store. That same year Zeckendorf contracted with Pei to build the twenty-five–story Mile High Center. Dallas oil millionaires Clinton and John Murchison bought the stuffy brick Denver Club and replaced it with a twenty-one–story high-rise. The new structures soon dwarfed the old Daniels and Fisher Tower, which stood as Denver's tallest building from 1911 until the Denver Club high-rise eclipsed it in 1952.[10]

City government officials, Chamber of Commerce members, and other business leaders feared the newcomers' increasing influence. The old guard, which included descendants of Denver's pioneer families such as Claude Boettcher, Gerald Hughes, and John Evans III, worked to maintain their power, but their tactics proved self-defeating. As president of the First National Bank from 1928 to 1959, John Evans III, great-grandson of the territorial governor whose name he bore, feared the risky speculation that characterized the city-building enterprises during the first part of the twentieth century, especially

the Moffat Railroad. Consequently, during the 1950s Evans tightened lend-
ing. Other banks followed suit, meaning that development capital continued
to come from out of state.[11]

The aggressive development strategies of investors like Zeckendorf and the
Murchisons convinced Denver's mayor, Quigg Newton, to focus on bringing
outside development, especially retail, into the city. Newton, city council
members, planners, and the business elite searched for ways to restore Denver to a place of prominence in the western economy and landscape and compete with Los Angeles, Dallas, Seattle, and Phoenix.[12] Between 1954 and 1963,
Newton's policies paid off. Retail sales increased 67 percent, and sales in the
service industry, including restaurants and hotel revenues, rose 123 percent
during the same period.[13] Newton also advocated a greater emphasis on bringing tourism to the state. Between 1950 and 1968, tourism surpassed mining
as the state's third-largest industry, following manufacturing and agriculture.
Revenue from tourism increased 418 percent during those twenty years, and
visitors to the state increased 303 percent.[14]

As the city government focused on attracting capital, tourism, and development to Denver, downtown's blighted conditions hurt the city's image.
Denver's business and civic leaders wanted to make downtown appealing to
investors as well as to conventions and visitors.[15] Their solution to the inner
city's decline was a comprehensive urban renewal policy. Beginning in 1957,
the Denver Planning Department, the Denver Urban Renewal Authority (DURA),
and a group of business owners called the Downtown Denver Improvement
Association (later the Downtown Denver Partnership) began reviewing plans
to revitalize downtown commerce by leveling entire city blocks and increasing warehouse and manufacturing space in lower downtown. One plan proposed creating a loop highway cutting through Market and Blake streets and
building a commercial development patterned after the shopping malls "prov-
ing to be so successful in suburban locations."[16] In the midst of the commercial section, the plan called for an airpark "in place of our Larimer Street
squalor" that would accommodate helicopters and all types of vertical take-
off aircraft. "Future air transportation into the heart of the city is certain, especially in Denver where air transportation is so important to the economy."[17]

Just southeast of the proposed airpark and lower downtown revitalization,
DURA proposed a 117-acre renewal project called Skyline to attract private
investment by eliminating "skid row, a major blighting influence in the area."[18]
Skyline followed the modern city planning model, mandating zoning regula-

The 1400 block of Larimer Street in 1960. (Denver Public Library Western History Department)

tion for different uses and dictating ways in which the project would work as a system.[19] Like the 1957 plan for lower downtown, Skyline called for a mammoth tear-down, clearing thirty blocks between 18th Street and Speer Boulevard, and between Larimer Street and Curtis Street. Although initially focused on housing, Skyline did not ultimately generate many residential facilities. One of the first proposals for Skyline included civic and cultural buildings, among them a downtown campus for the University of Colorado, a convention and cultural complex, an exhibition hall, and lots of parking garages.[20] Most of those projects were eventually built downtown, though none within the Skyline Urban Renewal District.

The Denver Planning Department approved DURA's Skyline plan in 1963, and a $6 million bond issue to fund the project went on the ballot in 1964. Although Skyline seemed to have support from the media, the bond issue failed. DURA and the planning board attributed the loss both to the high dollar amount and to a number of other bond initiatives on the same ballot.[21] DURA redefined Skyline's boundaries and uses and then began a major public relations campaign to coincide with the 1967 election. The new project guidelines included an entertainment and specialty district, and DURA persuaded the U.S. Department of Transportation to build a link from Interstate 25 to provide access to the Skyline district.[22] DURA made alliances with the mayor, the Denver Planning Department, and the newly created Denver Landmark Preservation Commission to gain support for Skyline funding. The strategy worked, and the Skyline Urban Renewal Project bond passed with 71 percent of the vote.[23]

By the time Skyline funding passed in 1967, one block of the project had already begun a transformation into something called "Larimer Square," thanks to Dana Crawford. Although her children were still young and her husband well employed, by 1963 Crawford was looking for an opportunity to work outside the home.[24] She read about Gaslight Square in St. Louis and began scouting for a location to create a similar district in Denver. According to Crawford, she wanted to create a place "where people of all backgrounds could celebrate their history and community."[25] She frequently visited Larimer Street to shop for antiques, and it occurred to her that the buildings themselves were antiques worthy of preservation.[26] After looking at a few other locations, Crawford decided that the 1400 block of Larimer Street fit her requirements.[27] That block fell under the jurisdiction of DURA, however, as the northwestern edge of the Skyline project. When she approached DURA with her ideas, the directors at DURA were skeptical but did not immediately impede her plan. Because Skyline was still in the initial approval phases, Crawford was able to begin developing "Larimer Square."

Although her initial inspiration was St. Louis's Gaslight Square, Crawford hoped to model Larimer Square on the more successful Ghirardelli Square in San Francisco, which was owned by a single corporation. Gaslight Square had trouble promoting the district because the multiple owners could not always agree on a course of action. Crawford realized that a single entity needed to acquire and manage the Larimer Square project.[28] Her initial inclination was to structure the project as a nonprofit corporation because she had nonprofit experience with the Denver Junior League and the Denver Art Museum. Most Denverites expected Crawford's work on Larimer Square to be a civic service, in keeping with the contemporary philanthropic role of upper-class women in the preservation movement. Crawford realized, however, that the buildings in Larimer Square would be more likely to be preserved if the project were profitable. By creating a for-profit corporation, Crawford was on the forefront of preservationists who linked historic preservation and development.[29]

To acquire the buildings on the 1400 block of Larimer Street, Crawford organized the corporation Larimer Square Inc. on 28 August 1964, with herself as president. The mission of the corporation was to purchase "the prop-

Dana Crawford sits atop bricks ready for the restoration of Larimer Square, 1965. (James O. Milmoe; courtesy of Thomas J. Noel)

erty on Larimer Street between 14th and 15th Streets; subsequently, to develop this property in an 'Historic Denver' motif, and to create an 'after 5' recreation center for Denver residents and visitors."[30] Many of the initial investors in Larimer Square Inc. were property owners on Larimer Street who traded equity in their buildings for shares of stock. Other early investors included Langdon Morris, the original architect on the project, and future U.S. representative Patricia Schroeder and her husband, James.[31] The corporation changed its name to Larimer Square Associates (LSA) in 1966, when stockholders Rike Wooten and Thomas Congdon became limited partners.[32] Within six months, the corporation acquired fifteen buildings on the 1400 block of Larimer, valued between $16,000 and $50,000 each. Most of the valuation was for the land—the appraisers found the buildings to be virtually worthless, although structurally sound.[33]

Crawford's motives in developing Larimer Square coincided with the goals of the city council, mayor, planning board, and the business establishment. Crawford wanted to stimulate commerce in the central business district.[34] In a column in the *Denver Post*, Crawford worried that Denver could become "a doughnut—with a concentration of low-income housing, crime, and decay at its center, surrounded by suburbs which might shun communitywide cooperation."[35] By merging historic preservation and economic development in Larimer Square, Crawford hoped to give people in the greater metropolitan area a reason to care about downtown.

Publicly, Crawford linked the profit motive and the civic service she performed in Larimer Square. In an interview in May 1965, a reporter for the *Denver Post* asked Crawford if her motivation in developing Larimer Square was preservation or profit. In her response, Crawford tied the two concepts together. She replied, "This is definitely a for-profit corporation . . . The people who are involved wanted a sound investment, of course. But our first motive is preservation. After all, this belongs to the people of Denver."[36] In an interview with the *Christian Science Monitor,* Crawford again linked the financial and cultural benefits of preservation on Larimer Street, saying, "We think Larimer Square will be here 100 years from now and paying both cultural and financial dividends to the city and to investors."[37]

Because Larimer Square was within Skyline's boundaries, Crawford needed support from the mayor and city council members to implement her development plans in opposition to DURA. To get their support, Crawford emphasized the benefits that preserving Larimer Square provided for the city. In 1965,

Crawford told the *Denver Post,* "Founders of Larimer Square are motivated to do something for the people of Denver to help them retain some of the frontier city's heritage."[38] Also in 1965, Crawford called a mayoral press conference to unveil Larimer Square. Mayor Tom Currigan supported Larimer Square, agreeing that preserving the block would benefit the city:

> Before the turn of the century, Denver was a gay and boisterous city, and its spirit was typified by Larimer Street. Recapturing that spirit of youthful Denver in this fashion and at the same time preserving some of our historic buildings is a marvelous concept. In addition, this plan, when it comes to fruition, will help stabilize the lower downtown area, improve the tax base, and become a source of pride for all Coloradoans.[39]

Other dignitaries, including Colorado Historical Society president Stephen H. Hart and DURA director Robert Cameron, also endorsed the project.

The plan did, however, have some opponents. One property owner on Larimer Square, Joseph Replin, refused to sell his property to the corporation.[40] The indigent men who inhabited Larimer Street also balked at both the Skyline Urban Renewal Project and Larimer Square, but their opposition was weak and disorganized. A few social workers, urban missionaries, and artists protested the displacement of the homeless. The folk singer U. Utah Phillips wrote the "Larimer Street Lament," the lyrics of which appeared in the IWW 1973 edition of *Songs for the Workers:*

> Your bulldozers rolling through my part of town,
> The iron ball swings and knocks it all down;
> You knocked down my flop-house, you knocked down my bars
> And you black-topped it over to park all your cars.
> (Chorus:) And where will I go? And where will I stay?
> When you've knocked down the skid road and hauled it away?
> I'll flag a fast rattler and ride it on down, boys,
> They're running the bums out of town.
> Old Maxie the tailor is closing his doors,
> There ain't nothing left in the second-hand stores;
> You knocked down my pawn shop and the big harbour light
> And the old Chinese Café that was open all night.
> (Chorus)
> You ran out the hookers who worked on the street
> And you built a big hall where the playboys can meet;
> My bookie joint closed when your cops pulled a raid,
> But you built a new hall for the stock market trade.

(Chorus)
These little storekeepers, they don't stand a chance,
With the big up-town bankers a-calling the dance,
With their suit-and-tie restaurants that's all owned by Greeks
And the counterfeit hippies and their plastic boutiques.
(Chorus)
Now I'm finding out there's just one kind of war:
It's the one going on 'tween the rich and the poor,
I don't know a lot about what you'd call class,
But the upper and middle can all kiss my ass.[41]

Even with a bard as eloquent as Phillips, the dissenters quieted down when missions opened between 20th and 23rd streets on Larimer, and the community moved seven blocks northeast.

Civic leaders and most Denver residents believed that the benefits of preserving Larimer Square outweighed such minor opposition. Larimer Square's importance to the city came from the block's connection to Denver's heritage.[42] In 1969 the Denver Landmark Preservation Commission established that emphasizing Denver's heritage was a crucial historic preservation goal. "Denver does, in our opinion, have a national responsibility for retaining some of the flavor of the old west, the excitement of the mining kings. The day of the trapper, the cowboy, the adventuring gold seekers is the day of America's growth and is the day in this country's history that is different from any other."[43] Denver's heritage gave the city a unique identity. Echoing Albuquerque's city planning director, Crawford wondered "what Denver will look like in twenty years. Will it have an individual style, or will it look like any city, USA?"[44] According to Crawford, Larimer Street symbolized Denver's frontier past.[45]

In order to link Larimer Square to Denver's "Wild West" heritage, Crawford emphasized that heritage over any other. Focusing on heritage sometimes at the expense of historical accuracy, she launched a media campaign extolling Larimer Street's importance to frontier Denver. Crawford initially wrote all of the promotional material for Larimer Square herself, and even after she hired an assistant, she still personally approved all advertisements and press releases.[46] According to these materials, Larimer Street was the most famous street in the West, a claim that is questionable at best. In a history of Larimer Street included in the first marketing packets, the author, most likely Crawford, wrote:

Denver has one of the most colorful, raucous, fascinating histories in America. Its rugged early days of gold and silver, boom or bust, rags to riches, will always capture the imagination of man. The antics of its now legendary city founders, the fur trappers, gold seekers, and adventurers, have inspired much of America's greatest folklore. Larimer Street in Denver was the most famous street in the West. The restaurants and hotels of its heyday were world-renowned. Stories of what happened when the greats and near-greats of the West strode up and down the streets filled volumes. And tales of what went on behind closed doors in the neighborhood shocked a nation.[47]

The language from this initial promotional packet appeared repeatedly in maps, fliers, economic feasibility reports, and other marketing proposals. For example, an undated marketing packet described Larimer Square as

a city block of 17 buildings on facing sides of Larimer Street—the most famous street in the west. Here are the sites and buildings where early Western outposts began and events stretching through the gold boom of the '50's and '60's, the silver boom of the '70's and '80's and the subsequent panic of the '90's wove the very fabric which makes Denver the city it is today.[48]

Similarly, a 1969 economic feasibility report compiled for Larimer Square Associates repeated the message:

In the last half of the 19th century Larimer Street in Denver was the most famous street in the West. The restaurants and hotels of its glamorous past were world-renowned. Stories of what happened when the greats and near-greats of the West strode down the streets filled volumes, and tales of what went on behind closed doors in the neighborhood shocked a nation.[49]

Finally, a tourist brochure for Larimer Square from between 1966 and 1968 read:

Denver has one of the most colorful, raucous, fascinating histories in America. Everyone who lives or visits here knows of the city's rugged early days of boom or bust, rags to riches in the eager search for gold and silver. At the heart of Denver's history, on the most famous street in the frontier west, stands Larimer Square . . . It's a fashionable place to browse and sip and dine in an atmosphere that faithfully reflects the elegance and gayety of Denver's heyday . . . The street is paved with stories of the nineteenth century.[50]

The Denver media quickly picked up the rhetoric, reinforcing the images of Denver's heritage. After Crawford unveiled the concept of Larimer Square

in 1965, both the *Denver Post* and the *Rocky Mountain News* praised her attempts to revitalize Denver's glory days. The *Denver Post* compared Crawford's
efforts on Larimer Street to Jacqueline Kennedy's restoration of the White
House.[51] The *Rocky Mountain News* exclaimed that the "joyous spirit that
characterized busy, brawling Larimer Street in frontier Denver a century ago
is about to be revived."[52] Crawford told the *Rocky Mountain News* that Larimer
Square Associates would recreate "the excitement that made Larimer Street
the talk of the nation in yesteryear."[53]

The media also emphasized the tourism potential for Larimer Square. *Rocky
Mountain News* reporter Robert L. Chase praised the preservation effort, saying, "Larimer Street was once the downtown Denver Main Street, and if this
group of individuals can restore some of that glory in shops, restaurants, cafés,
art and antique galleries . . . Larimer Square [will be] a showplace of the city,
rivaling those which attract throngs in Philadelphia, New York, San Francisco
and numerous other older cities in the country."[54] A special *Denver Post* tourism section claimed that Larimer Square provided something Denver had long
needed, "a good tourist attraction that reflects the city's colorful past, something
that would help keep visitors here a little longer." The *Post* told Denverites:

> You've probably experienced the difficulty in digging up sightseeing diversions
> for relatives and friends without hauling them off to the mountains. Give them
> a drive to Buffalo Bill's grave on Lookout Mountain, a quick look at Red Rocks
> and the inevitable drive to Central City. And while you could entertain them
> in the city there wasn't anything to show them that they couldn't see back home.
> Now we have Larimer Square as a first rate attraction good for an afternoon
> and/or evening's diversion.[55]

Conventions and Visitor's Bureau brochures reinforced the emphasis on
Larimer Square's "heritage" over its "history." A pamphlet from the early
1980s gushed,

> Here in Denver's most historic block, just walking down the street can become
> an adventure. The handsome Victorian buildings lend a sense of history to every
> shopping and dining experience. The colorful façades which line the block
> whisper tales of fancy ladies and derbied men; elegant dance halls and back
> room deals. Walking through a portico at dusk you may catch a faint rustle of
> stiff silks or a breath of some exotic perfume. Sit and have a drink on the very
> spot where Colorado's first legislators quenched parched throats with a few
> mid-session shots . . . Come. Touch the past in this neighborhood of legends.[56]

The early renovation of Larimer Square, 1968. Notice the recessed sidewalks. (Denver Public Library Western History Department)

Not surprisingly, no one in Denver was interested in preserving Larimer Street's heritage as skid row. Unlike the original Skid Road in Seattle, which reveled in its seediness, Larimer Street was completely "rehabilitated" to obliterate its derelict phase. An investors' package from 1965 admitted Larimer Street's blighted past but downplayed the presence of any bums or slums. Acknowledging that Larimer Street deteriorated as the business district moved south and east, the authors admitted only to having "marginal businesses" like plumbing contractors shops, a used commercial equipment dealer, and a saddle and harness store. They also stressed that the 1400 block of Larimer was situated "two long blocks" from the skid row district, and presented no problems of "human rehabilitation or policing."[57] In 1965, however, the 1400 block of Larimer Street had two bars, a mission, three low-rent hotels that also provided housing, and seven vacant, boarded buildings.[58] Whatever the facts of history, LSA wanted nothing to do with Larimer Street's skid-row identity.

Larimer Square Associates also distanced Larimer Street from skid row by prohibiting certain types of businesses. In 1966, when one of the tenants wanted to lease a building as a 3.2 beer "joint," Crawford insisted that the bar would not fit into the atmosphere of Larimer Square. "We are trying to preserve the cultural heritage of early Denver and we welcome property owners and tenants from this immediate neighborhood to join in this effort . . . However, we must consider the undesirable effect the proposed 3.2 beer and entertainment facility would have on the entire lower downtown area."[59] U. Utah Phillips, author of the "Larimer Street Lament," might say that a 3.2 beer bar would have done more to preserve the true cultural heritage of Larimer Street than the upscale boutiques Crawford hoped to attract.

Because the propaganda used by LSA and the media created an identity for Denver based on a glorified frontier heritage, the restoration of the buildings had to reinforce that identity. Similar to those in Old Town Albuquerque, the buildings on Larimer Street became symbols that reinforced Denver's heritage. In her initial announcement of Larimer Square, Crawford celebrated the buildings and the "real west" architecture they represented. When describing the architecture in an investors' package, LSA acknowledged that the buildings were vital to the creation of an "Early Denver" motif.[60] Even as founders of the historic district claimed that the buildings represented a previous era, Larimer Square in the 1970s looked considerably different than the city at the turn of the century. From the late nineteenth century until the advent of Larimer Square, buildings on Larimer Street looked like part of a big city. They sat right up next to the street. Fire escapes prominently adorned the fronts of buildings, and signs were big—the bigger the better. Sometimes store owners painted the signs on the side of the building, and other times they placed them on the roof. The invention of neon made signs on Larimer even more noticeable.[61]

By the time Larimer Square was finished ninety years later, however, the buildings had changed. They no longer abutted the street. Receding first floors and recessed entrances gave the block an atmosphere reminiscent of Old West covered sidewalks. The fire escapes disappeared, and some upper floors of buildings sported flower boxes. The historic district ordinance required business signs to be small, hanging directly over entrances as they do on small-town main streets. The ordinance prohibited signs on roofs, and there was no neon in sight.[62]

The streetscape of Larimer also changed with the creation of the historic district. In the 1880s, the block was unmistakably urban. Utility wires ran overhead, and large utility poles dotted the sidewalk. Streetcar tracks ran down the middle of the street, and carriages and later cars parked along the curb. After 1920, parking meters lined the street. The sidewalks were narrow, crowded, and bustling. The tall overhead streetlights brightly lit the block. The

Flower boxes on Larimer Square windows, 2000.

street was also dirty. Horse manure, coal dust, and the fluid results of chewing tobacco filled the streets and sidewalks. No vegetation grew at all along Larimer Street.[63]

The Larimer Square Historic District, however, transformed the block to remove the trappings of big city life. Antique-style lamps made to look like old-fashioned gaslights replaced the overhead streetlights. In a true bow to nostalgia, the city removed the parking meters (for a time), and visitors could park for free on the block. Banners like those welcoming visitors to small towns hung above the street, advertising whatever festival Larimer Square hosted. Large clocks, reminiscent of those on courthouse lawns, resided at either end of Larimer Square. Antique-looking wrought-iron signs marked the boundaries of the historic district. Larimer Street lost one full lane of traffic, as the city widened sidewalks to make room for benches along the block, allowing people to relax as they strolled. Finally, Larimer Square Associates lobbied the city to plant street trees, giving the block both the look and the feel of a park or town square. Larimer Square resembled a small western town rather than part of a high-tech city.

As Larimer Square took shape, Crawford and Larimer Square Associates found themselves in repeated conflict with the Denver Urban Renewal

Banners advertise Oktoberfest in Larimer Square, 2002.

Authority. Larimer Square fell completely within the boundaries of the Sky-line Urban Renewal District, which slated most of LSA's buildings for demo-lition.[64] Larimer Square was able to get a toehold in the area because LSA purchased the property in late 1964 and 1965, before voters approved Skyline's funding. DURA's 1967 plans designated the 1400 block of Larimer Street for "retail shops, restaurants, cultural and entertainment facilities, and profes-sional offices," but DURA and Larimer Square Associates had dramatically different ideas about the buildings housing those facilities.[65]

Although DURA director Robert Cameron claimed that the urban renewal authority was receptive to the idea of historic preservation, DURA and his-toric preservation advocates had a tense relationship at best. In 1967 the newly formed Denver Landmark Preservation Commission (DLPC) endorsed the Skyline Urban Renewal Project, but soon the cooperation between historic preservationists and urban renewal advocates deteriorated.[66] At a city council hearing concerning the Tabor Block at 16th and Larimer, conflict erupted. Although the building was arguably worthy of preservation as the last remain-ing structure built by Horace Tabor, the first building in Denver over two sto-ries, the first building in Denver to have an elevator, and an excellent example of nineteenth-century commercial architecture, DURA vice chairman Alex B. Holland said they found nothing significant about the building to merit saving

Benches and trees enhance the small-town atmosphere of Larimer Square, 2000.

it. The crux of the issue was money. Preservation of the building would have delayed federal urban renewal funds, so DURA destroyed the Tabor Block.[67]

DURA's burgeoning hostility toward historic preservation affected Larimer Square. DURA's directors scrutinized everything Larimer Square Associates did, and they frequently impeded building renovations.[68] In order to continue the building of Larimer Square unhindered, in 1971 Crawford and LSA approached the DLPC about designation as a historic district. Crawford was not initially an advocate of historic designation. She was wary of the design review process in the historic district, which made her fear that she could not rebuild the structures as she chose. She allied with the DLPC primarily for protection against DURA, but waited until she finished most of the major renovations before approaching the landmark commission so that it could not stop her plans.[69]

On 21 June 1971 the DLPC unanimously voted to designate Larimer Square Denver's first historic district.[70] Attorney Ben Klein, who leased 1421–1425 Larimer Street to Larimer Square Associates, raised the only objection during the proceedings. Klein opposed having his building included because it "is not original and has no architectural or historical significance."[71] The landmark commission responded that although individual buildings might not qualify as landmarks, "the group as a whole is significant in its value for preservation as part of the community."[72] Larimer Square became a designated National Register historic district two years later, on 7 May 1973.[73]

After that, the battles with DURA subsided but did not cease. DURA made Larimer Square Associates sign an Owner Participation Agreement, assuring that LSA would comply with all of the Skyline project's guidelines for remodeling old buildings. LSA also had to agree to follow the covenants of the Skyline Urban Renewal District.[74] Despite the Owner Participation Agreement and the designation of Larimer Square as a historic district, DURA continued to monitor the 1400 block of Larimer. Fifteen months after Larimer Square became a historic district, and thirteen months after the Owner Participation Agreement, maps of Skyline still showed Larimer Square as "proposed for acquisition."[75]

To ensure the economic success of Larimer Square, Crawford ran the venture like a shopping mall. To gain experience in mall management, Crawford volunteered to act as an apprentice to the manager of Denver's Belcaro Shopping Center for two months.[76] Larimer Square Associates patterned its leases after mall leases, retaining control over hours of business and aesthetics like displays, restaurant menus, and ads. Crawford demanded that her tenants be profitable and that they share the profits with Larimer Square Associates. A typical lease in the 1970s required the tenant to give LSA 6 percent of gross sales, or $1,750/month, whichever was more. The lease stipulated that a business must gross at least $400,000 annually after its third year, and for every year thereafter. If a tenant did not make enough money, Crawford had the option to terminate the lease.[77] Understandably, tenants who made money loved Crawford, while those who struggled frequently blamed her for their failure. In the words of Fred Thomas, the successful owner of Café Promenade, "She [Crawford] is a very good businesswoman, and you have to be a callous witch to be a very good businesswoman. I have great admiration and respect for her."[78] Small businesses that could not profit under LSA's stringent guidelines left Larimer Square and moved into lower downtown, starting a small retail community there, discussed in Chapter 5.[79]

Crawford was careful to pick the type of tenants that could prosper on Larimer Square. Initially, she courted high-end "quality" retailers that would enhance the project's "cultural, historical atmosphere," such as art galleries, book stores, flower shops, boutiques, tea and spice outlets, jewelry and watch shops, candy stores, and restaurants.[80] The first businesses to open on Larimer Square were the "gay '90's" themed restaurant Your Father's Mustache,

Gusterman Silversmiths, Blue Bottle Stained Glass, Poor Richard's Leather Goods, Le Chocolat Candy, and the Criterion Christmas Store.[81] Single-point businesses struggled on Larimer Square, however. Perhaps it was the strict lease terms, or perhaps it was competition from developments that opened in the late 1970s and 1980s, but many of the small businesses on Larimer Square folded or moved. By 1980, Crawford actively courted national chains. Between 1983 and 1986, Williams-Sonoma, Ann Taylor, Talbots, and Laura Ashley opened stores on Larimer Square, adding to the shopping mall atmosphere.[82]

Crawford understood that Larimer Square's profits had to come from both residents and tourists. To appeal to tourists, she advertised Larimer Square as one of the major attractions of the city. In market analyses and investors' packages, Crawford compiled figures on tourism and recreation in Denver and specified the amount of money each generated for the city. She estimated that half of Larimer Square's traffic came from tourists, and that 2.5 million people visited Larimer Square in 1968.[83] She also commissioned research to show that the recreation industry in Denver was on the rise and that Larimer Square competed for between 51.4 percent and 75.8 percent of every tourist dollar spent in Denver.[84]

If half of Larimer Square's visitors came from out of town, the other half lived in the metropolitan area. Because they arrived in cars, parking was a serious issue. Crawford analyzed traffic patterns and planned for parking spaces around Larimer Square. One market analysis showed that in 1963 and 1964 an average of 22,000 vehicles passed through the intersection of 15th and Larimer in a twenty-four-hour period, and that drivers had access to 3,000 parking spaces within easy walking distance of Larimer Square.[85] To add to that number, LSA purchased six lots on the 1400 block of Market Street, directly behind Larimer Square, and, ironically, tore down the historic buildings on those lots to make room for parking for potential customers.[86]

Although some small businesses struggled, Larimer Square was a hugely profitable real estate venture. In 1973 New York Life Insurance granted Larimer Square Associates a twenty-year long-term conventional loan for improvements and renovations, making Larimer Square the first historic district approved for such a conservative financing agreement in the business community.[87] Twenty years after Larimer Square Associates incorporated, property values had risen immensely. In 1985 the fifteen original properties that Crawford and LSA purchased, plus two others buildings purchased later, were now collectively worth $15 million. In 1965, buildings on Larimer Street leased for 11 cents per square foot. In 1985 that figure jumped to $20 per square foot.[88]

As Larimer Square thrived in the 1970s and 1980s, Dana Crawford faced criticism from the historic preservation community. Initially Crawford was nationally recognized as an authority on preservation, becoming involved with the National Trust for Historic Preservation in 1968, helping to found Historic Denver in 1970, and serving as a preservation consultant in other cities.[89] A 1982 controversy caused the media to brand her more of a developer than a preservationist, however. The controversy revolved around designating the individual buildings on Larimer Square as landmarks. Although the district had both Denver Landmark Preservation Commission and National Register designation, the individual buildings were by themselves not considered historic sites. In 1982, the city council passed a zoning ordinance allowing owners of historic properties in districts with height limitations to sell the air over their buildings to developers in other zoning locations. The council implemented these "transferable development rights" (TDRs) as an incentive for property owners to keep historic buildings rather than tear them down and build high-rises. Because the buildings in Larimer Square were part of a historic district and not individual landmarks, they were not eligible for TDRs. Crawford and Larimer Square Associates applied to the DLPC for individual designation of the buildings. Eventually ten of the buildings on the block qualified for landmark designation, but the media saw the whole application process as a greedy maneuver.[90]

The controversy over TDRs coincided with Crawford's announcement of a new planned development, New Larimer Square, across 14th Street from Larimer Square. New Larimer Square proposed a twenty-two–story residential building, a hotel, and ground-level retail shops. None of the development included historic buildings, and the high-rise apartments would have violated the historic district's height restrictions that Crawford herself struggled to establish. Worse yet, the high rise would have blocked Larimer Square's mountain views, something fiercely guarded by most Denver residents. Compounding these sins in the public's opinion, Crawford and LSA applied for $5 million in urban renewal funds to implement the $56 million project. Both daily newspapers, the DLPC, and historic preservationists throughout the city condemned the plan as a ploy to use public funds for private gain. Mayor Federico Peña opposed it, and Crawford did not even have the support of many of her LSA partners. Eventually she dropped the plan.[91]

Realizing that they had taken Larimer Square as far as they could, Crawford and Larimer Square Associates offered the property for sale in 1986. LSA initially asked $15 million, but it ultimately sold to the Hahn Company, a real estate development company from San Diego, for $14.5 million, including 25,000 square feet of TDRs. The Hahn Company also operated the nearby Tivoli complex, an 1881 brewery converted into shops and entertainment facilities.[92] Larimer Square sold again in 1993, and this time a local group headed by developer Jeffrey Hermanson bought the property. In 1993 the Hahn Company asked between $9 million and $10 million for Larimer Square, taking a considerable loss from what it paid Larimer Square Associates.[93]

After the sale of Larimer Square, Crawford became involved with real estate development in the soon-to-be historic district of LoDo, in lower downtown Denver, and in the Central Platte Valley, just north of LoDo. In 1983 the *Denver Post*'s *Empire Magazine* deemed Crawford the most powerful woman in Denver, and her control over property on Larimer Street and in lower downtown made her one of the most influential developers in the Rocky Mountain region. The success of Larimer Square convinced the city planning department to incorporate historic preservation into downtown development, which led ultimately to the creation of the Lower Downtown Historic District, discussed in Chapter 5. Crawford's reputation as a historic preservationist did not fare so well, however. Although Colorado Preservation Inc. sponsors the annual "Dana Crawford Awards" for preservation projects, Crawford's form of preservation was criticized by preservation purists who felt that her aggressive for-profit business strategies weakened the civic-minded nobility of the preservation cause.[94]

Despite criticism, Crawford changed the trajectory of city planning in Denver and created a civic identity that resonated with residents and tourists. With the help of the Denver Landmark Preservation Commission, Mayor Tom Currigan, the city council, the Denver media, and her partners at Larimer Square Associates, Crawford emphasized Denver's Wild West heritage in Larimer Square, which provided Denverites with a vision of a great future based on an exciting, adventure-filled past. During the 1980s, Larimer Square became the focal point of the city. It was consistently one of the top tourist attractions in the region through the 1990s, frequently surpassing the Denver Mint and Buffalo Bill's Grave.[95] In the 1990s, when the Colorado Avalanche won the Stanley Cup and the Denver Broncos won two consecutive Super Bowls, people from across the state congregated in Larimer Square. The district attracted visitors and suburban residents because it purported to take people back to another time, no matter how invented that heritage was. Patrons continue to visit Larimer Square because they can shop, dine, and socialize in the very buildings that made Larimer Street "the most famous street in the West."

3

OF BUMS AND BUSINESSMEN:

SEATTLE'S PIONEER SQUARE

It is late summer 2000 in Seattle. In Pioneer Square, the city's first historic district, a police officer approaches a group of grizzled men sitting on a bench, sipping something from a brown paper bag. The officer writes them a citation for public drinking, and the group moves on. Nearby, a young couple watches the scene from a sidewalk café. The man wears a goatee, sport shirt, and Dockers; the woman is in a fashionable pantsuit. The couple bemusedly observes the policeman write the bums a ticket for drinking wine as they sip a glass of merlot and discuss the dot-com industry, never noticing the irony of the situation. The actors in this scene represent the diversity of constituencies who jockeyed for power in the Pioneer Square Historic District. In preserving Pioneer Square, Seattle's city council, planning commission, social service advocates, and prodevelopment coalitions all struggled to define a civic identity for Seattle, with mixed success.

Pioneer Square was the birthplace of the city of Seattle. The first Euro-American settlers arrived in the marshy tidal basin in 1852 and platted the fledgling town on the only flat spot along the coast, up against a series of steep timber-covered hills. Despite a location prone to flooding, geographic isolation, and fierce competition from Tacoma to the south, Seattle managed to prosper. The determination of Seattle's founders to build a great city against all odds gave birth to a perception of civic stubbornness known as the "Seattle Spirit."[1] Pioneer Henry Yesler embodied the Seattle Spirit when he built a sawmill to make the less-than-perfect location profitable. The road between Yesler's mill on the waterfront and the trees on top of the hill became known as the "Skid Road" because lumberjacks skidded the cut timbers down a path to the mill. The building boom in San Francisco during the 1850s created a demand for lumber, and Yesler's mill prospered, shipping Seattle trees to California gold towns.

The mill also divided the city in two, separating the land claims of pioneers A. A. Denny and Doc Maynard. Both Denny and Maynard designed street grids for the city, with Denny's running along the compass points and Maynard's running along the shore. The two men filed their plats simultaneously, so the city adopted both. The competing street grids created a triangular piece of land where First Avenue intersected Skid Road, officially named Yesler Way. Although geometrically incorrect, the triangle became known as Pioneer Square.[2] The area quickly became the center of commerce for the young city.

Seattle's growth experienced a major setback on 6 June 1889, when an overturned pot of glue started the catastrophic Seattle fire. The wooden town burned quickly, and the fire destroyed twenty-five blocks and more than 120 acres of the business district. Seattle's civic leaders used the disaster as an opportunity to make the city even stronger, immediately passing an ordinance requiring the central business district rebuilt in brick. Architect Elmer Fisher designed most of the new buildings, and within two years of the fire Seattle-ites had reestablished their town. The municipal government also determined to solve the flooding problem caused by the city's location in the tidal basin. Over the next ten years, the city backfilled low-lying areas and terraced the streets up the hill, raising the street level and creating a subterranean floor to most buildings, called the "underground."

Seattle had barely finished rebuilding when the Klondike gold rush began in 1897. Pioneer Square boomed as it became the "jumping-off" point for fortune seekers heading into the northern wilderness of Alaska. An overwhelm-

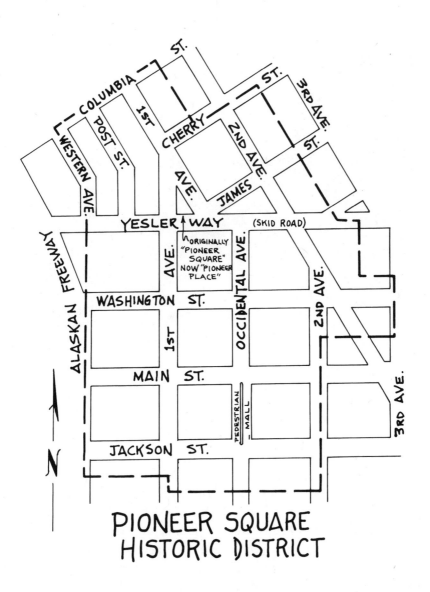

PIONEER SQUARE
HISTORIC DISTRICT

Triangular Pioneer Square at the intersection of First Avenue, James Street, and Yesler Way, c. 1900. (Manuscripts, Special Collections, University Archives, University of Washington Library, neg. no. UW8571)

ingly male contingent of miners, merchants, sailors, and adventurers got their stake in Pioneer Square, many returning to the area when their luck did not pan out "up north." Pioneer Square's boom did not last long into the twentieth century, however. To make more land available for settlement, the city began a comprehensive grading of the hills north of the district, particularly Denny Hill. By 1910 the flattened Denny Hill area attracted development north of the original downtown, and the central business district moved. Pioneer Square fell upon hard times and became a haven for unemployed miners, longshoremen, and lumbermen waiting for the next boom.[3]

During the Great Depression, the single men inhabiting Pioneer Square formed a community of their own. These men tended to be unemployed, single, and alcoholic, prompting a local pastor to observe, "Yesler Way was once a skid road down which logs were pushed to Henry Yesler's sawmill on the waterfront. Today it is a skid road down which human souls go sliding to hell."[4] The concentration of indigents drew missions, soup kitchens, and city social services to Pioneer Square to help the bums. As the old skid road became as-

Pioneer Square's warehouses, 1931. (Manuscripts, Special Collections,
University Archives, University of Washington Library, neg. no. ACurtis 58220)

sociated with men down on their luck, it gave rise to the term *skid row* to
describe blighted sections of cities nationwide.[5]

Pioneer Square's social deterioration mirrored its physical decline. A 1948
earthquake damaged many of the district's structures, prompting the planning department to tighten building codes. The more stringent codes condemned many buildings that survived the quake, and those that passed the
stricter inspections had to have the ornamentation removed and keep the upper
stories vacant because of earthquake danger. The deteriorating physical condition exacerbated the ailing social conditions, and Pioneer Square languished
in disuse and disarray for the next twenty years.[6]

After 1940, Seattle's economy boomed again, although Pioneer Square
remained insulated from the prosperity. The Boeing Corporation brought a
surge of people and capital to Seattle during and after World War II. Founded
in 1916 by William Boeing, the company became the bedrock of Seattle's
economy. For example, the value of all goods manufactured in Seattle in 1939

Skid Road patrons congregating under the pergola in Pioneer Square, 1960. (Seattle Municipal Archives)

totaled $70 million, but five years later, in 1944, Boeing alone manufactured $560 million worth of merchandise. Between 1952 and 1965 Boeing developed the 707, 727, 737, and the immense 747, allowing the corporation to stand alone in the field of commercial passenger aircraft.[7]

Boeing's prosperity brought a rush of aerospace workers to the Pacific Northwest. The new residents came predominantly from the Midwest and Northeast, and most worked for Boeing or supporting industries. In 1947 Boeing employed one out of every five King County manufacturing workers; ten years later, the corporation employed one out of every two.[8] The newcomers moved into the suburbs ringing Seattle's city limits. Boeing's locations encouraged suburbanization. Because the corporation needed plenty of space around its facilities for test runways, Boeing spread its manufacturing plants around the metropolitan area.[9]

Suburbanization changed the geographic, demographic, and commercial patterns of Seattle. Residential neighborhoods sprawled farther and farther away from downtown.[10] Professionals coming to work for Boeing had more education and higher income than the native middle class, composed mainly of skilled tradesmen and middle managers who still lived within the city lim-its.[11] Suburban residents lived in larger, more valuable homes, had more chil-dren, earned higher incomes, and owned their own cars.[12] Commercial services moved to the suburbs, too. In 1946, the Bellevue Square Shopping Center opened east of the central business district with a branch of Frederick and Nelson, a prominent downtown department store. Northgate, one of the nation's first suburban malls, opened in 1950 with a branch of the downtown store Bon Marché. Northgate also offered a theater, hospital, bank, and dry cleaners, competing with the central business district for more than just re-tail dollars.[13] The increasing number of suburban retail centers challenged the commercial supremacy of Seattle's central business district. While down-town gross sales rose 5 percent between 1948 and 1954, sales in the rest of the metropolitan area increased over 50 percent. In addition, premium down-town retail sites in 1956 commanded only half the market price of an equiva-lent site thirty years earlier, whereas outlying commercial land values increased to ten times their former value.[14] Downtown Seattle's appearance changed, too, as modern and International-style skyscrapers, especially the Norton Building, the Washington Building, and the Seattle Main Public Library, in-corporated standardized building styles, materials, and glass exteriors.[15] Ac-cording to historian Roger Sale, changes in the metropolitan area left Seattle residents with "no sense of street or meeting place, no image or school worth remembering, no sense of Seattle as a city."[16]

In order to revitalize downtown, city planners and business owners turned to urban renewal strategies. During the late 1950s, business leaders formed the Central Association of Seattle, entering into an informal partnership with the city planning department to attract private investment and federal urban renewal funds.[17] The Seattle Center, site of the 1962 World's Fair and home of the Space Needle, represented the most prominent legacy of Seattle's urban renewal plans. Architects and planners for the World's Fair, also known as the Century 21 Exposition, sought to compete with suburban malls and en-tertainment complexes.[18] City planners cleared old homes in the blighted Warren neighborhood, just north of downtown, to create the project. They closed the streets to automobile traffic and built a large suburban-style cul-tural complex, complete with theaters, green spaces, and pedestrian malls.

Century 21 provided a forward-looking vision for Seattle. The planners and business leaders who conceptualized the Seattle Center sought to create a futuristic identity for the city, positioning it as the urban blueprint for the twenty-first century. The fair was a financial success and brought visitors to the region, but they rarely ventured beyond Century 21's complex. Rather than make the central business district competitive with the suburbs, the Century 21 Exposition created a suburban-style enclave within the city and failed to define an accepted civic identity (with identity being a socially constructed, mutually agreed-upon concept). Century 21 provided a possible vision for Seattle's future, but it never gained broad support from Seattle residents as an agreed-upon identity.[19]

Although Century 21's traffic did not spill over to the central business district, the number of visitors encouraged the Central Association of Seattle and the city's planning commission to sponsor an urban renewal plan for downtown. Washington's state legislature passed an urban renewal law in 1957 that gave the city the power of eminent domain. With this law and the financial success of Century 21 in mind, members of the city council and the Central Association of Seattle commissioned the Monson Plan in 1963.[20] Officially titled *Comprehensive Plan for Central Business District Seattle*, written by Donald Monson, the plan redesigned downtown in a suburban image.[21] The Monson Plan patterned the entire downtown after a shopping mall. The central business district would house the retail core, and parking garages and an access road would replace blighted fringe areas like Pioneer Square and the Pike Place Market.[22]

The plan spared triangular Pioneer Square from demolition, however. Now called Pioneer Place, the public space had been the focus of preservation efforts by area business leaders since the mid-1950s. In 1954 the Pioneer Businessmen's Association, composed of merchants near Pioneer Square, along with the Seattle Chapter of the American Institute of Architects and the Seattle Junior Chamber of Commerce, sponsored a design competition to preserve Pioneer Place. The groups hoped that a redesigned Pioneer Place would stimulate tourist activity. University of Washington architecture professor Victor Steinbrueck won the design competition with a plan for a commemorative park, a museum at the corner of First Avenue and Cherry Street, a walking bridge, and sunken landscaping.[23] The plan never received funding from the city, however, but the Monson Plan incorporated similar provisions to restore Pioneer Place.[24]

The Central Association of Seattle supported the effort to restore Pioneer Place as long as it brought retail dollars into downtown. The executive vice president of the Central Association claimed, "We think the economic potential is there [to restore Pioneer Place] . . . We need more tourist attractions in Seattle."[25] In 1966 a group of private investors affiliated with the Central Association commissioned architect John Graham Jr., designer of Northgate Shopping Center, to develop a retail plan for Pioneer Square. Graham's design advocated tearing down most of the buildings south of Yesler Way and creating multiple mixed-use "superblocks" with high-rise office buildings, parking garages, pedestrian plazas, and retail shops.[26] The Graham Plan recommended a "compact yet varied" Old Town area around Pioneer Place and suggested that some of the unique ornamentation be taken off of old buildings before demolition and then put in a museum as a way to preserve the area's architectural heritage.[27]

While the planning department and the Central Association commissioned plans to "renew" Pioneer Square, private individuals quietly bought and restored a few of the old buildings in the least desirable part of the district, far south of Yesler Way. In 1962 architect Ralph Anderson paid $30,000 for the three-story Jackson Building on the corner of First Avenue and Jackson Street. Anderson had wanted to buy a building since 1959 but found city building codes and earthquake guidelines too restrictive to make restoration profitable. After purchasing the Jackson Building, he remodeled it piecemeal to avoid complying with the "unreasonable" engineering guidelines. Once he refurbished the building, Anderson rented the first floor to an interior decorator, created office space on the second floor, and made the third floor into an apartment.[28]

In 1965 Anderson's friend and gallery owner Richard White took a long-term lease on the nearby Liberty Building, remodeled it, and opened an art gallery. The following year Anderson bought the adjacent four-story Union Trust Building for $75,000 and began renovations. In December of 1968 White bought the four-story Globe Building in the same block. By 1969 White and Anderson together controlled most of the buildings in the block bordered by South Jackson Street, South First Avenue, South Main Street, and Occidental Avenue. White, Anderson, and other property owners worked to beautify the district, planting street trees in the medians because the "underground" floors of buildings kept them from planting along the sidewalks.[29]

As Anderson and White rehabilitated the district, the area became a haven for other artists, architects, interior designers, and rug merchants who knew the developers and liked the aesthetics of the old buildings. Young professionals, who enjoyed the proximity to downtown, also moved in. The low rents in Pioneer Square allowed businesses to afford larger spaces than in the

Street trees along Occidental Avenue, 2002. (Rebekah Harvey)

central business district. Additionally, the old buildings provided artists with lofts where they could work and live close to the galleries that would show their art.[30]

Journalist Bill Speidel also contributed to the revitalization of Pioneer Square with the establishment of Underground Seattle. Speidel, who worked in Pioneer Square and wrote a history of early Seattle, became fascinated with the area under Seattle's streets. When the city terraced the streets at the turn of the twentieth century to reduce flooding, the resulting raised roads caused the first floors of older buildings to be buried. The city planning department condemned the "underground" in the 1910s because it was infested with rats. Speidel petitioned the city to open the old caverns so he could give historic tours of the underground, but the city refused because of liability issues. After several failed attempts to secure insurance coverage, Speidel finally got Lloyd's of London to insure the endeavor, and he began Underground Seattle in 1965. The tours wove through the submerged portions of the buildings, emphasizing Seattle's seamy past filled with gamblers, madams, murders, corruption, and poor sanitation. Speidel's tours brought tourists into Pioneer Square and increased interest in the district among residents, many of whom had moved to Seattle in the previous two decades.[31]

Bill Speidel's Underground Seattle tours start in the Pioneer Building on Pioneer Square. (Rebekah Harvey)

Investments by Anderson, White, and Speidel prompted more development in the district during the 1960s. By 1975, $10 million had gone into restoring Pioneer Square, $8 million of which came from private investors.[32] Property values increased, sometimes by as much as five times: before Richard White opened his gallery in the Liberty Building, space rented for eighty cents per square foot. After White refurbished the building, space rented for $4 per square foot.[33] The renaissance caused demographic changes in the neighborhood. Between 1967 and 1969, two-thirds of the residents of Skid Road moved out of the flophouses as businesspeople bought the buildings to renovate them for office space, and commercial enterprises occupied what had once been low-income housing.[34]

As private investment in Pioneer Square increased, property owners lobbied the mayor and city council members to implement a zoning ordinance to protect the buildings from demolition and neglect. Attempts to obtain city zoning protection began in 1962, after developers tore down the historic Hotel Seattle, in the heart of Pioneer Square, to build a parking garage. Locals called the resulting structure the "Sinking Ship" garage because its triangular shape and sunken appearance resembled the bow of an ocean liner. The Sinking Ship encapsulated fears that Pioneer Square would become a gigantic parking lot for downtown and motivated preservationists to take action.[35] Throughout the 1960s, groups like Allied Arts of Seattle and the Seattle Chapter of the American Institute of Architects joined Anderson, Speidel, and other individuals to lobby for a municipal historic preservation law. In 1969 preservationists successfully nominated Pioneer Square to the National Register of Historic Places.[36]

Until 1967, however, requests for city preservation fell on deaf ears. Mayor J. D. "Dorm" Braman and most city council members generally supported urban renewal projects over historic preservation.[37] Because urban renewal plans brought federal funding, Braman urged the speedy implementation of the 1966 Graham Plan. Indeed, Braman alienated members of the planning commission when he applied for Housing and Urban Development funding without the prior approval of the planning department.[38] In 1967 Braman's office also applied for money from the federal Model Cities Program, a program designed to improve conditions of urban life by integrating social, economic, and physical reforms.[39] To rein in Braman's eagerness, the planning commission drafted a historic preservation ordinance for Pioneer Square in 1967, outlining design guidelines and stipulating a review process. Despite multiple revisions and hearings between 1967 and 1969, the ordinance failed to pass.[40]

Support for Pioneer Square's preservation widened after the composition of Seattle's city council shifted. Prior to 1967 the council consisted of older, conservative men allied with downtown business interests. In 1967, however, a group called Choose an Effective City Council (CHECC) emerged as a force in Seattle politics. CHECC represented part of a national movement toward civic activism. Most of the founding CHECC members had attended college in the East and returned to Seattle invigorated by the reform impulses of the Kennedy and Johnson administrations.[41] CHECC activists lived in old neighborhoods near downtown and wanted to make Seattle's municipal government more responsive to issues such as community revitalization and historic preservation. In the 1967 election, three CHECC-supported candidates, Phyllis Lamphere, Tim Hill, and Sam Smith, won city council seats. In 1969 CHECC successfully backed mayoral candidate Wes Uhlman, who advocated historic preservation in Pioneer Square.[42]

The newly elected city council members, already predisposed to historic preservation, wanted to duplicate the success of historic preservation projects in other cities. In 1970 Denver's Larimer Square and San Francisco's historic preservation projects provided successful examples of districts that brought development to blighted areas. That spring, council members traveled to San Francisco and toured Ghirardelli Square, Jackson Square, and the Cannery, hearing economic projections from San Francisco planners. San Francisco's optimistic financial outlook convinced council members who might not have supported historic preservation for its aesthetic merits to consider preservation as a way to attract investment and economic development.[43]

The Central Association of Seattle vehemently opposed a preservation law, however, even though few of the association's members had businesses in Pioneer Square. During April 1970 the newspapers widely reported the dispute between the city council and the Central Association. The latter opposed the size of the district, the design review process, and the power of the historic preservation ordinance to deny demolition permits.[44] Association members tried to block the ordinance by arguing that it was tantamount to a taking of property. The Central Association also claimed that a poll of Pioneer Square property owners showed that 80 percent did not support historic preservation, but members of the Pioneer Square Association and city council discounted the results because the survey was skewed to elicit a negative response.[45]

Two significant Pioneer Square property owners joined the Central Association in opposition to the Pioneer Square Historic District. Sam Israel and Jack Buttnick, who between them owned almost twenty buildings, resented the city's intrusion into their business. Israel derogatorily called the preservationists "do-gooders" and claimed that the buildings "are just junk" and that anyone trying to restore them was "just plain crazy."[46]

Despite the opposition, the city council unanimously passed the Pioneer Square Historic Preservation Ordinance on 27 April 1970.[47] The boundaries of the district stretched far beyond triangular Pioneer Place; it ran from Columbia Street on the north to a line one-half block south of Jackson Street on the south, and from Western Avenue on the West to a jagged line between First and Second Avenues and between Second Avenue and Occidental Avenue on the east.[48] The council enlarged the district in 1973, during construction of the Kingdome, to give the district a buffer between its borders and the stadium.[49]

The combination of city legislation, federal funding, and private initiative meant that multiple agencies had jurisdiction over the administration of Pioneer Square. The city planning department formed the Pioneer Square Historic Preservation Board, which oversaw the design review process. When building began on the King County Stadium (Kingdome) south of Pioneer Square, the planning commission, known after 1970 as the Department of Community Development (DCD), also established the Pioneer Square Special Review Board to mitigate the stadium's impact on the historic district.[50] Because the federal Model Cities Program required citizen participation, the city chartered the Historic Seattle Preservation and Development Authority to provide a forum for residential involvement.[51] The Model Cities Program also sanctioned the formation of the Skid Road Community Council, which enhanced social services for the area's indigents, and the Skid Road Labor Cooperative, which employed street people to work on Model Cities improvements.[52] The Pioneer Square Association represented the private preservationists involved in Pioneer Square, including business and property owners.[53]

Although the struggle to preserve Pioneer Square had populist overtones, the preservation ordinance transferred power from one elite coalition to another.[54] The groups supporting historic preservation, including Allied Arts of Seattle, the Seattle Chapter of the American Institute of Architects, the Junior League, and the Pacific Society of Landscape Architects, claimed to be saving Pioneer Square for "the people" rather than "the Interests."[55] The historic preservation ordinance did not give power to "the people," however, but rather transferred power from the business elite to the cultural elite. Artists and architects had already implemented most of the redevelopment in Pioneer Square. Design review provisions gave architects increased influence over planning and design, weakening the influence of downtown business leaders. Although the elite groups vying for power in Pioneer Square disagreed on exactly how to develop the district, they acknowledged that the area needed renovation to attract capital and development.[56]

To attract investors and consumers, the groups administering Pioneer Square advertised the district as an important part of Seattle's heritage.[57] Because Pioneer Square was part of the original town site, the civic identity it symbolized resonated with Seattle residents more than the futuristic vision of Century 21. Politicians and civic leaders used propaganda to link Pioneer Square with the booster idealism of the "Seattle Spirit." When Seattle experienced a recession in the early 1970s, Mayor Wes Uhlman claimed,

> it is not entirely coincidental that the renaissance of Pioneer Square began just about the time the bottom dropped out of the local economy in 1969 and 1970. The rich history of Pioneer Square provided something substantive to cling to during those troubled times. When the very survival of the city seemed

to be at stake, the identity of Seattle represented by those old bricks and stones seemed to give new hope and a focus of action as a united community.[58]

City Councilman Michael Hildt equated Pioneer Square's preservation with the "Seattle Spirit" that allowed the city to become the premier city of the Northwest.[59] Seattle historian Walt Crowley claimed that the "citizen pioneers" who led the preservation effort saw in the old buildings "Seattle's true soul, and fought hard to save it."[60] Wes Uhlman also equated Pioneer Square with Seattle's soul, claiming that the city chose to preserve the district "not only because it was economically smarter, but because there was a psychological and spiritual benefit to it as well."[61]

Members of the cultural elite, especially prominent architects, agreed that Pioneer Square represented an important part of Seattle's identity. Victor Steinbrueck argued that the buildings in the district were symbols for the important historical events that took place in them.[62] Ralph Anderson believed that the buildings themselves forged Seattle's identity. Anderson, credited with creating a Northwestern regional style of architecture, understandably believed that Pioneer Square's architecture made the district unique. Anderson claimed, "Maybe I'm provincial, but I like a region to have a definite character, an identity. I would like to keep that identity and have it reflected in architecture rather than universalize it so that you might be in St. Louis or Tallahassee."[63]

Because Pioneer Square was the city's birthplace, members of city council and the Department of Community Development sought to make physical improvements that emphasized, and in some cases recreated, the district's heritage as the cradle of the Seattle Spirit.[64] The DCD adopted a master plan in 1974, calling for the city to allocate $300,000 per year for improvements between 1972 and 1978.[65] The money provided maintenance and upgrades to sidewalks, better store access, benches, street trees, and historic period street lamps.[66] For a few years during the 1970s, the city's police department even had its daytime beat cops wear 1910-style uniforms to fit into the heritage of the district.[67] To oversee the plan's implementation, the DCD hired a full-time district manager.[68] As a reaction to uncooperative property owners like Sam Israel and Jack Buttnick, the city council passed a "Minimum Maintenance Ordinance" in 1974, requiring owners of historic buildings to keep the buildings in good repair. If an owner could not maintain the building, the city set aside funds to make repairs for the owner in return for a lien against the property.[69]

Antique-looking lamps, benches, and flower baskets in Pioneer Square, 2002. (Rebekah Harvey)

The purpose of the emphasis on Seattle's heritage was to attract customers, both tourists and locals. Although the master plan purported "to promote the district, and its historic setting, as a unique community embodying a mix of businesses, people, services, housing, economic, and social groups," the DCD also intended Pioneer Square to compete with Northgate and Southcenter malls.[70] The master plan calculated the distance consumers had to walk between stores, allocated shopping "activity zones," and compared rents for retail businesses and restaurants with manufacturing and wholesale uses. The plan retained residential uses but promoted a mix of low, middle, and upper-income housing to give the area a broader retail "clientele."[71]

Emphasizing retail development, a 1972 article in the *Seattle Post-Intelligencer* claimed that "Seattle's newest shopping center doesn't have controlled temperature or a covered mall. It does have an abundance of one-of-a-kind, quality stores and restaurants, however, and that's why the Pioneer Square area is fast becoming a favorite destination for local shoppers."[72] When an ordinance expanded the boundaries of Pioneer Square in 1973, one of its purposes was to "protect and enhance the City's attraction to tourists and visitors."[73]

The efforts to highlight and recreate Seattle's heritage in Pioneer Square faced obstacles, however, because the district celebrated *two* heritages. The National Register of Historic Places reflected both traditions, listing its official name as the "Pioneer Square/Skid Road Historic District." The tradition created by city council and the planning commission, codified in the 1974 master plan, emphasized the glorious Pioneer Square heritage while ignoring the notorious Skid Road history. The Pioneer Square heritage celebrated the Seattle Spirit and highlighted Victorian architectural symbols and the dramatic story of Seattle's founding.

In contrast, some reformers, activists, and long-time residents fought to preserve Pioneer Square's infamous tradition as Skid Road. Locals honored the seedy image of Pioneer Square as a symbol of Seattle's egalitarian past.[74] Bill Speidel's Underground Seattle tours reinforced the notorious heritage by glamorizing the shady characters who populated Skid Road. Although most cities had a "skid row," Pioneer Square was the *original* Skid Road, representative of the working-class lumberjacks, longshoremen, and miners who made Seattle's past colorful.[75] By romanticizing the skid roaders, activists argued that the indigents in Pioneer Square were a vital and constant part of Seattle's heritage.[76]

The two competing heritages confused efforts to establish an agreed-upon identity. Most plans for the historic district reflected this civic schizophrenia. The zoning ordinance preserved Seattle's "historic heritage" and "attracted visitors to the City" while also safeguarding the rights of the derelicts to stay in the district.[77] Indeed, city policy dictated that "bums and businessmen" could coexist.[78]

Early preservationists like Anderson, White, and Speidel accepted and even promoted the district's Skid Road identity, since they never intended to dislocate the bums. According to Anderson, the early preservationists felt the bums had a right to be there because they were part of the district's heritage. Anderson said that his goal in renovating buildings was to save the architecture, not to turn the area into a tourist trap.[79] Fellow preservationist Richard White felt the bums provided the district with a benefit. "I think the men just standing around here at night may deter vandals."[80] Architect Victor Steinbrueck claimed that "human renewal" in the district should come before rehabilitation of the buildings, and that preservation should also provide services for the Skid Road residents.[81] City Councilman Bruce Chapman reiterated that it was city policy to provide social services for the skid roaders, not to just relocate them. He stated that the panhandlers were harmless and if the tourists did not like them, they should go elsewhere.[82] In his 1981 tourist guide to the district, historian Walt Crowley begins with a section entitled "A Word about the Locals":

> Pioneer Square is not a walled-off amusement park or an antiseptic shopping mall. It is a living neighborhood in the heart of Seattle's downtown, and as such it is home, workplace, market, and social center for many different types and classes of people. Some are elderly, poor, or just down on their luck . . . Visitors should understand this and use the same common sense they would use exploring any unfamiliar territory.[83]

Bill Speidel had a realistic strategy for tolerating the bums. Speidel always kept quarters in his pocket for the panhandlers. "They ask for twenty-five cents for coffee and I tell them my quarters are only for beer and wine . . . 'Don't give me any of that coffee crap,' I tell them."[84]

In the years immediately following the creation of the historic district, the city council, Pioneer Square Association, property owners, and developers deemphasized the Skid Road past and focused on promoting the "Seattle Spirit." From approximately 1965 to 1978, the emphasis on the booster heritage, coupled with capital improvements and building renovations, created a nascent heritage tourism attraction. When the Conventions and Visitor's Bureau advertised Pioneer Square's revitalized image, the types of businesses in the area shifted, reflecting an expectation of impending tourist crowds.[85] For example, in 1965 the district contained taverns, low-cost "lodgings," second-hand stores, heavy equipment manufacturers, liquor stores, pawnbrokers, and missions.[86] In 1969, even before historic designation, the upscale restaurant Brasserie Pittsbourg heralded the transition to a new visitor-oriented economy when it moved into the Pioneer Building on Pioneer Place Park.[87] By 1970 book stores, antiques shops, a men's furnishings store, and a gasthaus-style restaurant coexisted with the Salvation Army store, barbershops, and flophouses in the district.[88]

Property values experienced a corresponding boost in Pioneer Square between 1970 and 1974, increasing two and a half times, faster than anywhere else in the metropolitan area.[89] Land closer to the central business district, specifically north of Yesler Way along First Avenue, experienced the greatest appreciation, but renovated buildings elsewhere in the district also gained value. In 1970 Ralph Anderson and some partners purchased the Grand Central Building, a former low-income hotel, and renovated it into a retail arcade. Rental rates in that building rose from five cents per square foot before redevelopment to $7 per square foot afterwards.[90]

Despite the dramatic increase in property values, Pioneer Square still offered economically efficient office space for young professionals just starting in business. Even the most elaborately renovated office facility in an old building cost about half of new construction, making the area appealing to businesses without huge profit margins—art galleries, antique dealers, and young lawyers, architects, and accountants. By the early 1980s the movement of young professionals into Pioneer Square coincided with the national movement of young professionals into downtown residences, so office space in Pioneer Square offered the yuppies a workplace close to their home.[91]

The gentrification of Pioneer Square initially caused displacement of the skid roaders. Room rents began to rise even before the historic district designation. In eighteen months between 1968 and 1969, the price of a room went from $7 a week to over $9 a week.[92] The number of residential properties declined as well. Between 1965 and 1972, sixty-one hotels and apartments closed or were demolished. The number of residential units dropped from 3,478 in 1960 to only 1,053 in 1973.[93] The area's resident population fell from

The Grand Central retail arcade, 2002. (Rebekah Harvey)

2,286 in 1960 to 921 in 1970.[94] A reporter for the *Los Angeles Times* lamented the disappearance of the bums, noting, "Where phalanxes of derelicts originally wove in boozy abandon, Mercer Island matrons now contemplate original art in a gallery that finished sealing its windows only a week before. Where did the bums go?"[95]

The bums did not go far. Reflecting a fondness for the skid roaders' role in Pioneer Square's heritage, mission owners, social welfare workers, and nostalgic residents worried that Seattleites would forget the indigents if they left their home turf in Pioneer Square.[96] Pioneer Square was not just *any* skid row—it was the *original* Skid Road, and therefore the bums played an integral role in the area's heritage. In contrast to Denver's Larimer Square, Seattle's city agencies stepped up their efforts to help the transients as the area gentrified. Because official city policy stated that "bums and businessmen" could coexist, the city government facilitated social services in the district whenever possible. The missions, which owned their buildings, received property tax credits from the city and continued to operate.[97] During the late 1970s, indigents in Pioneer Square increased, creating tension between developers and social service workers and contributing to the district's decline as a retail center in the early 1980s. Articles about Pioneer Square continually commented on the bums' detrimental effects on commerce, and the juxtaposition between men getting ticketed for drinking Mad Dog on the street while young couples drank Rothschild in sidewalk cafés became a cliché.[98]

The homeless in the late 1970s and 1980s were different from bums in previous decades. Whereas the skid roaders of the 1950s and 1960s had alcohol problems, more of the street people in the late 1970s and 1980s were mentally ill and used illegal drugs, which made them violent.[99] Between 1975 and 1979, as other crime in the district stayed steady, aggravated assaults doubled from 35 in 1975 to 72 in 1979.[100] Concerns over crime increased further in 1979, when bums assaulted François Kissel, the owner of Brasserie Pittsbourg, as he left the popular restaurant.[101]

Despite the Skid Road heritage of Pioneer Square, suburban shoppers, tourists, and business owners did not appreciate the bums as "living history." As developers tried to rehabilitate Pioneer Square into a first-class tourist destination, transients deterred businesses from locating in the district. When the Westin Hotel chain moved into Seattle, it chose to locate north of downtown rather than in Pioneer Square, citing the derelict problem.[102] Merchants complained to city council and the Pioneer Square Historic Preservation Board that bums on the sidewalk offended potential customers, but the city generally refused to increase police patrols. The police could do nothing about the indigents anyway, because public drunkenness was merely a violation, not a crime.[103] The lack of police action further alienated business interest in the district. Business owners and economic developers argued that if Pioneer Square was to prosper commercially, "bums and businessmen" could *not* coexist.

Yet the city still refused to relocate the social services that attracted the homeless to Pioneer Square. The city council, DCD, Historic Seattle Preservation and Development Authority, and the historic preservation ordinance all had stipulations to keep the district "economically and socially diverse," a euphemism for providing for the bums.[104] Prominent preservationists like Bill Speidel advocated the continued presence of the derelicts in the district. The bums had been there first, after all, and were part of Seattle's heritage.[105] The executive director of Historic Seattle, Lawson Elliott, summed up the dilemma perfectly when he said, "Everybody thinks they own the place. The new guy who comes down here and spends $200,000 thinks he has a proprietary role, and he's probably right. He does. The guy that's stood there on the street corner and watched people go by for twenty years thinks he has a proprietary role, and he's probably right, too."[106] Despite their adverse effect on business, the bums were there to stay.

The city council aggravated the struggle to attract investment when, in the 1980s, it decreased funding improvements in Pioneer Square. When reform-minded Wes Uhlman was mayor between 1970 and 1978, the city spent an average of $300,000 yearly in the historic district and employed a full-time district manager to coordinate improvements.[107] After the more politically and fiscally conservative Charles Royer took office in 1978, city funding stopped. Between 1978 and 1980, the city sponsored no capital improvement projects, and it changed the position of district manager from full time to part time.[108] Immediately after leaving office, Uhlman voiced his concerns by warning Royer of the district's decline without financial support. Private investment depended on city funding, and without it, "Pioneer Square will be forgotten and treated like the tail of the downtown dog," Uhlman said.[109] Seattle developer Bruce Lorig confirmed Uhlman's fear, telling the Pioneer Square Historic Preservation Board that the restrictions in Pioneer Square without corresponding governmental funding deterred private-sector investment and hindered development.[110]

Initially thought to be a boon to Pioneer Square, the Kingdome also had an adverse affect on the historic district. The stadium created congestion and traffic at game times, making an already difficult parking situation virtually impossible. Fans attending games changed the restaurant trade in the district, patronizing drop-in style restaurants before the game and nightclubs afterwards. Finer dining establishments like Brasserie Pittsbourg struggled for customers. Indeed, many restaurants witnessed a decline in traffic on game nights, as people from other parts of Seattle chose to avoid the Kingdome surroundings altogether.[111] Dome-oriented sports shops sprang up in Pioneer

Square to take advantage of the promise of increased traffic. When patrons did not materialize, however, merchants closed shop, causing high turnover.[112]

As retail businesses continued to decline in the early 1980s, the DCD sought to generate more residential usage in Pioneer Square. Building owners, merchants, city planning officials, and developers planned a diverse twenty-four–hour community.[113] A change in federal funding also facilitated the usage shift. In 1981 the U.S. Congress reduced tax incentives for restoring old buildings but increased the amount of funding available for urban housing projects.[114]

The emphasis on housing created another little boom for Pioneer Square after 1985. One of the first residential projects in Pioneer Square was the Olympic Block, just south of Pioneer Place. Built on the site of the collapsed Olympic Building, the new Olympic Block started construction in 1984 and provided nineteen middle- and upper-income condominium units, in addition to some ground-floor retail development.[115] Other developers offered condominiums and luxury apartments, drawing a diversity of income levels to the district. Because of the four major missions in Pioneer Square, however, the income level of the district remained skewed to the lower end.[116]

The shift to residential usage in Pioneer Square marked a new phase in the district's history. Ralph Anderson and Bruce Chapman both separately categorized the district's preservation in three phases. Phase one, from 1962 to 1970, witnessed private investment and individual development. Property owners and civic leaders accepted and even promoted both of the district's identities. Phase two began with the designation of the historic district in 1970 and ended when Wes Uhlman left office in 1978. Generous municipal and federal funding, infrastructural improvements, and increased entrepreneurship characterized this period. Business leaders glorified the Seattle Spirit, although the official policy still claimed that bums and businessmen could coexist. During phase three, from 1978 to 1986, the district's Skid Road identity persisted, marking the decline of Pioneer Square as a retail center for downtown and the beginning of the district as a mixed-use residential area, which it remains today.[117]

Although the diverse groups representing Pioneer Square agreed that the district defined Seattle's identity, they could not choose which heritage to recreate. Because so many entities owned property or controlled funding, no centralized power appeared to dictate an appropriate tradition. Contemporary commercially successful historic districts celebrated traditions related to the district's, and the city's, heritage, but the groups in Pioneer Square never agreed on which heritage to symbolically represent. The most tangible and obvious identity was that of the original Skid Road, an identity that also made the district truly unique. That identity deterred the development of the area as a retail center, however, and diluted the symbolic power of the booster identity in Pioneer Square. As Seattleites struggled to find an identity in Pioneer Square, they were able to look north to find another definition of civic heritage emerging in the Pike Place Market.

"AN HONEST PLACE IN A PHONY TIME": PIKE PLACE MARKET, SEATTLE

[The Pike Place Market] reveals the face of truth. Its roughness
reminds me of Seattle's beginnings, its lusty past, the vitality that
gave it national notice long ago. It is an honest place in a phony time.
—Fred Bassetti, Seattle architect

Clinging to a hillside on the northwestern edge of downtown
Seattle, the Pike Place Market has a carnival atmosphere. The smell of fresh
seafood, ripe fruits and vegetables, a panoply of floral arrangements, and masses
of humanity mingle with sounds of fishmongers tossing salmon and yelling at
passing crowds. Elderly men, suburban housewives, burned-out hippies, and
well-dressed businesspeople literally rub elbows as they vie for space in the
crowded arcade. Artists and artisans add to the atmosphere, and tourists mill

about, taking in the spectacle. The diversity and seeming authenticity of Pike Place Market is the hallmark of Seattle, the city's top tourist attraction, and the center of Seattle's civic identity.

Like many inner-city treasures, the Pike Place Market was threatened by an urban renewal plan in the 1960s. The plan proposed surrounding the core of the market with a luxury hotel, convention center, and condominiums. The prospect of changing the market mobilized the citizenry in a campaign to "save" its unique function and atmosphere, although the campaign itself blurred the distinction between "saving" and "destroying" the market. The battle culminated in 1971 with a citizens' initiative to preserve the market that passed with overwhelming support. The struggle over the market, however, was really a battle over who had the power to shape Seattle's actual and symbolic landscape—the downtown business elite, embodied by the city council and the Central Association of Seattle, or the emerging cultural elite claiming to speak for "the people."[1] In the end, the Pike Place Market remained, yet it was neither the historical market nor the high-end development proposed by urban renewal. Instead, it simulated a nostalgic farmers' market. Outwardly, the market represented an early form of individualistic capitalism that preserved a laissez-faire atmosphere, but it took quasi-socialist city controls to maintain this business structure.

The Pike Place Market is the oldest continually operating farmers' market in the United States.[2] It was organized during the Progressive Era (roughly 1890–1913) as a reaction to the unscrupulous practices of produce jobbers and wholesalers. Responding to public outcries for control on food prices, the Seattle City Council formed the public market along narrow Pike Place on 17 August 1907. From its beginning the Pike Place Market was an overwhelming success. The first day, farmers sold out of their produce before they even parked their wagons. During the market's early years, patrons arrived on foot or by boat, carriage, bicycle, or streetcar. The shoppers were predominantly women, and they came from all parts of the city, all social classes, and all ethnic backgrounds, creating a diversity in the market rarely seen in other parts of the city.[3] The ethnic diversity of the market's customers reflected the diversity in farmers. King County had over 3,000 farms by 1906, and European and Japanese immigrants occupied more than half of them. Within the market, patrons could hear Norwegian, Swedish, Finnish, German, Italian, Serbo-Croatian, Tagalog (from the Philippines), Chinese, Japanese, and even Chinook languages.[4]

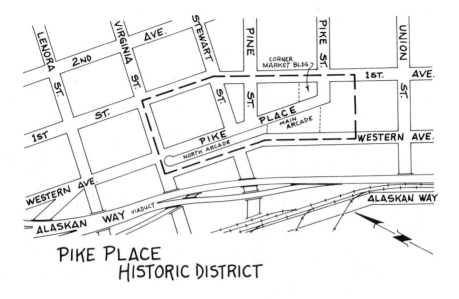

PIKE PLACE
HISTORIC DISTRICT

A young architect named Frank Goodwin saw a great opportunity in the city's public market. After witnessing the crowds on the first market day, he purchased land along the west side of Pike Place, between First and Western avenues, north of Pike Street. Goodwin quickly constructed the Main Arcade building to provide farmers shelter when peddling their wares. The building had seventy-six stalls, and Goodwin gave top priority to farmers and gardeners marketing their own produce. When the Main Arcade opened later in 1907, the city held a ceremony dedicating the market to the people of Seattle. Between 1911 and 1916, Goodwin added new buildings. He built a labyrinth below the Main Arcade that tunneled down to Western Avenue on the waterfront, as well as the Sanitary Market along Pike Place, the Corner Market at First Avenue and Pike Street, and the Economy Market across the street. As construction progressed, Goodwin formed a management corporation named the Public Market and Department Store Company.[5]

When the Pike Place Market celebrated its tenth anniversary in 1917, it was already an important part of Seattle's civic identity. The city had 340,000 people, and at least one-third of the population had been born in or emigrated to Seattle after the market's creation.[6] The Pike Place Market prices on produce became the going rate, limiting what food vendors in other parts of the city could charge.[7] When the city wanted to remove farmers from Pike Place in 1920 to make room

The Corner Market at Pike Street and First Avenue, 1912. (Manuscripts, Special Collections, University Archives, University of Washington Library, neg. no. ACurtis 24655)

for cars, citizens fought to save the landmark. City council members suggested another location for the market, but patrons protested. The Public Market and Department Store Company, now called the Pike Place Market Company and owned by Frank Goodwin's nephew, Arthur, helped solve the problem by expanding the Main Arcade and donating the added space to the city in 1924. This north arcade became known as the Municipal Market Building.[8]

The Pike Place Market witnessed its heyday in the 1930s, when demand for inexpensive produce meant that more farmers sold truck crops directly to the public. The number of yearly permits the Health Department issued to market vendors hit an all-time high of 628 in 1932 at the height of the Great Depression.[9] At the same time, the market became a haven for unemployed men who lived in nearby cheap hotels and sought part-time or seasonal work. Businesses catering to single men, such as adult book stores and pool halls, lined First Avenue, adjacent to the market.[10]

Ownership of the market buildings changed during the 1930s. A decade earlier an Italian immigrant named Joe Desimone signed a long-term lease for space in the Main Arcade building. During the 1930s Desimone began buying shares of stock in the Pike Place Market Company. In 1941 Arthur Goodwin sold out, making Desimone the primary owner of the market. Desimone and his heirs owned the majority of the market buildings until the city purchased them during restoration in the 1970s.[11]

Unlike the rest of the city, the market's economy did not boom during World War II. Japanese Americans represented the largest group of market vendors—60 percent—prior to the war. One-sixth of all Japanese Americans lived in Washington state, and most were truck farmers. Anti-Japanese sentiment at the beginning of the war kept many consumers from purchasing produce from Japanese farmers. When a fire gutted the Sanitary Market eight days after the bombing of Pearl Harbor, vendors and customers became suspicious of Japanese-American merchants. The eventual internment of Japanese Americans nearly killed business in the market. In their absence, licenses to farmers plummeted from 515 in 1939 to merely 196 in 1943.[12]

The market community also declined during the war. Hotels that had served as residences to the semi-transient male population working on the ships and docks lost their clientele. Men who had been living in the area were now merely passing through on their way overseas. As the hotels lost their regular business, some became brothels to maintain income. The most notable whorehouse in the market was the LaSalle Hotel, adjacent to the Main Arcade, which operated from 1942 to 1951.[13]

The market never bounced back after the war. Few Japanese Americans resumed farming after returning from the internment camps, primarily because they no longer owned their land. Suburbanization also reduced the amount of land available for farming, and rezoning claimed former stretches of farmland for commercial or industrial uses. The need for a farmers' market decreased, too, since suburbanites could go to supermarkets and get fresh produce trucked in along the new interstate highway system. The national Marshall Plan also changed the nature of farming. Farmers selling directly to the government grew a single crop with migrant labor, decreasing the amount of truck crops grown in the region.[14]

By the time the city council and the Central Association of Seattle commissioned the *Comprehensive Plan for Central Business District Seattle* (known as the Monson Plan) in 1963, the Pike Place Market buildings badly needed repairs to wiring, plumbing, paint, and facades. The market no longer generated income for the city. Revenue from stall rentals declined 21 percent

The back of the Stewart House, with Trudy and Leonora's Barber Shop in the foreground, 1967. The run-down condition of the buildings was typical of the market during the 1960s. (Seattle Municipal Archives)

between 1951 and 1955 while annual expenses for upkeep and sanitation rose 68 percent. City council members considered letting the market's lease lapse in 1957 but gave in to public pressure and reluctantly renewed. The Desimone family could not justify huge investments in upkeep, either, because of declining profits from permit rentals.[15] The number of vendors decreased drastically as well, with stall rentals reaching an all-time low of forty-two in 1969.[16]

The community tax base did not offer the city much hope of funding repairs or improvements. The market neighborhood housed predominantly elderly, white, working-class, single men with no family ties who opted to live there because of inexpensive rent and the male-oriented culture of taverns and poolrooms nearby. Although poor, the market neighborhood differed from the "Skid Road" population in Seattle's Pioneer Square. Whereas Pioneer Square's demographics consisted of relatively young alcoholics, drug addicts, and derelicts, the Pike Place Market community contained elderly pensioners who did not have an excessive problem with alcoholism or addiction.[17]

Despite dilapidated facilities and a declining neighborhood, customers continued to patronize Pike Place Market. Although suburban shopping cen-

The Corner Market in decline, 1972.
(Seattle Municipal Archives)

ters stole some of the market's business, residents throughout Seattle still came
to the market for the freshest produce, fish, or specialty items. During the
1960s, daily retail sales in the market averaged $55 per square foot, and al-
though this amount was much lower than a rehabilitated district like Ghirardelli
Square in San Francisco, it was much higher than anyone in Seattle's planning department expected.[18] Eighty percent of the market's business came
from the neighborhoods closest to downtown, but only 15 percent came from
within walking distance, meaning most customers could afford to ride a bus
or drive. Twenty percent of the market's clientele shopped there at least once
a week.[19] According to market observers, the customers were from all ethnic and economic backgrounds, keeping with market tradition. African Americans living downtown and Asians from the International District to the south
shopped alongside housewives from the affluent areas of Washington Park,
the Broadmoor, and the Highlands.[20]

Despite steady customers, downtown businesspeople lobbied the city to
do something about the deteriorating physical conditions of Pike Place Market. In order to deal with decaying urban areas, Washington's state legislature

passed an urban renewal law in 1957 that gave the city the power of eminent domain to take control and redevelop the area. With this law in mind, members of city council and the Central Association of Seattle in 1963 commissioned the aforementioned Monson Plan.[21] The Monson Plan proposed the total elimination of the market.

The Monson Plan was not the first attempt to do away with the market, however. In 1950, as a solution to traffic problems, Seattle civil and structural engineer Harlan Edwards suggested demolishing Pike Place Market and replacing it with a seven-story landscaped parking garage and shops. Immediately, advocates of the market's dingy realism began fighting to save the place. Internationally renowned artist Mark Tobey set the tone for later fights to save the market when he said, "Landmarks with human dimensions are being torn down to be replaced by structures that appear never to have been touched by human hands. There seems a talent today for picking the most beautiful and personal places to destroy—what might be called an aesthetic destructive sense."[22]

The Monson Plan had nearly the same specifications for the market as Edwards's plan. Under the provisions of the Monson Plan, the city would authorize a private developer to bulldoze 12.5 acres between First Avenue and Western. In this space, the plan proposed a terraced garage holding 3,000 cars, a luxury hotel, several high-rise office buildings, and a downtown park containing a rebuilt market as "a visitor and tourist attraction quite equal to the Los Angeles Farmer's Market," according to Central Association president Ben Ehrlichman.[23] The Central Association of Seattle and the Seattle Urban Renewal Enterprise (SURE) jointly produced a feasibility study in 1964 that was based on the Monson Plan. The study reinforced the Monson Plan's design and confirmed that the plan qualified for federal urban renewal funding. The city council approved the plan in January 1965. The plan then continued on to the federal department of Housing and Urban Development (HUD), which granted preliminary funding in December 1966.[24] The new urban renewal project became known as Pike Plaza.

To get control of the market, however, the city had to condemn property, since Joe Desimone's will prohibited his heirs from selling it. The city, therefore, had to make a case for blight and condemnation to get federal funding. Structural studies commissioned by the city found that 90 percent of the market buildings warranted clearance and that 89 percent of existing structures within the Pike Plaza project did not meet the city's health and safety regulations.[25] The city also had reports from the city's fire, health, and planning departments confirming that the market was a rat-infested, congested, dilapidated firetrap.[26]

Business in the market fared better than the structures, however. The market continued to function as a "strong magnet" for downtown, and newspaper pundits and research analysts suggested keeping it as the focal point of any urban renewal plan. The market did not necessarily need to be kept in its original buildings, however. A study by Development Research Associates found that "the public" valued the "essence" of the market because of the "atmosphere stimulated by the merchandising methods" and the "personal attributes of the merchants in the area."[27]

As the city formalized development plans, Seattle mayor J. D. "Dorm" Braman believed that the key to the Pike Plaza project was private capital. Despite urban renewal funds, the mayor worried that the area would become an "urban renewal wasteland" without large investors. Braman had witnessed other cities that used urban renewal funds to clear land and then waited in vain for either private funds or more public funds to arrive. In order to avoid the Pike Plaza land lying empty for years, he urged twenty local investors and prominent business leaders to form the Central Park Plaza Corporation. The group incorporated in April 1966 and immediately began buying available property in and around the redevelopment area.[28]

With federal funding and private investors in place, the city planning department, known after 1970 as the Department of Community Development (DCD), finalized urban renewal designs. Planners sought to attract affluent people living in the suburbs. Mayor Braman summarized this objective in an address to the city council, claiming that

> what we are trying to do here is to respond to what is . . . the exodus of people living in the heart and core of our cities. This has led to the abandonment, as far as housing is concerned, of the core portion of almost every city in the country, which is followed then by people of lesser income and lesser ability to carry the burden of the city's operations, and it has resulted in terrible blight . . . What we are trying to do here is to restore this property to the highest best use, which is to encourage the return to Seattle of many of the people of high income, the people who have taken their brains and their money and their ability to [contribute to the] tax base and left the environs of Seattle and gone across the lake or to the north or south of us . . . One way or another, we are going to have to encourage these people to come back in Seattle, and one of the ways to do it . . . [is] to redevelop this wonderful, beautiful living property

so that people of high income . . . return to Seattle their brains and their money and their tax base.[29]

The approved design for Pike Plaza reflected the need to bring high-end shoppers and tourists to the area. The plan cleared the land between First and Western avenues and University and Lenora streets to make way for hotels, luxury apartments, better parking facilities, open space, and a connection between the central business district and the waterfront. Because research showed that the market's function still drew people to the area, most drafts featured a retail development where the Main Arcade stood. High-rise apartments and hotels surrounding the retail area were proposed, and the shopping space was to be new, glossy, and bright.[30]

The grand plans for Pike Plaza were not without opposition. Following the lead of artist Mark Tobey, a group of Seattle citizens joined together to save the shabby, yet livable, character of the market from the expansive schemes of the city. When the first Pike Plaza redevelopment plans appeared in 1964, artists, architects, students, and professionals formed a group called Friends of the Market. Most of the organizers belonged to Allied Arts of Seattle, an organization dedicated to artistic endeavors, and many, like Ralph Anderson, were already involved in restoring Pioneer Square (see Chapter 3).[31] Friends of the Market formed in 1965, headed by Seattle attorney Robert Ashley and University of Washington architectural professor Victor Steinbrueck.

Between 1965 and 1968 the Friends of the Market promoted the seedy market as it was. According to the Friends, the market was a classic example of public space, where people of all backgrounds and classes mingled. The Friends of the Market opened an office on Pike Place and sold copies of Mark Tobey's book *World of a Market* and Steinbrueck's two books of market scenes, *Seattle Cityscape* and *Market Sketchbook*. The store carried shopping bags, books with recipes from market merchants, and market buttons. The Friends of the Market sought to save the class diversity of the market and to sell the vision that the market could function as the cornerstone of downtown Seattle without being rebuilt.[32]

Steinbrueck was the undeniable leader of the Friends of the Market. He had a predisposition toward safeguarding the rights of, in his words, "the working man." Steinbrueck's middle name was "Eugene," after famed labor leader and socialist Eugene V. Debs. Born in North Dakota, he moved as a child to Georgetown, Washington, where his father worked as a machinist during World

Pike Place Market hero Victor Steinbrueck, shown in a 1965 portrait and leading a march to save the market in 1971. (*Seattle Post-Intelligencer* Collection, Seattle Museum of History and Industry)

War I. According to Steinbrueck, "Georgetown was a poor, working-class neighborhood. I was very conscious of the difficulties of working people."[33] Steinbrueck's influence led the Friends of the Market to turn their opposition to Pike Plaza into a populist struggle of "the little people" against the "business interests."

Steinbrueck himself was not against progress. He codesigned Seattle's most prominent symbol of progress, the Space Needle. He realized, however, that the addition of affluent tourists and luxury apartment dwellers would irrevocably change Pike Place Market. He believed that the market was more than the physical structures that housed produce; it was, he felt, "a series of experiences building on each other not limited to just the core."[34] As he crusaded to preserve the experience of the market, Steinbrueck became a tireless and ruthless activist, likened to both Gandhi and Genghis Khan.[35] His merry band of students, lawyers, architects, artists, and housing activists sought to convince the city that their plan was too disjointed and schizophrenic to benefit either the market or the central business district. Instead, Steinbrueck and the Friends of the Market argued that the future lay in the seedy remnants of the past.[36] To that end, the Friends of the Market wrote letters to the editors of local newspapers and talked to the national media about the market's virtues. They gave tours of the market and promoted it to members of city council, the DCD, church groups, and service organizations. Their lobbying paid off, as they persuaded the city council and the Central Association of Seattle to modify the Pike Plaza design in 1968.[37]

As part of the compromise, city council held a design competition. Architects submitted their vision for the Pike Plaza project, and the Department of Community Development chose one of them. Although Steinbrueck submitted a plan on behalf of the Friends of the Market, the DCD chose a design drawn by architects John Morse and Paul Kirk. Both Morse and Kirk had ties to the downtown business establishment; Morse belonged to the Central Association of Seattle. The choice of the Morse/Kirk design appealed to the downtown interests but immediately made the Friends of the Market suspicious.[38]

Unlike earlier plans, the Morse/Kirk design advocated keeping some of the market's buildings. A 1968 draft of the plan stated that the design would maintain the market's appearance *and* function. Morse and Kirk acknowledged that the market should be preserved not just for sentimental reasons but also because it was economically healthy.[39] The design included rehabilitating the

Sanitary Market, Economy Market, and Corner Market structures, all of which were slated for clearance in previous plans. Additionally, Morse and Kirk kept the Leland and LaSalle hotels, turning them into studio apartments with market functions on the ground level. Signage was to be "identification and not advertisement" in keeping with market tradition, and the plan kept the famous "Public Market" marquee. Landscaping was open for easy public access, and the plan called for pieces of public art throughout.[40]

Had this been the entire plan, the Friends of the Market might have been satisfied. The rest of the design, however, stipulated that the surrounding area be totally rebuilt along the guidelines set forth in the Monson Plan. The market would be nestled into an area accommodating a 4,000-car parking garage, a 32-story apartment building for low-income and elderly residents, four 28-story luxury apartment buildings, 300,000 square feet of office space, and a hockey arena. A pedestrian bridge stretched from First Avenue to a point on the roof of the Main Arcade so that walkers could take advantage of a westward view of Elliott Bay.[41]

The Morse/Kirk design fostered a safe environment for female shoppers, marking a departure from recent conditions in the market. As was noted earlier, since the days of the Great Depression the market had been overwhelmingly male both in population and in culture. Although never explicitly stated, the Morse/Kirk design catered to female shoppers and tourists by offering a renewed, clean, safe environment.[42] Indeed, every drawing of the Morse/Kirk plan showed middle-class women strolling, browsing, and purchasing in the market, compared to Steinbrueck's *Market Sketchbook*, which showed mainly men.[43]

The Friends of the Market feared that the proposed design was unsympathetic to the spirit of the market and that farmers would not be able to afford rents in the new upscale area.[44] They also worried that the market would not survive out of context. According to Steinbrueck, "It is most unrealistic to expect a low income market, or anything resembling what we care so much about, to survive under the new elegantized [sic] total situation which is quite unsympathetic."[45] An article in the *Seattle Times* gave an excellent summation of the concerns market advocates had about the changes:

Can the sellers of day-old bread, week-old fruit and economy grade meat keep drawing the urban poor to patronize their stands under the shadow of the first-class, 600–room hotel to be built down the street? How conscious of their clothes and physical condition will the workingmen and pensioners who depend on the market for entertainment as much as foodstuffs become with luxury highrise apartment towers just a couple of blocks away down the street? Just how much protective coloration does the jumble of First Avenue give to the market's people? How much of it is necessary to keep the market as the same blend of something-for-everyone that it is now?[46]

The Friends of the Market's opposition to the proposed design outraged Mayor Braman, who generally sided with the business interests and who had been relieved when the Morse/Kirk design proved so sympathetic to the market. Upon realizing that the Friends would not support the design, or "Scheme 23," as it became known, Braman set the antagonistic tone for the rest of the debates by calling Steinbrueck and the Friends "nitpickers." In a statement to the city council in 1968, Braman claimed that he would not let the Friends of the Market stand in the way of the $80 million urban renewal plan. Braman called the Pike Place Market a "decadent, somnolent fire trap" and said that the city would relocate the 400 residents, mostly elderly, single men, to other parts of the city. "We don't have to leave these people in the middle of this choice area, and as far as I'm concerned we're not going to leave them there," he said. Braman criticized the Friends of the Market for "nitpicking on behalf of people living in unpainted houses, who are not paying taxes and not contributing a thing."[47] Braman's rhetoric countered Steinbrueck's concern for "the working man" and reinforced the class overtones prevalent in the debate over the market's future.

The Friends of the Market organized petitions opposing the Morse/Kirk design and eventually garnered 53,000 signatures.[48] The elected city council members could not ignore this much opposition, so they held public hearings on Pike Plaza before adopting the plan. Over six weeks in the spring of 1969, the hearings unfolded like a courtroom drama. They began with numerous city experts, all of whom made a case for clearing as much of the Pike Plaza area as possible. The assistant director of the Environmental Board of the King County Health Department talked about the unsanitary conditions, claiming the market neighborhood was infested with rats and cockroaches and that poor sewage removal made disease rampant. Fire Marshal Stephen H. MacPherson testified that the mayor's assessment of the market as a firetrap was essentially correct. The number of multiple-alarm fires in the market was far higher than any other similar-sized area of the city. The city's structural engineer testified that most of the buildings were unable to be rehabilitated and therefore should be condemned and removed.[49]

Steinbrueck cross-examined each of the city's experts. During these cross-examinations, he exhibited a dramatic flair comparable to Perry Mason or Matlock. In challenging the structural engineer, Steinbrueck went through a list of buildings in the market, asking the engineer to elaborate on the condition of each structure. The engineer protested that he could not answer questions about specific buildings without the report in front of him, but Steinbrueck persisted. He pointed out that minor repairs like paint and plumbing would change a building's designation from demolition status to merely substandard, which allowed for rehabilitation. Steinbrueck's style was to not really ask questions but rather to carry on a monologue that left the expert speechless. When committee chairperson Phyllis Lamphere challenged Steinbrueck for not actually asking questions, Steinbrueck began adding the phrase, "isn't that right?" to the end of his diatribes.[50]

After the city's experts presented their case for demolition and removal, Paul Kirk and John Morse gave an extensive explanation of their proposal. Again, Steinbrueck cross-examined the two men. John Morse's answers to Steinbrueck's questions illustrated that the goals of Friends of the Market and city council members were in reality quite similar. When Steinbrueck asked Morse how he reconciled high-income apartments with the low-income environment of the market, Morse's answer sounded like it could have come from Friends of the Market literature. Morse replied, "The history of the Market has been a mingling of people from Broadmoor and people from other areas coming down into the Market to shop and we think this is the main thing about the Market. It hasn't been a single structure or a single class that made the Market work."[51] Steinbrueck and Morse seemed to disagree more on exactly which buildings were part of the market than on the goal for the market itself.[52]

After being put off for weeks, the Friends of the Market finally made their formal presentation. Steinbrueck, of course, led the way. His argument used the familiar framework of competing class interests. The idea that "the people" were fighting "the interests" became the most prevalent interpretation of the struggle to save Pike Place Market.[53] The Friends of the Market submitted the petition with 53,000 signatures on it, showing widespread popular support for preservation of the market.[54] Steinbrueck also claimed that the thrift shops, taverns, and cafés served working people who could not afford to go elsewhere for their food and entertainment. During the proceedings, a low-income resident of the market neighborhood named Merle Haug testified, echoing perfectly the Friends' position. "Is Urban Renewal supposed to be out to get rid of . . . the low income and move in the high income?" Haug asked. "Mayor Braman said that he was going to try to raise the tax base. It looks to me like he is going to move in a high income tax base from another part of the city to move it down to the Market just because it [has] a view. Now, is that Urban Renewal, or is it just taking the dirt and scraping it away?"[55] During the Friends' presentation, a man identified as Dr. Spradley stood up to speak on behalf of the indigent in the market. When Chairperson Lamphere asked him if he was a member of the Friends of the Market, Steinbrueck answered for the doctor, saying that he was not an official member, "but if he is a friend of the people, he is obviously a friend of the Market."[56] The city council hearings were the first step toward the legacy of the market's preservation as a "people's victory."

Less noticed by the press, but equally present, was the Friends of the Market's argument that Pike Place Market must be preserved to safeguard Seattle's identity. Architect and Friends of the Market member Ibsen Nelson read a statement to the council arguing that the market was unique to Seattle. "As public markets go," Nelson read, "there is not another market in any U.S. city as extensive or as unique as Seattle's Pike Place Market. Nor is there any feature of this city more important to the identity and vitality of Seattle as a regional urban center."[57] The Friends of the Market showed Mark Tobey's artwork and had citizens testify as to what the market meant to them as Seattle residents. The faculty of the University of Washington School of Architecture and Urban Planning submitted a letter supporting the market as the center of life in the city. The Friends read Fred Bassetti's statement quoted at the beginning of this chapter, arguing that the market's place in Seattle's history was irreplaceable. Finally, the Friends of the Market brought travel agents to the hearing to testify that the market was a popular visitor attraction and a symbol of Seattle.[58]

During the course of the city council hearings, the newspapers shifted their editorial opinions slightly. At the beginning of the hearings in March 1969, editorials in the *Seattle Post-Intelligencer* supported the urban renewal plan and claimed that the Friends of the Market had taken an "unreasonable position" in opposition to it.[59] By late April, editorials in that paper still claimed to support the urban renewal plan overall but urged the city to consider the suggestions of Steinbrueck, Nelson, and Bassetti for keeping more of the market intact.[60]

Despite the media's subtle shift toward supporting preservation, despite the 53,000 citizens supporting preservation, and despite the Friends of the Market's compelling testimony, the Seattle City Council unanimously approved the Morse/Kirk design in August 1969. Council members still believed the plan was a reasonable compromise between preservationists and developers and that it had the greatest likelihood of receiving HUD funding. The basis for their decision was the testimony that over 70 percent of the market's structures could not be rehabilitated. The resulting ordinance also cited inappropriate uses and traffic congestion problems as the basis for proceeding with Scheme 23. In addition, it claimed that the Morse/Kirk design would allow the city to attract both federal and private development funds.[61]

The city council did not completely ignore the Friends of the Market's concerns. The wording of the final urban renewal plan showed great sensitivity to the market and the impact of redevelopment. The plan acknowledged that "the focal point of the project is the Pike Place Market which is a unique and historic cluster of public produce stalls, meat and fish shops, second-hand stores, and a myriad of other retail services. While the Market itself has deteriorated, it has become institutionalized and remains as a major activity center in the city."[62] The council conceded that it would do as much as possible to preserve the market.

The Friends of the Market did not want to compromise, however. Once the city council approved the Morse/Kirk design, Steinbrueck and the Friends shifted into high gear, trying a number of strategies to keep the urban renewal plan from going into effect. Steinbrueck wrote letters protesting the urban renewal plan to anyone who would listen—the mayor, city council members, the HUD office in Washington, Lady Bird Johnson, and even President Richard Nixon. He wrote editorials in the Seattle daily papers decrying the city's economic agenda in Pike Plaza. Between November 1970 and May 1971, Steinbrueck and the Friends of the Market inundated the media with press releases opposing the urban renewal plan. The press releases, presumably written by Steinbrueck, called the city's urban renewal plan a "big lie" and decried the expectation of HUD money as a "pathetic hope for survival" for a project the Friends claimed was floundering. Steinbrueck also pointed out that there was no guarantee that the farmers could remain in the market and thus could be "cheated out of their way of life."[63]

As part of his crusade, Steinbrueck turned to the state and federal historic preservation agencies for help. In 1969 he nominated seven acres of Pike Place

Market to be included on the National Register of Historic Places. The district was placed on the register in February 1970. The designation prompted the Friends of the Market to suggest that the Department of Community Development reconsider its HUD application for Pike Plaza, since historic sites generally did not qualify for urban renewal funds. Instead, the department's Urban Renewal Division lobbied the state historic preservation office to change the boundaries of the district rather than potentially lose HUD funding. The state historic preservation officer, Charles H. Odegaard, made the recommendation, and the National Park Service reduced the size of the district from seven acres to 1.7 acres, incorporating just the Main Arcade and the Corner Market.[64]

The reduction of the size of the historic district at first appeared to be a devastating blow to the Friends of the Market, who along with Allied Arts of Seattle, the Washington Environmental Council, Victor Steinbrueck, Ralph Anderson, and a number of market merchants filed a lawsuit against Odegaard. The suit claimed that Odegaard "without good cause, arbitrarily and by mere administrative fiat, removed merely the entire Public Market district from the National Register."[65] The suit never went to trial.

Although initially devastating, the reduction of the market's National Register designation did have a positive, if unintended, consequence. The fact that the Department of Community Development and the Central Association of Seattle were willing to acknowledge and work with a 1.7-acre historic district symbolized a shift in the conception of preservation's role in the urban renewal plan. The DCD agreed to work within the guidelines of a historic district. Mayor Wes Uhlman, who replaced Dorm Braman in 1970 partially because of his moderate stance toward the Pike Place Market, even suggested a city ordinance, similar to the one just enacted in Pioneer Square, protecting the district.[66]

The city's willingness to incorporate historic preservation did not appease Steinbrueck and the Friends; if anything, it made them more determined to implement their vision of the market's future. When HUD approved $10.6 million for the Pike Plaza Redevelopment Plan (Scheme 23) in May 1971, the Friends took their crusade directly to the public, launching an initiative campaign to establish a seven-acre Market Historic District. To get the initiative on the ballot, the Friends needed 15,560 signatures. In June 1971 the Friends of the Market filed a petition with over 25,000 signatures.[67] Initiative 1 went on the ballot that November.

The Friends of the Market designed Initiative 1 to do two things. First, it would establish a seven-acre Pike Place Market historic district within the larger, twenty-two–acre urban renewal area. Second, it would create a Market Historical Commission to oversee structural and design changes. Ironically, the initiative really did not differ that much from the plan already proposed by the city council and Mayor Uhlman. The city's plan established a design review board for development projects in the central business district. Initiative 1 really just enlarged the size of the district from 1.7 acres to seven acres and created a historical design commission specific to the market, rather than a city-wide review board.[68]

The similarities in the positions of those supporting and those opposing Initiative 1 set up a confusing campaign. The Friends of the Market, which represented Seattle's cultural elite, students, and activists, opposed the mayor, city council, Desimone family, and the Central Association of Seattle. Newspapers, broadcast media, and election propaganda tried to frame the debate in familiar class terms. An article in the *Seattle Post-Intelligencer* exemplified the rhetoric surrounding Initiative 1 when it quoted Victor Steinbrueck saying that the urban renewal plan was a land grab for private investors who did not care about the "little man" inhabiting the market. City planners countered that the plan rewarded investors willing to risk their money to get rid of downtown blight. When Steinbrueck questioned the "humanness" of dislocating the market population, a city councilman countered that the derelicts neither voted nor paid taxes.[69]

Despite the seeming polarity in views, the groups on the opposite sides of Initiative 1 agreed that the market should be preserved; they merely disagreed on how best to preserve it.[70] The opponents of Initiative 1 supported private development of the market supplemented by government funds. Indeed, James Braman, the son of the former mayor and the head of the Department of Community Development, claimed that the formation of the seven-acre historic district would endanger HUD funding for the entire twenty-two–acre Pike Plaza Urban Renewal Development, which in turn would prompt investors to withdraw $150 million in potential investment funds. Steinbrueck and the Friends of the Market, however, countered that the Pike Plaza plan would kill the market and the people using it by making them victims of "poisonous affluence," despite provisions in the urban renewal plan to provide low-income housing and mixed-use retail outlets.[71]

In September 1971 the Alliance for a Living Market joined the Friends of the Market in the fight to pass Initiative 1. A doctor named Jack Bagdade founded the Alliance after joining the Friends of the Market. He felt the Friends were too artsy and academic to appeal to a broad range of voters, so Bagdade began the Alliance to reach more politically astute, younger voters. The Alliance consisted mostly of activists from CHECC (Choose an Effective City Council), young attorneys, and representatives of market businesses, as opposed to the artists, architects, students, and professors who populated the Friends of the Market. Bagdade brought attorney and CHECC activist Tim Manring into the Alliance, and under Manring's guidance, the Alliance framed opposition to the Pike Plaza Urban Renewal Plan in economic terms. The Alliance showed that the recession of 1970–1971 made the city's assumptions about urban renewal outdated and negated the optimistic projections of the Central Park Plaza Corporation.[72] Manring focused on community outreach, working with television stations and newspapers, making presentations to the city council, and talking to citizen's groups to garner support for Initiative 1.[73]

In August 1971 a group confusingly called the Committee to Save the Market (CSM) formed in opposition to the Friends of the Market. This new committee purported to represent market merchants and property owners, with Reid M. Lowell of Lowell's Restaurant and Jerry Wagner of the Pure Food Market serving as committee cochairs. Richard Desimone, representative of the Desimone family interests, supported the committee. The CSM backed Scheme 23 with the addition of a 1.7-acre historic district in the market's core.[74]

During the summer of 1971 the struggle over the fate of the Pike Place Market filled the Seattle media. The Friends of the Market took out full-page and double-page ads in both papers to denounce the urban renewal plan, using great drama to make their point. One broadside issued by the Friends read,

> Citizens of Seattle and King County: In the name of common decency, and the tradition and heritage of our region, the Friends of the Market summon you to our cause . . . the central business MERCHANTS OF GREED are using URBAN RENEWAL to MURDER THE MARKET BY STRANGULATION AND RAPE THROUGH DEMOLITION AND DISRUPTION . . . BY TAKING THE heart of the market to give life to their swank hotel and luxury apartment developments (capitals in original).[75]

The Friends of the Market also argued for passage of Initiative 1 on the basis that the Pike Place Market was an integral part of Seattle's heritage. In a series of four ads, the first paragraph of each established the market as a cornerstone of Seattle's identity. The first in the series began:

Spend an afternoon down at the Pike Place Market. And see for yourself. You'll find it much like it was in 1907 when it was built. For over 60 years, its vendors have been hawking their wares. For over 60 years, Seattle has delighted in its fine, often home-grown food at better-than-store prices. And for over 60 years, its European open market flavor has given *Seattle a one-of-a-kind* place (italics added).[76]

The Committee to Save the Market fought back by accusing the Friends of the Market and the Alliance for a Living Market of strangling the market to death by depriving it of much-needed funding. The CSM claimed that without the HUD money from the urban renewal plan, the market would continue to decay. It was the CSM, according to its own literature, and not the Friends of the Market, that had the true solution to the market's problems.[77]

Because both sides of the initiative struggle claimed to be doing the same thing, CHECC tried to sort out the confusion. In September 1971, CHECC activists called on the Friends of the Market, the Alliance for a Living Market, and the Committee to Save the Market to reveal their funding sources. The Friends of the Market and the Alliance for a Living Market immediately complied, showing that they got funding mostly in small chunks from members and other individuals. The Committee to Save the Market declined, however, making it look as if its organizers had something to hide. Finally, after three requests the CSM complied. With the exception of the Desimone family's Pike Place Public Markets Inc., CSM's funding sources read like a roll call of the downtown business establishment. The largest supporters of CSM included Sea First Bank, Washington International Hotels, Safeco, the Central Park Plaza Corporation, and Frederick and Nelson Department Stores.[78] Although the CSM claimed to represent thirty-seven market merchants, none of the money came from them.[79]

On 2 November 1971, Initiative 1 passed with 76,369 votes in favor, 53,264 votes against.[80] The initiative created a seven-acre historic district out of the market and a twelve-member historic district commission to oversee the restoration. The night of the election, James Braman of the DCD made an appearance at the Friends of the Markets' victory celebration with his wrists wrapped in bandages stained with fake blood. In his concession speech Braman said, "The people have spoken," and he vowed to work with the Friends of the Market to preserve Pike Place.[81]

Within a month, council members passed an ordinance reflecting the voters' mandate in Initiative 1. The ordinance stated:

It is deemed essential by the people of the City of Seattle that the cultural, economic, and historical qualities relating to the Pike Place Markets [sic] and the surrounding area, and an harmonious outward appearance and market uses which preserve property values and attracts residents and tourists be preserved and encouraged.[82]

The ordinance emphasized that the *use* of the market was the most important aspect of preservation. The "meet the producer" philosophy had been a hallmark of the Friends of the Market's campaign, and now a city ordinance protected that economic function, making the market unique among historic districts around the country.[83]

The twelve-member Market Historical Commission (MHC) established by the ordinance oversaw the market's design and restoration. The members of the commission represented a cross-section of groups interested in the market, consisting of two members each from Friends of the Market, the Seattle Chapter of the American Institute of Architects, and Allied Arts of Seattle; two market property owners; two market merchants; and two market-area residents.[84]

The victory of Initiative 1 codified the Pike Place Market as a public rather than private place. The market had always been both, with private buildings housing public functions. The debate over Pike Plaza was largely a struggle over which "public" the market would serve and which identity to promote. The city council and mayor advocated allowing private interests to dictate the market's future identity.[85] Initiative 1 advocated a public vision of the market with a populist identity. According to Seattle historian Roger Sale, the passage of Initiative 1 went a step beyond activism to border on socialism. "What in effect the election said was that the Market did not belong to its owners, or to the city government, but to the people. It was the perfect expression of . . . the old populist feeling, because it made clear that on the edge of the new frontier was the past."[86]

The success of Initiative 1 stemmed partially from the economic and social climate of Seattle in 1971. The citizens' initiative happened amidst a milieu of social protest, especially against Establishment interests in inner cities. Between 1963, when the Monson Plan appeared, and 1971, urban renewal promoters faced increased public awareness and involvement in Seattle's civic decisions.[87] Initiative 1's success marked the end of the cozy, paternalistic team of downtown businesses, major editorialists, and city hall that dominated politics in 1958, when the Central Association of Seattle formed. The social unrest of the 1960s, the Vietnam War, and the economic recession in Seattle in 1970–1971 intervened to foster a new activism and a new set of players on the city's planning stage.[88]

The victory of historic preservation in both Pioneer Square and the Pike Place Market did not represent a populist victory as much as a transfer of planning power from a business elite, namely the Central Association of Seattle, to a cultural elite composed of architects like Steinbrueck, Fred Bassetti, and Ralph Anderson, along with artists, students, and urban design professionals. Seattle's business elite recognized the importance of the market's economic function to the reinvigoration of the central business district, but they did not value the market's structure or design. The cultural elite, however, realized the significance of design, livability, historical associations, and identity within the market. They emphasized those aspects of the market over its economic potential.[89]

In addition to competing visions of the physical form of the city, the economic elite and the cultural elite had competing visions of the symbolic form of the city. Mayor Braman, city council members, and the Central Association of Seattle envisioned Pike Plaza creating an identity for Seattle as a modern world-class city, able to compete with any city in California or the East. This was the identity offered by Century 21 and the Space Needle.[90] The Friends of the Market, however, believed that Seattle's future resided in the past. According to the Friends, Seattle's identity was the *historic* market, as it was during its heyday in the Depression. Mark Tobey's artwork and Steinbrueck's *Market Sketchbook* served as the primary texts for this identity. In Steinbrueck's book, the run-down, haphazard buildings and the seedy, colorful characters who patronized them *were* the market. They embodied the historic, social, and aesthetic identity of Seattle and, if destroyed, could never be recreated. Many of the greatest catchphrases describing the market came from Friends of the Market members in the early days of their crusade. Mark Tobey's description of the market as "the heart and soul of Seattle" was widely quoted in the press, and Fred Bassetti's statement that the market was an "honest place in a phony time" became a slogan for the Initiative 1 struggle.[91]

The Friends of the Market argued that the Pike Place Market was unique to Seattle. The market, after all, gave Seattle an identity different from Portland's, San Francisco's, or any other West Coast city's. Irving Clark, a board member of the Friends of the Market, described the market's influence on Seattle, saying,

What American city do you like most to visit? Isn't it true that it is those cities that have unique character? San Francisco or New York, or Washington D.C., or Boston . . . they are all distinct ones from the other, and they are all unique . . . In Seattle, it would be money ahead if we maintain a definite and unique feeling. When you have a friend visit you from another city, where do you take that person? . . . I suggest that first and foremost you take him to the Market.[92]

In press releases, the Friends of the Market described the identity encapsulated in the market as an "intangible benefit," something "to which a monetary value cannot be assigned."[93] The *Seattle Times* ran an article right before the election on Initiative 1, titled "Unique Identity," in which *Washington Post* writer Wolf Von Eckardt argued that citizens should vote "yes" for Initiative 1. The article began, "November 2 Seattle will vote along with some mundane political matters on whether to keep its soul and an irreplaceable piece of Americana—the Pike Place Market."[94] An article from the *Seattle Post-Intelligencer* six years later claimed that "the Pike Place Market is the very essence of life [in Seattle] . . . The people of the market are the people of Seattle."[95] A promotional calendar from the period featured one of Steinbrueck's sketches of the market, accompanied by a caption that read,

> Born in Seattle's pioneer days, the colorful Pike Place Market has survived for fifty years with virtually no change in its character and flavor. This oasis of authenticity in the modern city of concrete, steel, and super-efficient marketing is an important part of Seattle's remaining charm—a feature that keeps ours from becoming just another impersonal metropolis.[96]

Finally, historian Roger Sale, writing in 1976, claimed, "For many people the Public Market *is* Seattle, its one great city achievement, the place they love most, the place they take visitors first."[97]

Why was the market a symbol of Seattle's identity? Unlike other districts discussed in this book, it was not the location of the city's birthplace. Yet the Pike Place Market encapsulated an egalitarianism inherent in Seattle's history. The market's ethnic diversity and working-class demographics reinforced Seattle's working-class, populist roots. During the first decades of the twentieth century, an ethos of populist reform subsumed the city-building impulse of the "Seattle Spirit." Middle-class reformers became radicalized, ironically, because living conditions for the middle and working classes were not that bad, so they had time and resources to devote to improvements. During the Progressive Era, citizens voted to make Seattle one of the first publicly owned ports in the United States. The city also formed the nation's first municipally owned power generating system, and the formation of Pike Place Market itself represented the populist spirit in the city. The high-water mark of Seattle's radical reform came after World War I, with the Great Strike of 1919.[98] Between 1920 and 1970, however, conservative business-oriented groups gained power in the city council, diluting Seattle's populist strain. To Seattle residents, Pike Place Market seemed to be the last remaining arena of the Progressive spirit.[99]

The business practices in the market reinforced its identity. In a world of globalization, corporate consolidation, and impersonal advertising, the "meet the producer" marketing hearkened back to a simpler agrarian era. The Friends of the Market argued that the buildings and surroundings were secondary to the personal marketing embodied by the market. The market linked function and place, so that changing the buildings would irreparably change the use. In a press release from 1970, the Friends of the Market claimed that the uniqueness of the market lay in its symbol of "the American tradition of small independent businessmen operating with enterprise and with service and personal involvement."[100] In Steinbrueck's notes for *Market Sketchbook*, he wrote, "The market has promoted itself because it fulfills needs—it has not needed phony advertising and development to sell its wares. It sells by value alone . . . People are attracted because it is a real place in a too-artificial world. There is little pretence—only the directness of simple people."[101] The National Register of Historic Places designation form claimed that the market was significant because it was a "living example of free enterprise and free marketing oriented to the small businessman . . . The market provides a living heritage of food marketing in its simplest form where the producer meets the consumer directly . . . The Pike Place marketing district is a living organism continually viable in the tradition of its simple beginnings."[102]

The victory of Initiative 1 meant keeping the market exactly as it always had been, renovating the buildings while preserving the economic model. At the first meeting of the newly created Market Historical Commission, the commissioners outlined four points they considered on all subsequent decisions:

1. The Market is a place for the farmer to sell his produce.
2. The Market is a place for the sale of every kind of food product.

3. The Market is a place where citizens in the low and moderate income groups can find food, goods and services, and residences.

4. The Market is and will always be a place with the flavor of a widely varied shopping area.[103]

The members of the Market Historical Commission realized they had a daunting task before them. The MHC stood "with one foot in the past and one foot in the future, charged with preserving the special quality of the market, and with planning for the future, preserving and upgrading structures, and dealing with all of the aspirations, desires, and proposals of the many owners and tenants within the District."[104] In order to be true to the "historic" functions of the market, the Market Historical Commission agreed to promote the sale of fruit, produce, flowers, meat, fish, poultry, and dry groceries, as well as support food sales at restaurants and cafés. It also agreed to promote uses that catered to pedestrians.[105]

Because the historic district resided entirely within the twenty-two–acre urban renewal area, the MHC and Friends of the Market had to follow the guidelines of the Urban Renewal Division of the Department of Community Development. The Pike Place Market was one of the first historic preservation projects to be carried out under the guidelines of urban renewal and with urban renewal funds. Traditionally, urban renewal was the antithesis of historic preservation. No model existed for the marriage of the two, which frequently led to jurisdictional struggles between city agencies. The division of authority ultimately gave the Market Historical Commission jurisdiction over all the rehabilitation work within the seven-acre historic district; the Department of Community Development's Urban Renewal Division oversaw implementation of the rest of the urban renewal plan.[106]

To add to the jurisdictional confusion, the plans for the market were also subject to the requirements set forth by the Federal Urban Renewal Program, which sometimes did not correspond with local goals for preserving the market. The fact that the Market Historical Commission preserved a use—marketing—also hindered communication between federal representatives and local program administrators. Use preservation had never been done before, and HUD tried to suppress funding. Seattle benefited from the fact that the Pike Place urban renewal project was one of the last projects funded in the country, however. Because HUD phased out urban renewal as national policy by the 1970s, the Pike Place project was able to negotiate the amount of money they could spend on building rehabilitation.[107]

Federal funding became vital to the project. From 1972 until the completion of the project in the 1980s, federal expenditures, including urban renewal and HUD funds, totaled between $50 million and $60 million.[108] Washington senator Warren Magnuson proved instrumental in securing funding for the Pike Place project. As a supporter of the Friends of the Market, Magnuson promised that if Initiative 1 passed, he would use his position on the Senate Appropriations Committee to ensure that the Pike Plaza urban renewal funds were not lost. Magnuson not only delivered the original $28 million but also secured an additional $10.6 million in block grants, $2 million in federal rehabilitation loans, and $2.5 million for public works and street repairs, plus funding and loans from HUD. The dependence on urban renewal funds dictated that some of urban renewal's goals be incorporated into the final plan. Consequently, the market was renovated and refurbished, cleaned, and polished, rather than restored to the gritty realism advocated by the Friends of the Market.

State restrictions also influenced the rehabilitation of the market. Washington state law required that the city act as the urban renewal agency but prohibited the city from actually developing land. Thus the Department of Community Development could use urban renewal funds to buy land, combine land into parcels, and sell land to private developers, but it could not develop land itself. To ensure that private developers would not fill the void, the Friends of the Market, the Alliance for a Living Market, and members of Allied Arts of Seattle suggested forming a public corporation, called the Pike Place Preservation and Development Authority (PDA). Chartered in June 1973, the PDA restored the market and followed the guidelines of the urban renewal project, but also had the freedom of a private body to take out mortgages on buildings and engage in development functions. Ultimately, the PDA assumed landlord functions for the city-owned properties within the renewal area. By 1981 the agency had an operating budget of over $2 million, and its duties included acting as leasing agent, providing janitorial services, collecting rents, performing building maintenance, coordinating security, and overseeing parking.[109]

The multiple agencies involved in the market's rehabilitation meant compromising plans to fit the overlapping sets of guidelines and objectives. As each new plan came before city council for approval, Victor Steinbrueck opposed elements of it. Steinbrueck and the Friends of the Market felt compelled to ensure that any final plan honored the public mandate codified by Initiative 1 and did not try to make the market too fancy. Absolute compliance with the intent of the citizens' initiative was not always practical, however, and Steinbrueck soon became disillusioned with his victory. He claimed that "we won the battle, and then we put the enemy in charge of administering the peace."[110] Out of frustration, Steinbrueck resigned from the Market Historical Commission in 1975.[111] By 1978 he openly criticized the market's rehabilitation. In an article in the *Seattle Post-Intelligencer*, he lamented the number of people in the market who "looked and sounded like they were from California and New York and Montana and Cleveland." Steinbrueck observed that they were not buying, but merely spectating. "It is not the Market of 1971, nor of Mark Tobey, nor of mine. It is the Market of the developer, the tourist bureau, and of 1978. Oh, well!"[112]

Steinbrueck's assessment of the market was, of course, absolutely accurate. Despite an early commitment to keep the market exactly as it was, the very preservation of it transformed the market into something completely different. Whereas the initial rehabilitation goals outlined appropriate uses and ways to maintain the market's uniqueness, later goals added an emphasis on attracting tourists and appealing to shoppers. For example, the first two goals listed in the rehabilitation guidelines sounded consistent with the Friends of the Market's vision. They were to "attract farmers/sellers and support their continued roles in the Market" and "induce diversity among Market-related businesses while maintaining the predominance of the food supply function of the Market."[113] The third and fourth goals sounded more like something from Scheme 23, however. Goal three was to "enhance the Market as a regional attraction," and the fourth goal was to "maintain and expand features of the Market which appeal to a broad cross-section of all people living in Seattle and the region."[114]

The market's rehabilitation process changed the businesses in the area. Despite a mandate to preserve the structures, the city and the PDA demolished twenty-eight buildings that they claimed were too structurally unsound to repair.[115] Once rehabilitation began, businesses had to be relocated during construction and renovation. Smaller businesses did not run enough of a profit margin to survive the upheaval. Of the original 250 businesses in the market when preservation began, 119, fewer than half, returned after restoration. The other 131 businesses either relocated outside of the project area (with the PDA paying relocation expenses) or went out of business.[116] Additionally, rents rose in the newly refurbished buildings. By 1977, rents in renovated areas increased 60 percent over pre-preservation rates.[117] Private development nearby also added to rising rents, pricing many merchants out of the market.[118]

When urban renewal and historic preservation finished with the Pike Place Market in 1983, it was a completely different place than it had been in 1971. Despite good intentions, the PDA created a district designed by elites, not the "little people."[119] The first director of the PDA, George Rolfe, recognized this phenomenon. "It is a curious reversal that the idea of a traditional Market— 1930s style, meat and vegetables for low-income people—does not come from low-income people today. It comes from the upper and middle income who want to sample what life was like then."[120] Rolfe's observation perfectly described the new identity of Pike Place Market. It was an area created by elites to simulate an egalitarian, working-class environment. According to John Turnbull, also a PDA director, the PDA acted as a "local police power" to ensure that the market was a "socialist controlled economy."[121]

The socialist power was a benevolent one, however. The PDA programs for low-income residents in the community were much more extensive than those planned by city council. The PDA used HUD grants and loans to convert old hotels and flophouses into subsidized apartments, and it urged the city to build forty-three market-rate rentals, which prompted private developers to build apartments in the neighborhood. The PDA also focused on community services, establishing a free clinic, a senior center, a food bank, a child care center, and a café providing subsidized, low-cost meals. The district even got its own newspaper—the *Pike Place Market News*—and a charitable foundation to underwrite the public programs offered in the district.[122]

Benevolent or not, in rebuilding the market, the PDA and the MHC invented a tradition in Pike Place.[123] The market actually had not been a farmers' market for years. During the 1950s and 1960s, craftspeople and merchants of manufactured goods filled space vacated by the declining number of farmers. Public perception still demanded a farmers' market, however, and that image was so important that even retail produce vendors who trucked their goods from California put signs over their stalls advertising "local, fresh-picked daily" produce.[124] The PDA acknowledged that the market's most important function was as a reminder of the way a traditional marketplace operated.[125]

Because the Pike Place Market had not actually been a farmers' market for years, the PDA and the MHC had to re-create it as one. According to PDA director John Turnbull, the PDA promoted "internal inconsistencies and acts

The Public Market marquee, 2002. (Rebekah Harvey)

of randomness" to provide the proper environment for the market.[126] The market they created was a premodern market, the "essence of penny capitalism . . . that is extremely important in this time of corporate giants . . . It is a beautiful way to get business and keep business that is individual."[127] The PDA and MHC created elaborate usage guidelines, dictating what percentage of a store's business could come from manufactured goods, what percentage could come from tourist-oriented goods, and what percentage must come from home-grown or homemade goods.[128] The agencies decided that no national chains could sell goods in the market.[129] In general, the guidelines emphasized the sale of fresh produce, fish, and other grocery items.[130]

The physical structures of the market were less important than their use. All design guidelines corresponded with usage guidelines. For example, to keep the mixed-use character of the market, the Pike Place urban renewal plan dictated different uses on different floors, so that retail, wholesale, storage, residential, and restaurants would all be in the same building.[131] The plan also broke the historic district into zones, and each zone determined not only the design elements of the various buildings but also the acceptable methods of merchandising, the types of display cases allowed, the available paint colors for the interior of the shop, and preferred lighting methods. The plan discouraged the use of fluorescent lighting and suggested that merchants phase it out in favor of incandescent bulbs.[132]

Starbucks is the only national chain allowed in the market
because this is the original location. (Rebekah Harvey)

By re-creating Pike Place Market as a farmers' market, the PDA and MHC
hearkened back to a time when a "market" was a physical location and not a
global economic system. Indeed, beginning with Friends of the Market and
ending with the PDA, all agencies involved in the preservation of the market
denied greater capitalistic forces to preserve Pike Place as a locale. Rather than
defer to the economic conditions of development espoused by the Central
Association of Seattle, the Friends of the Market and the PDA stubbornly created a place apart, and they tried to regulate the use of the market to keep it
from succumbing to the most potent market force in postwar Seattle: tourism.
The identity preserved in the Pike Place Market symbolized an earlier form of
capitalism where producers sold merchandise directly to the consumer.[133]

Maintaining the market as a community-based farmers' market was not always easy, however. Getting the merchants to adhere to the guidelines was one of the biggest challenges. According to a chairman of the MHC, "It was necessary to exert some muscle to insure that the merchants didn't allow themselves to be seduced into the whole Madison Avenue supermarket hype."[134] One hardware store in the market repeatedly violated the historic district guidelines by selling more Seattle key chains and coffee mugs than nuts and bolts.[135] In 1982 City Councilman Michael Hildt challenged the usage guidelines. The Hildt Amendment, as the measure became known, allowed artists and craftspeople into the market to "provide a variety of goods and services particularly to Seattle residents but also to visitors."[136] By 1996, there were 175 craftspeople registered with the PDA, compared to 125 farmers.[137]

Despite efforts to keep farmers in the Pike Place Market, measures like the Hildt Amendment, plus larger capitalist forces, changed the space usage considerably during the years of preservation. In 1974, for example, wholesale uses accounted for 23 percent of the available space. By 1982 only 8 percent of the space was wholesale. Conversely, 16 percent of the market in 1974 was retail, whereas by 1982 that number had jumped to 56 percent.[138] The types of businesses in the market differed from those Steinbrueck and the Friends of the Market sought to save, too. Until 1970 nearly all market businesses were community based—produce vendors, thrift shops, optometrists, shoe repair shops, hardware stores, print shops, and dressmakers. By 1980 gift shops, toy stores, antiques, boutiques, gem stores, and imports greatly outnumbered produce vendors.[139]

One of the biggest dilemmas facing the PDA and the MHC was that there were not enough farmers to sell produce in the market. King County simply no longer supported family farms. To combat this problem, the PDA started farmer-support programs to keep farmers economically viable and to promote new farms. The program encouraged corporate farmers to direct-market some of their excess produce in the Pike Place Market. The PDA-sponsored Farmer Liaison Program consisted of a city-hired representative who helped farmers plan and develop spin-off programs, attracted new farmers to the market, provided marketing assistance to farmers, and worked with farmer advocacy groups. The Revolving Loan Program provided loans for new farmers who could not get commercial loans, enabling them to buy equipment, seeds, and fertilizer. To ensure that the farmers were not part of a corporate farming struc-

Tourists and locals in the Pike Place Market, 2002. (Rebekah Harvey)

ture, a PDA representative visited every farm yearly.[140] The PDA also organized a farmer-consumer co-op known as the Bulk Commodities Exchange.
The co-op sponsored the purchase of fresh produce from small local farms
and its resale in bulk to restaurants and buying clubs. These initiatives did help
bring farmers into the market. The number of farmers selling produce increased from sixty in 1976 to eighty in 1983. Still, despite the PDA's best efforts, the bulk of the produce sold in the Pike Place Market came from central
Washington, east of the Cascade Mountains.[141]

Tourism provided another dilemma for the governing bodies of the market. The successful completion of the urban renewal plan meant that there
were more produce stands, more stalls for craftspeople, and more restaurant
and deli space. The expanded goods and services combined with the nostalgic
feel of the market attracted more visitors.[142] Market merchants catered to
tourists by changing their hours. The market was originally open until 6 or
7 p.m. six days a week. To attract more visitors, merchants started opening on
Sundays, but to keep from having to hire more employees, they closed at
5 p.m. on weekdays. The new schedule favored visitors who could come during the weekday (usually tourists) while penalizing people who had to come
to the market after work.[143] These changes led to more tourists. Whereas in

The restored Corner Market, 2002. The difference in the buildings before and after renovation is really minimal. (Rebekah Harvey)

1973 only 7 percent of market merchants reported 400 customers in an average business day, by 1982, 26 percent of merchants reported at least that many customers, and 13 percent anticipated over 800 customers per day, far greater than the local demand could generate.[144]

By the early 1990s the Pike Place Market was Seattle's leading tourist attraction.[145] It was also one of the most prominent symbols of the city. Visitors came in droves to sample the experience they believed was unique to Seattle. In this regard, the supporters of the market succeeded in using it to create a civic identity in Seattle. Pictures of the market grace the covers of visitors guides, tourist maps, and booster brochures. After the Space Needle, the Pike Place Market is the most recognizable man-made symbol of Seattle.

Unfortunately, the market's very success threatens to destroy it. The volume of tourists in the market keeps the locals at bay. In 1996 John Pastier of *Historic Preservation* magazine wrote an article criticizing tourism in the market. Pastier claimed that the market was losing its authenticity and becoming just another "festival marketplace." Pastier continued, "as tourism grows, it dilutes the market's authenticity and interferes with the purposes for which it was founded and which led an enlightened generation of preservationists and community advocates to save it from a more overt form of destruction." The success of tourism would lead, Pastier warned, to a "slippery slope" that

Pike Place, lined with market buildings, 2002. (Rebekah Harvey)

would choke out farmers and produce sellers to make way for merchants who catered to tourists. [146]

The rise of tourism in the market—and the struggle to control it—showed the difficulty of regulating market forces, in every sense of the word. By denying the capitalistic structures at work in post–World War II American life, the PDA, Urban Renewal Division, and MHC created the Pike Place Market as a place where consumption was limited to a single point-of-purchase event, rather than a way of life.[147] Yet by choosing who could sell their wares in the market and what goods merchants could sell, the PDA set up an artificial model of capitalism that simply could not exist without outside regulation. The PDA had to control the whole process, from the point of production to the point of consumption, in order to keep the market independent of the forces of standardization, consolidation, and globalization.

The success of the Pike Place Market seemed to many observers to be a Pyrrhic victory. Steinbrueck saw the handwriting on the wall in 1975, when he resigned from the MHC in protest. By resigning, however, Steinbrueck relinquished his ability to shape the ultimate creation of the market. The compromises that came from the political and economic realities of joining a public development corporation with the city's urban renewal office to get federal money meant that the market became more like Scheme 23 than Steinbrueck's market. In an act of possible reconciliation, Seattle's city council in 1985 named the park at the north end of the market "Steinbrueck Park," perhaps to recall the crusader's vision for the place.

Yet the market succeeded in providing Seattle with a civic identity. The farmers' market, and the nostalgia it invokes, have indeed become symbols of the city. In the tradition of Mark Tobey and Victor Steinbrueck, artists sit among the vegetable stands and paint scenes of the market to sell to visitors. Pictures of the neon "Public Market" sign adorn the covers of visitors' guides in hotel rooms, and produce vendors in the market sell cloth shopping bags with colorful stencils of market scenes for tourists to bring home. Along with the Space Needle and Mount Rainier, images of the Pike Place Market have become synonymous with Seattle.

IF YOU PRESERVE IT,

THEY WILL COME:

LOWER DOWNTOWN, DENVER

Adjacent to Larimer Square in Denver, Lower Downtown is the center of the city's social life. Pedestrians move easily between Larimer Square and "LoDo," as the district is called. In the evening, the streets fill with young singles hopping the bars that occupy old warehouses, couples dining on loading-docks-turned-patios, and tourists sitting on historic-looking benches, enjoying the huge flower pots along the street and soaking up the historic ambience. Denver's light rail system transports visitors into the district from the suburbs, and the 16th Street Mall, the city's commercial pedestrian thoroughfare, terminates in the middle of Lower Downtown, dropping shoppers into the district. Coors Field, home of the Colorado Rockies baseball team, sits at one edge of LoDo, and the Pepsi Center, where the Colorado Avalanche hockey team and the Denver Nuggets basketball team play, sits at the other. Together, the venues flood the district with sports fans year round.

Unlike Seattle's Pike Place Market, which preserved the historic use of the district, the Lower Downtown Historic District was an elaborate adaptive re-use project that created a mixed-use neighborhood out of Denver's old warehouse district. In the late 1980s, Denver's city government, business leaders, and historic preservationists fought to save Lower Downtown as a way to revitalize the central business district. The campaign for Lower Downtown marked a dramatic shift in the city's policy on historic preservation from the 1960s, when Dana Crawford fought the Denver Urban Renewal Authority (DURA) to preserve Larimer Square. During the Lower Downtown campaign, the city council, the Denver Landmark Preservation Commission, a nonprofit preservation organization called Historic Denver, and a group of Denver business-people called the Downtown Denver Partnership joined forces to overcome opposition from property owners and create a historic district in Lower Downtown. Influenced by urban renewal–funded preservation projects like Seattle's Pike Place Market, advocates believed that the historic preservation of Lower Downtown was the best way to bring suburban residents, tourists, and other visitors into the central business district, and they lobbied for the establishment of a historic district on the grounds that Lower Downtown's old buildings could serve as an extension of the civic identity already created in Larimer Square.

Lower Downtown was the birthplace of Denver. Situated just northeast of Larimer Square, the district's informal borders were the South Platte River, Cherry Creek, Larimer Street, and 20th Street. As noted in Chapter 2, General William Larimer claimed this area as the Denver City Town Company, and it was the first area settled after Denver's 1858 gold rush. Pioneers used lumber from the cottonwood trees lining the rivers as the first building material, but a devastating fire in 1863, followed by a flood in 1864, prompted settlers to rebuild in brick. Even before Larimer Street's heyday, Blake Street and Market Street became Denver's main thoroughfares, filled with saloons, brothels, gambling halls, boarding houses, general stores, banks, and blacksmiths. Entrepreneur Walter Scott Cheesman's drugstore sat at the corner of 15th and Blake, and the area also housed the Clark and Gruber Mint, the Kountze Brothers Bank (later Colorado National Bank), and the original Daniels Dry Goods Store.[1]

The arrival of the railroad in 1870 changed the commercial pattern in Lower Downtown. After 1881, Union Station sat near the river at the edge of the

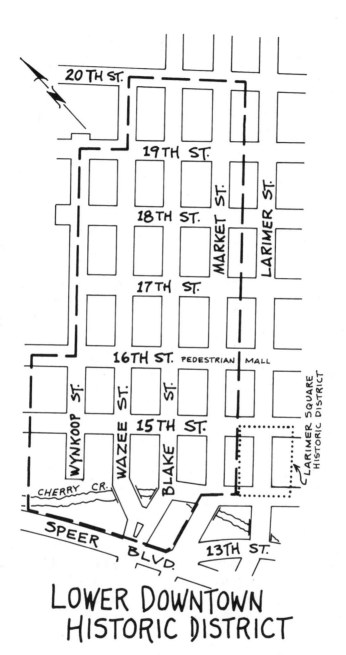

LOWER DOWNTOWN
HISTORIC DISTRICT

district, and over the next sixty years warehouses and wholesale businesses grew along the tracks. Retail establishments moved first to Larimer Street, then to 16th Street, while Blake, Wazee, and Market streets became staging areas for meat, produce, ores, and raw materials waiting to be shipped to other parts of the nation.[2] Between 1880 and 1893, mineral rushes and railroad commerce created explosive growth in Denver, and 17th Street, which terminated at Union Station, became known as the "Wall Street of the West." Hotels popped up along 17th Street to cater to rail passengers.[3] The arrival of the railroad also changed Lower Downtown's appearance, as pressed and cast metals became more readily available building materials, allowing for more ornate Victorian brick warehouses.[4]

Lower Downtown's fortunes fell with the repeal of the Sherman Silver Purchase Act in 1893. Although the ensuing depression affected the entire nation, it devastated silver-producing states like Colorado. Building in Denver virtually stopped until after World War I, and then most commercial development moved along the streetcar lines out of the central business district.[5] Construction of the interstate highway system after World War II led to a further decline in rail traffic, causing the abandonment of many of Lower Downtown's old warehouses. The city built raised viaducts over the rail yards and the South Platte River, connecting Lower Downtown's street grid to the interstate. Lower Downtown, like adjacent Larimer Street, became skid row. Transients took up residence in the empty warehouses, frequently vandalizing the buildings and causing fires. The viaducts created a dark no-man's land, and the streets under the raised roadways became havens for bums and derelicts. The once posh hotels that catered to Victorian rail passengers found new life as flophouses.[6]

As it had done with Larimer Square, DURA slated most of Lower Downtown for demolition. As early as 1944, an architectural plan for the city proposed widening Market Street through Lower Downtown to four lanes, bulldozing the buildings in the district to make room for the expanded roadway, and turning the alley between Market Street and Blake Street into parking.[7] In 1958 the Denver Planning Department issued a series of bulletins outlining proposals for Lower Downtown, and each one called for the complete razing of the district. One planning bulletin claimed that the rail center around Union Station was the "key to the entire downtown economy" and proposed constructing a Lower Downtown expressway to connect the warehouse district with the new Valley Highway, Interstate 25. According to the

Warehouses along Wynkoop Street in Lower Downtown, 1936. (Denver Public Library Western History Department)

planning bulletin, easier access would bring more manufacturing and industrial employment to Lower Downtown, increasing the tax base. The new expressway would have obliterated Wazee, Market, Larimer, and Lawrence streets, while Blake Street and Arapahoe Street would have been widened to four lanes each.[8]

A combination of limited city finances, shifting priorities, and boundary quirks saved Lower Downtown from becoming a highway. When DURA ultimately set the Skyline Urban Renewal Project's boundaries in 1964, it missed most of Lower Downtown, although Larimer Street fell within the project. The funding of the massive Skyline project left the city without the finances to implement other major urban design changes. Meanwhile, Larimer Square became a historic district, and its success caused DURA and city planners to reconsider demolition plans in Lower Downtown.[9] In fact, the Denver city council changed Lower Downtown's zoning in 1974 to "provide for and encourage the preservation and vitality of older areas that are significant because of their architectural, historical, and economic value."[10] The district was zoned for industrial and manufacturing, which prohibited any other uses. Prompted by the success of Larimer Square and pressure from a few Lower Downtown property owners, the city created a new zoning category, B–7 mixed use, allowing for commercial, retail, and residential development. The new zoning area covered approximately twenty blocks from 20th Street to Speer Boulevard, and from Wynkoop Street to the alley between Market and Larimer streets.[11]

The 1974 rezoning created a wave of private development in Lower Downtown. Potential developers, impressed with increased property values in Larimer Square, saw opportunities for adaptive reuse of Lower Downtown's historic warehouses. As the Skyline Urban Renewal Project tore down historic buildings along Lawrence and Larimer streets to restore commerce, more sensitive developers worked on using neighboring historic buildings to achieve the same purpose. According to an article in the *Denver Post*'s *Empire Magazine,* "The alley that divides central downtown from lower downtown Denver [the Market/Larimer alley] is a Royal Gorge. On one side rise the towers of the Skyline Urban Renewal Project . . . Northwest of that alley, construction is just as vigorous. But instead of tall towers being raised, two- and three-story antiques are being restored."[12]

Ironically, the people driving the earliest restoration projects in Lower Downtown usually did not come from Denver. Locals were too prejudiced against Lower Downtown to see any value in the neighborhood, but transplants recognized the potential in the run-down old warehouses. One of the earliest developers was Bill Saslow, who came to Denver from Boston in 1971. Saslow was a leading activist for the creation of the B–7 zoning category, recognizing that development in Lower Downtown depended on a variety of uses. In 1974 Saslow and partners Allan Reiver and Peter Dominick Jr. renovated Market Street Mall at 18th and Market streets, gutting it to create 28,000 square feet of retail and office space. By the 1980s it held establishments including art galleries, a travel agency, an interior design studio, and a theater. Saslow also developed the Blake Street Bath and Racquet Club in the 1700 block of Blake Street, which contained second-floor condominiums, ground-floor office and retail space, and a swimming pool and tennis court along the back alley. Allan Reiver, a transplant from Houston who arrived in Denver in 1970, developed Market Center, an office complex at 17th and Market. Local Peter Dominick Jr. also renovated office and retail space in Lower Downtown, notably the Wazee Exchange Building at 19th and Wazee. Together, the "Wazee Three," as they called their partnership, influenced the restoration of more than two dozen structures in Lower Downtown. By 1981 a vice president of First Denver Mortgage Company estimated that private developers like the Wazee Three

The Blake Street Bath and Racquet Club at 18th and Blake Street, one of the earliest mixed-use renewal projects in LoDo. (Bill Saslow)

had rehabilitated 865,000 square feet of office space in Lower Downtown at an estimated cost of over $29 million.[13]

Although not the pioneer in Lower Downtown that she had been in Larimer Square, Dana Crawford joined the effort to revitalize the area in the early 1980s. In 1981 Crawford and developer Charles Callaway bought the Oxford Hotel at 17th and Wazee. The Oxford was one of Lower Downtown's architectural jewels, designed by Frank Edbrooke, the architect who later built the famous Brown Palace Hotel at the other end of downtown. The Oxford closed for remodeling in 1979, but the project stalled for lack of funds until Crawford and Callaway got involved and shepherded the $12 million restoration to completion.[14] Crawford also joined a partnership to buy the Ice House, once a warehouse and cold storage facility for a local dairy. Crawford and partners restored the Ice House into a design center that became the artistic anchor of Lower Downtown.[15]

The business owners and historic preservationists working to revitalize Lower Downtown recognized that the district would never be a viable retail or residential center unless the transients, bums, and other "undesirables" were moved out. During the 1970s, Colorado's Supreme Court rescinded the law that made public drunkenness a crime, so police could do little to keep the homeless and drunks off the streets. In response, property owners led by

Bill Saslow, the association of Denver businesses called Downtown Denver Inc. (later the Downtown Denver Partnership), and Denver General Hospital cooperatively formed an organization called "Denver C.A.R.E.S." Established in 1978, the name stood for Comprehensive Alcohol Rehabilitation Emergency Services. The program operated vans, driven by Denver General Hospital personnel, who patrolled the streets looking for public drunkenness. If van drivers spotted someone intoxicated on the street who posed a danger to themselves or others, they took him or her to the city's detoxification center. The vans had police radios in them in case one of the bums did not want to be moved and was causing a disturbance. Although the detoxification unit only kept the drunks for three days, they usually found new haunts when they sobered up. The program helped remove the derelicts from Lower Downtown, and it still runs today.[16]

Despite private investments, zoning changes, and other civic improvements, Lower Downtown witnessed a blitzkrieg of demolitions in the early 1980s. Denver's oil boom in the late 1970s inspired developers to look for cheap office space near the 17th Street financial district. Speculators bought property and tore down historic buildings to make way for new office space and parking lots. The demolitions prompted an amendment to the B–7 zoning ordinance in 1982, increasing the density of Lower Downtown and allowing owners of historic buildings to sell their unused development rights to builders of higher-density projects elsewhere. The value of the transferable development rights gave historic property owners an additional asset, providing an incentive to restore old buildings rather than tear them down.[17]

The zoning amendment failed to slow down demolitions, however. Between 1981 and 1988, between 20 and 25 percent of the buildings in the district met the wrecking ball.[18] Historic preservationists and downtown business activists realized that incentives to private developers were not enough to preserve the old buildings. Historic Denver, an organization formed in 1970 to save the house of Molly Brown of *Titanic* fame, became interested in Lower Downtown during the 1980s. In addition to the Molly Brown House, Historic Denver worked to save other structures, including an old brothel known as the Navarre, the Paramount Theater, and a block of working-class homes in the Auraria Higher Education Center. Historic Denver joined the Downtown Denver Partnership (DDP) to campaign for a historic district in Lower Downtown as a way to protect the area's "critical mass" of historic structures.[19] As early as 1981, these groups lobbied city council for a mixed-use historic district like Larimer Square, but on a larger scale and with the housing component.[20]

DDP and Historic Denver did not make much progress, however, until 1983, when Denver voters elected Federico Peña mayor. Peña came into office with an ambitious revitalization agenda for Denver. His campaign slogan, "Imagine a great city," set the tone for his administration. Peña sought to reverse the flood of tax dollars, investment capital, and retail revenue out of the central business district.[21] The 16th Street Mall was nearing completion when Peña took office, and that project started the revival of Denver's downtown. Peña's other priorities included a convention center for Denver, a new airport, and a downtown residential neighborhood. He realized that downtown Denver must be a twenty-four–hour community, which meant attracting residents. Peña's civic agenda and willingness to make substantial changes prompted the first serious efforts at city-mandated preservation in Lower Downtown and inspired journalists and city council members to try to enhance Denver's "livability."[22]

Peña's first priority was building a convention center. One of the proposed locations was behind Union Station. Initially, preservationists opposed this site because they feared that development would lead to the demolition of more historic buildings in Lower Downtown. However, Historic Denver and DDP realized that they could trade their support of the convention center for guarantees of support for historic preservation from the city planning office. The property owners in Lower Downtown also backed preservation, realizing that the combined convention center and historic district would increase business.[23] To keep their part of the bargain, Historic Denver president Lane Ittleson wrote a letter to members urging them to support the Union Station convention center site. According to Ittleson's letter, "the new convention center represents a unique opportunity to realize the full potential of lower downtown. We find that for almost the first time, property owners and preservationists are in agreement about the best and most desirable use for lower downtown."[24]

Unfortunately, voters defeated the Union Station convention center proposal, and the friendly coalition of business interests, preservationists, city government, and property owners dissolved.[25] By early 1986, one-quarter of the property in Lower Downtown was for sale, as speculators who hoped to profit from the proposed convention center bailed out once the market softened. The sale of the old buildings raised preservationists' fears that more demolitions would follow as new owners, less sensitive to the area's historic character, might tear down buildings. Ittleson, however, saw the rejection of the Union Station site for the convention center as a positive thing. Without high dollar options, Ittleson believed property owners would turn to preservation instead of development.[26] Still, the preservation community actively sought some sort of ordinance to protect Lower Downtown.

The first step toward a historic preservation ordinance in Lower Downtown came in 1985, when Peña ordered the drafting of a downtown master plan. Representatives from the business community, the city planning community, and the historic preservation community drafted the Downtown Area Plan and presented it formally in 1986. One crucial member of the Downtown Area Plan drafting committee was Lisa Purdy, a planning consultant with ties to both Historic Denver and the Downtown Denver Partnership. Although the Downtown Area Plan included provisions for a new airport, a light rail system, and revitalization of various districts of Denver, Purdy ensured a prominent place for the preservation of Lower Downtown.[27] Purdy and the other authors of the Downtown Area Plan envisioned Lower Downtown serving as the artistic center of the city, complete with galleries, public art projects, a design center at the Ice House, architects' offices, and downtown housing. The plan proposed using the old warehouses for lofts, which appealed to artists and architects and also provided an efficient use of the warehouses' interior. The plan's residential component gave the central business district the desired round-the-clock community, providing a market for retail and community-based businesses.[28] To strengthen the urban community, the plan also called for new traffic patterns to promote pedestrian activity. The most controversial part of the plan, however, was demolition control. Preservationists, supported by Mayor Peña, insisted on a demolition moratorium in Lower Downtown to protect the remaining historic structures.[29]

In 1986 the city council approved the Downtown Area Plan, but a separate ordinance needed to pass the council to establish Lower Downtown as a historic district.[30] To solidify the council's support, the preservation community had to convince the citizens of Denver that the old skid row was worth preserving. Because Denverites had a bias against the dilapidated old warehouses, the proponents of historic preservation had to make the district appealing to people accustomed to avoiding the area. To that end, business leaders with the Downtown Denver Partnership, preservationists, and leaders of Historic Denver argued that Lower Downtown's tie to Denver's heritage made the area vital to the city's future identity.[31]

Supporters of the historic district believed that Lower Downtown could answer the criticism that Denver had nothing unique about it. In a 1978 article in the *Rocky Mountain Journal*, for example, Lower Downtown property owner Peter Dominick Jr. asked, "Why, with all its potential, is Denver cloaked in mediocrity? All that icing, but no cake." He argued that Denver had nothing in its urban environment to make it special and keep tourists in town. Most Denverites, Dominick claimed, thought of the mountains as their primary asset and did not believe that the built environment could compete with the natural beauty of the landscape.[32] Similarly, Mayor Peña noted that the building boom of the early 1980s left the city nondescript. According to the mayor, "Some people . . . criticized our buildings downtown. They said they looked like Houston."[33] To answer these charges, Richard C. D. Fleming, CEO of the Downtown Denver Partnership, argued that Denver needed to project a unique image.[34] Fleming claimed that preserving Lower Downtown would "wake up the 'sleeping giant' of promise in Denver, find its pulse, and make the downtown its heart."[35] Similarly, *Denver Post* columnist Bill Hornby claimed that "a great deal of livability for residents as well as our invitation to visitors lies in our Western heritage . . . Denver must carefully preserve its historic heritage."[36]

Lower Downtown not only distinguished Denver from other cities but also set downtown apart from the suburbs. Like most western cities after World War II, Denver's retail and residential development grew outside the city limits. Denver's sprawl looked, architecturally and commercially, like any other city, and thus diluted the city's civic identity.[37] Former Denver city planning director and former Historic Denver president Jennifer Moulton said, "Denver has no point of difference other than [Lower] Downtown. Everything else we've done in the last twenty years looked like it could have been done anywhere . . . We have no identity other than Lower Downtown."[38] Lisa Purdy echoed this sentiment by saying, "Lower downtown is what separates us from the suburbs. It is a unique asset. If it gets wiped out, we've got nothing. We're like anywhere else."[39] Bill Mosher of DDP agreed, claiming that "downtown needs to be unique and different from the suburbs." He noticed that business owners felt "they have to be *more* like the suburbs. But if part of your advantage is being unique and different, that means capitalizing on your historic heritage."[40] The urban design plan that supplemented the Downtown Area Plan emphasized that Lower Downtown made the city different from the suburbs. According to the plan, "Lower downtown is the only concentration of urban historic buildings in the region. Denver can be distinguished from its surrounding suburbs because of these historic roots."[41]

The unique heritage of Lower Downtown had less to do with the architecture than it did with a sense that history *happened* there. Although some of the buildings were designed by renowned Denver architects, they were fairly typical of most Victorian-era western cities. However, the events and people associated with the buildings and the district, such as Wyatt Earp, Bat Masterson, Buffalo Bill, Big Bill Haywood, and Horace and Baby Doe Tabor, made the district an integral part of Denver's communal past and an accepted symbol of the city's heritage.

Proponents of establishing a historic district in Lower Downtown also argued that the unique identity encapsulated in the old buildings gave Denver an economic asset to spark revitalization of the entire central business district. During city council hearings on Lower Downtown, Peña's aid Tom Gougeon informed council members that creating a historic district in Lower Downtown was more important to Denver's economy than either the convention center or a new airport, both projects aggressively pushed by the Peña administration. Gougeon told the council, "I've never told you any of those is the single most important issue for the city, but I'm telling you that historic designation for Lower Downtown is."[42] According to Peña, historic designation for Lower Downtown was "the best opportunity to kick off the revitalization of downtown Denver."[43] The Downtown Area Plan claimed that the district was a "market asset" and advocated the preservation and development of the district because it would "stimulate new economic demand in Lower Downtown."

When observers claimed that Denver had nothing unique except Lower Downtown, they implicitly included Larimer Square. Indeed, prior to the implementation of the Skyline project and Dana Crawford's restoration of Larimer Square, Larimer Street was part of Lower Downtown. When Purdy, Moulton, Peña, and other preservationists referred to Lower Downtown's role in making Denver unique, they inherently acknowledged that Larimer Square already provided the basis for Denver's identity. Because of its proximity, much of Lower Downtown's symbolic power was an extension of the identity Dana Crawford established in Larimer Square twenty years earlier. Preserving the entire warehouse district expanded on Larimer Square's heritage and added a community dimension.[44]

Preservationists predicted that a historic district in Lower Downtown would attract consumers to the central business district. The authors of the Downtown Area Plan called for Lower Downtown to be "marketed and managed as a cohesive whole" to consumers, developers, and tenants. Preservation, the Downtown Area Plan continued, would create a special "market draw" in Lower Downtown for residents and tourists, and the district as a whole would become "one of Denver's great landmarks—the not-to-be-missed place."[45] The urban design plan for Lower Downtown reinforced the economic potential of the district, claiming that the area gave Denver a unique "market niche" to attract visitors.[46] Members of the media also saw value in preserving Lower Downtown. Journalists cited commercially successful historic districts in other cities and pointed out that a strong association with the past would bring tourist dollars in the future.[47]

The heritage Denver sought to preserve was *not* warehouses and manufacturing plants, however. In order for Lower Downtown to promote the revitalization of the central business district, city planners, the mayor's office, preservationists, and business interests had to create a new identity in Lower Downtown that maintained a link to Denver's history without promoting the district's actual use. According to Richard Fleming of the Downtown Denver Partnership, people should think of downtown Denver "as they do Faneuil Hall in Boston, an urban remake that draws more customers than Disneyland."[48] The "urban remake" Fleming proposed took the form of a manufactured heritage in Lower Downtown, outlined by the Downtown Area Plan.[49] Bill Mosher of the Downtown Denver Partnership acknowledged the attempt to create a tradition in the Downtown Area Plan, claiming "all the emphasis on Denver's historic fabric is not accidental."[50] In standard adaptive reuse form, the authors of the Downtown Area Plan used Lower Downtown's old warehouses to invoke nostalgia for Denver's frontier heritage while designating a new usage for the buildings to create a new identity. The Downtown Area Plan called for the replacement of an old industrial area with a bohemian urban village, using the old buildings as a backdrop to invoke historic credibility.

The most important part of Lower Downtown's identity was the large number of nineteenth-century buildings together in one geographical area. Because few of the structures were noteworthy by themselves, preservation proponents needed to save the "critical mass" of buildings. Demolition had taken its toll, however, and preservationists wanted to inspire new development that would be compatible with the historic buildings. Consequently, the demolition moratorium coupled with design guidelines would regulate changes and ensure compatible infill development. According to the plan, the design guidelines would "create a unified overall image" in the district.[51]

Around the buildings, the Downtown Area Plan suggested creating a pedestrian-friendly neighborhood. Like Larimer Square, Lower Downtown sought to recreate a small-town atmosphere by emphasizing pedestrian access. The Downtown Area Plan proposed historic landscaping, street furniture, and light fixtures that reinforced the "urban village" image.[52] The urban design plan also suggested keeping the alleyways intact, not only for their historic functions of deliveries or trash removal but also to "maintain the rhythm of buildings" and prevent development of entire blocks, thus ensuring "unique pedestrian passages" between buildings.[53]

The proposed historic preservation ordinance emphasized the new use outlined in the Downtown Area Plan and the urban design plan. The Denver Landmark Preservation Commission acknowledged the importance of the new heritage in its recommendation to city council. The DLPC approved preservation in Lower Downtown because the concentration of old buildings would "foster civic pride in the beauty and accomplishments of the past" as well as "protect and enhance the city's attraction to tourists and visitors" and "promote the use of outstanding historical or architectural structures . . . for education, stimulation and welfare of the people of the city."[54] The proposed historic district ordinance echoed this sentiment, claiming that Lower Downtown "should be developed or preserved according to a plan based on an historic, cultural, and architectural *motif*" (emphasis added).[55]

Despite the promises of economic revitalization and a unique market niche, Lower Downtown's preservation met with stiff opposition from the district's property owners. Only four property owners supported the historic preservation ordinance, with most vocally opposed. The property owners focused their opposition on the design review and demolition restrictions, which Bill Saslow called "arbitrary" and "draconian." Property owners objected to the formation of a Lower Downtown design review board, believing it duplicated the Denver Landmark Preservation Commission. Because of the overwhelming number of demolitions in the 1980s, the mayor's office and preservationists advocated demolition restrictions to keep the "critical mass" of buildings intact.[56] Most of the property owners dismissed the threat of demolition, however. Bill Saslow and Allan Reiver reminded the preservationists that they, the property owners, had been the first to see the value in the old buildings, and that they generally supported historic preservation. The property owners felt that the moratorium on demolitions carried preservation too far, however, and infringed on their property rights.[57]

Ironically, one of the most outspoken opponents of the historic district was none other than Dana Crawford. Although Crawford advocated maintaining the historic character of the district, she disagreed with the demolition restriction, and her experience with DURA in Larimer Square made her wary of any design review guidelines. Crawford also was promoting a high-rise development on the edge of the district, and she feared that design review guidelines might hinder that project. Her stance on historic preservation in Lower Downtown showed that Crawford used historic preservation as a means to an end, rather than as an end in itself. One source claimed Crawford was "more of a preservation-minded developer than a development-minded preservationist."[58]

The state's economy reinforced opposition to the historic district. The Rocky Mountain states witnessed a deep recession during the 1980s.[59] Speculators overbuilt downtown office space during the oil boom of the late 1970s, and when the market busted five years later, entire high-rises sat vacant. Downtown land prices declined by as much as 80 percent, and office vacancies exceeded 25 percent by 1987.[60] Like many downtown property owners, Lower Downtown developers experienced foreclosures, repossessions, and bankruptcies. Some property owners felt they needed to sell their run-down buildings to avoid bankruptcy, and design and demolition restrictions dramatically reduced the value of their property.[61]

Opposition from the property owners jeopardized the passage of the Lower Downtown Historic District ordinance. Despite support from the mayor's office, the Office of Planning and Community Development (formerly the Denver Planning Department), the Downtown Denver Partnership, and Historic Denver, property owners had great influence on city council's decision whether or not to preserve a district. Indeed, opposition from property owners usually stopped historic designation. There was, however, one precedent for preservation against an owner's opposition; it occurred when the Denver Landmarks Preservation Commission designated the Mayan Theater on South Broadway in 1985 over the owner's objections.[62] Knowing that opposition from Lower Downtown property owners could block the ordinance, preservationists went straight to the public, working to garner city-wide support to ensure city council's approval.[63]

Preservation advocates spent more than a year stumping for the creation of the Lower Downtown Historic District, using the district's importance to Denver's identity as the key selling point and painting a picture of the type of community Lower Downtown could be. Lisa Purdy spoke to civic groups on a daily basis, having breakfast or lunch meetings with the Junior League of

Denver, the Garden Club, women's organizations and other preservation-friendly groups.[64] Jennifer Moulton, working on behalf of Historic Denver and the Downtown Denver Partnership, collected success stories and precedents from adaptive reuse projects across the country to prove that property values increased with preservation.[65] Property owners fought back, signing petitions protesting the historic district and hiring lawyers to declare the historic district ordinance unconstitutional on the grounds that it was tantamount to a taking of property.[66] The struggle to implement the Lower Downtown Historic District ordinance was, according to people on both sides of the issue, a "bloodletting."[67]

When the city council began its hearings on Lower Downtown, preservationists realized that their efforts had paid off. The majority of people who spoke at the hearings advocated the historic district, citing Lower Downtown's significance to Denver's identity and heritage and the district's potential to bring suburban dwellers downtown. The property owners who testified, however, opposed the formation of the historic district because of the accursed demolition restrictions. Property owners also testified that the design review board in Lower Downtown duplicated the functions of the DLPC and the Office of Planning and Community Development.[68] The property owners did not make a convincing case, however, and after four months of hearings, the council passed the Lower Downtown Historic District ordinance by a final vote of ten to three.[69]

With the historic district established, Historic Denver, the Downtown Denver Partnership, the mayor's office, and the Office of Planning and Community Development implemented programs to diffuse the property owners' dissatisfaction. The city planning office agreed to sponsor an economic impact study in the district every two years. To jump-start investment, DDP opened the Lower Downtown Business Support Office, which marketed the area to potential investors. The Business Support Office also administered a revolving loan program funded by the National Trust for Historic Preservation, Historic Denver, and downtown business interests. Property owners could get loans to cover improvements to keep them in compliance with the historic district guidelines.[70] The Office of Planning and Community Development also agreed to provide infrastructural improvements like benches, flower pots, and trash containers, as well as street maintenance and repairs, funded by a 1989 bond issue.[71] The Department of Transportation removed the viaducts, diverting traffic and adding tunnels, bridges, and new streets along the river.[72]

The state and federal governments aided improvements in Lower Downtown by giving property owners in the district rehabilitation tax credits and state tax cuts for investments that led to job creation.[73] The Lower Downtown Historic District also got support from an unlikely source—the Denver Urban Renewal Agency. Ironically, DURA had changed its stance on historic preservation since the battles with Dana Crawford over Larimer Square and had become one of the most important proponents of historic preservation in Denver. DURA earmarked some of its funds to give tax increment financing to buildings in Lower Downtown. As of 1996 DURA played a critical role in thirteen major rehabilitations in the district that totaled $174 million.[74]

Soon after the establishment of the historic district, Lower Downtown took on a new identity—"LoDo." Coined by *Denver Post* columnist Dick Kreck, "LoDo" was, of course, a play on the name of the artists' district of SoHo in New York City. The new nickname perfectly symbolized the identity that preservation advocates sought to create for Lower Downtown.[75] Envisioned as an urban village, LoDo symbolized Denver's new standard of livability, as residents dwelled in the middle of an off-beat, artistic urban neighborhood. Creators of LoDo believed the area would define a new lifestyle for Denver. LoDo's combination of bohemian businesses, urban residences, and art galleries, literally built on the foundations of Denver's heritage, defined Denver's civic identity for the new millennium.[76]

Despite intentions of groups wanting to create an urban village, LoDo took on a life of its own. Historic designation led to a boom in the district that even preservation supporters did not imagine. In the first two years after designation, LoDo's twenty blocks witnessed fourteen new, significant construction projects and 114 new businesses.[77] Contrary to property owners' fears that the historic district would deflate property values, it actually stabilized the real estate market. With city support, investors felt more confident to proceed with improvements. Brad Segal, coordinator of the Lower Downtown Business Support Office, estimated that in LoDo's first year as a historic district, $40 million in new investments came into the area, along with forty new businesses and 150 new jobs.[78] The required economic impact statements in 1990 and 1992 showed that Lower Downtown prospered better than the rest of downtown Denver. After 1992, the city quit requiring the statements.[79]

One of the first successful adaptive reuse projects in LoDo was the Wynkoop Brewing Company. Located in the 1899 J. S. Brown Mercantile Building, the brewpub was the first in the city and among the first in the nation. Owner John Hickenlooper converted the old warehouse into a restaurant and brewery, with lofts in the upper floors. Although the initial prospects of the Wynkoop Brewing

The Wynkoop Brewing Company, 2002.

Company looked so bad that Hickenlooper's own mother refused to invest in the venture, the bar immediately became a popular destination and brought suburbanites into Lower Downtown.[80] The brewery's success helped to propel Hickenlooper into the mayor's office in 2003.

The success of the Wynkoop Brewing Company and its lofts prompted Dana Crawford to get into the residential market. Crawford developed the Edbrooke Lofts from the Davis Brothers Warehouse at 1450 Wynkoop. When every unit in the project sold before construction began, Crawford allowed that historic preservation in Lower Downtown was a good idea after all. Crawford also revitalized the former Brecht Candy Company at 1333 Wazee Street into the Acme Lofts.[81]

The lofts over the Wynkoop Brewing Company and Crawford's Edbrooke Lofts started a residential boom in LoDo. During the 1980s, only 5 percent of Denver's workforce lived within 10 miles of downtown, well below the national average of 20 percent, signaling a strong, untapped market for housing close to the central business district.[82] However, the Skyline Urban Renewal Project's apartments failed to provide the desired increase in population.[83] Lower Downtown was the logical place for urban housing, since the historic character of

The Brecht Candy Company on 12th and Wazee, 1910. (Denver Public Library Western History Department)

the buildings made it a desirable neighborhood, and the scale of the buildings promoted a pedestrian-friendly environment.[84] Reinforcing the initial vision for Lower Downtown as a center for the arts, lofts became the district's prevailing type of housing.

Lofts began as living quarters in old industrial buildings with large windows and a minimum of interior walls. New York's SoHo popularized the style, and lofts became preferred by artists who needed the space to do double duty as home and studio. Lofts' popularity stemmed from the union of the real estate market and the art market, and they appealed to the Bourgeois Bohemians (Bobos) who were quickly becoming the new elite.[85] As lofts became popular with people other than artists, the market in LoDo boomed, changing the housing demographic by creating more single-family dwellings and fewer single-room occupancy hotels. Metro Denver residents reversed a century-long trend by moving from the suburbs into the city. Downtown housing experienced the biggest increase in Denver's history between 1990 and 1996, with LoDo's resident population growing by more than 20 percent.[86]

Because of soaring property values, community-based businesses could not keep up with the growing population in LoDo. In 1999 the district had 1,450 residents, but no grocery stores. A small market opened at 16th and Blake in late 1999 but closed within two years, and the large supermarkets, such as King Soopers and Safeway, continued to assert that there were still not enough

The Brecht Candy Company's rebirth as the Acme Lofts, 2002.

residents in LoDo to warrant opening a store.[87] That meant that district residents, many of whom used their cars infrequently, had to drive to find a grocery store. There were also no dry cleaners, drug stores, or hardware stores in LoDo for almost a decade after its establishment. This did not appear to deter potential residents, however, and LoDo continued to grow.[88]

The popularity of lofts was only one reason for Lower Downtown's dramatic rise in property values. In 1995, Coors Field, home of the expansion major-league Colorado Rockies baseball team, opened on the edge of the historic district. The architects of the stadium designed the building to be sensitive to the architectural tradition, historic character, and pedestrian scale of the district. The stadium has a sunken playing field so that its bleachers do not tower too high over the street. The brick construction, reminiscent of old-fashioned ball parks, reflects the building materials of the warehouse district, and replicas of columbines, Colorado's state flower, adorn the top edge of the stadium.[89]

Coors Field proved to be a mixed blessing for Lower Downtown. Economically, the stadium brought a rush of business to LoDo. Between January and June of 1995, the first year the stadium was open, the historic district logged $60 million in taxable sales. By comparison, the district had registered $73.3 million in sales for the entire year of 1994. These numbers reflect only retail sales to people staying in Denver. Anything purchased and shipped out of state would be additional.[90] Some observers attributed the economic boom in LoDo to the arrival of the stadium, but preservationists countered that the revival of LoDo began with the establishment of the historic district, and Coors Field merely accelerated a trend already in place.[91]

The stadium did, however, change the character of the historic district. The presence of the baseball field attracted sports bars, night clubs, and upscale restaurants and bistros to Lower Downtown.[92] The increasing number of entertainment establishments created a district very different from the one envisioned by preservation lobbyists. Instead of a center for the arts, LoDo became the city's hottest night spot, with over fifty bars and restaurants by 1995.[93] The changes in LoDo led *Denver Post* columnist Dick Kreck to observe,

> This is not the way we envisioned it. Lower Downtown was supposed to be an urban village, a place where residents would live in renovated warehouses and stroll to small shops, galleries, and boutiques. What we have is a party-hearty zone full of sports bars, restaurants, and coffee filling stations. It is beginning to wear.[94]

Because the sports bars, many of them national chains, were willing to pay top dollar for space near the stadium, small businesses and independent art galleries could not compete. The artistic and design center of the city slowly moved out of Lower Downtown to the emerging Golden Triangle district two miles to the south.[95]

The high concentration of bars and restaurants led to tension between the owners of entertainment establishments and residents. Property owners worried about the commercialization of the area and feared that the rising costs of lofts would drive middle-income residents out of the district. Residents also

Coors Field sits at the edge of Lower Downtown, bringing fans and money into the district.

grew tired of dealing with rowdy baseball fans. Suburbanites coming to Coors Field did not always realize that people lived in the old warehouses. LoDo dwellers told horror stories of drunken baseball fans urinating on cars, sleeping on terraces, and vomiting in the entrances of million-dollar lofts.[96] When a huge entertainment complex called Planet LoDo tried to enter the neighborhood in July 1996, residents lobbied the city to deny the liquor license. Planet LoDo proposed locating in an area highly concentrated with housing. Residents worried that the block-sized bar would bring noise, traffic, and crime into a part of the neighborhood that, because it was not near Coors Field, had fewer problems with those things. When the city council denied Planet LoDo's liquor license, residents petitioned to get a moratorium on new liquor licenses in LoDo, but because of the B–7 zoning, no use could be prohibited. At best, residents hoped to achieve a favorable balance between residential, retail, and entertainment uses.[97]

As the character of the neighborhood changed, residents depended on design guidelines to give them control over booming development. By the mid-1990s, loft builders renovated most of the existing warehouses, meaning later developers had to build new construction, which was expensive and therefore dictated higher-yield uses, usually bars and restaurants.[98] In order to maintain LoDo's character, interest groups and the neighborhood association joined forces to create a neighborhood development plan in 1996. The plan set height limits on buildings, decreased densities, replaced traffic lights with stop signs, and proposed converting some of the one-way streets to two-way traffic to enhance the district's pedestrian accessibility.[99]

Despite the lingering tension between residents and entertainment establishments in LoDo, the economic success of the historic district prompted development in adjacent regions of downtown. The late 1990s saw Six Flags Elitch Gardens amusement park and the Pepsi Center, home of the Denver Nuggets and Colorado Avalanche, establish themselves on the edge of LoDo. Lofts are currently under construction in the Central Platte Valley, and the Regional Transportation District (RTD) extended its light-rail service to Union Station to accommodate the area.[100] LoDo was one of Denver's top three tourist attractions every year from 1997 to 2001, beating the Colorado Rockies, Buffalo Bill's Grave, the Denver Mint, and Coors Brewery.[101] Truly, the proponents of the Lower Downtown Historic District succeeded in creating a livable city and revitalizing the central business district.

The establishment of the Lower Downtown Historic District also commodified and disseminated Denver's identity. National broadcasts of Colorado Rockies games routinely showed the historic district and the lifestyle it represented for Denver. The created identity in LoDo is so obvious as to be subtle. The city planners and historic preservationists who created a mixed-use neighborhood in the city never considered using the old buildings for their historic functions. Instead, LoDo was a large-scale recycling project, finding new ways to adapt the old warehouses to contemporary uses. Today, the neighborhood in the old manufacturing district serves to manufacture Denver's civic identity as a big city with a small-town atmosphere, showcasing Denver's heritage while ensuring its economic future.

Epilogue

       The five historic districts in this study exemplified the way historic preservation activists created civic identities in western cities. Despite differences in interest groups, funding sources, and motivations, historic preservation advocates in all five districts exaggerated the city's heritage or invented traditions to define, commodify, and disseminate a city's identity. Whereas Albuquerque's city commission used architectural symbols to invent a tradition in Old Town, Dana Crawford in Denver's Larimer Square reinforced architectural cues with a shrewd use of the media. In Seattle, historic preservation illustrated a struggle between multiple groups using the city's history to legitimize their vision of Seattle's identity. In both Pioneer Square and the Pike Place Market, business elites, cultural elites, city officials, social activists, and historic preservationists used political rhetoric to claim control of the physical and symbolic landscape. Finally, in Lower Downtown, Denver, the city government used historic preservation as part of an adaptive reuse strategy to create an image of a friendly, livable city, redefining urban living in the West.

       The success of each district's civic identity depended on the number of decision makers involved in the process. Districts with a single owner or *strong* governing agency created civic identities more effectively than districts where multiple agencies jockeyed for control. Old Town and LoDo had powerful city ordinances and design review boards that tightly controlled economic and architectural decisions, and therefore identity formation. In Larimer Square and the Pike Place Market, a single entity owned the entire district, supported by governmental bodies, allowing the owners to dictate which heritage to preserve. Consequently, these four districts succeeded in establishing civic identities. In contrast, Pioneer Square's multiplicity of interest groups prohibited any single entity from having the power to create a tradition that resonated with a single heritage.

       The preservation of these five districts had unintended consequences in each case. Whereas historic preservation began in opposition to urban renewal, by the 1980s historic preservation *became* urban renewal. Historic preservation reinforced the shift in city planning policy from a modernist to a postmodernist strategy by allowing for subdistricting and neighborhood difference. Historic preservation assumed an urban renewal function by attracting investors and consumers downtown. Albuquerque's city commission spent city funds to update services and pave streets in Old Town, and federal urban renewal money contributed to the rehabilitation of Pioneer Square, the Pike Place Market, and Lower Downtown. In Larimer Square and the Pike Place Market, where preservationists seemingly opposed urban renewal advocates, the participants disagreed on the buildings occupying the revitalized district, not the need for revitalization.

The preservation of each district transformed them, however, changing their racial/ethnic, class, and gender composition. Although Albuquerque's city commission created Old Town as a Hispanic village, the establishment of the historic district usurped Hispanic political and cultural authority in Old Town. Larimer Square changed from a working- and lower-class male neighborhood of flophouses and taverns into a block-long shopping mall, attracting mostly white suburban women and families. In Pioneer Square, historic preservation brought upscale restaurants and young professionals into the neighborhood with skid road indigents, but middle-class patrons failed to reconcile themselves with the presence of bums as living history. The Pike Place Market became an area completely different from the one envisioned by supporters, creating a primitive capitalist ecology under the auspices of preserving the historic market. Lower Downtown changed from the dark and deserted warehouse district to Denver's most popular entertainment and tourist destination, transforming the city's skid row into an upscale mixed-use neighborhood.

Like all capitalist endeavors, locally designated historic districts worked because they filled a market niche. Although criticized for faking authenticity, commodifying history, and masking shifts in power relationships, historic districts provided benefits for visitors and residents alike. Historic districts created clean, safe space within cities, which appealed to suburbanites, especially women. The districts provided consumers with a pleasant and memorable place in which to spend leisure time and consume products in an atmosphere that was unique to that city.

As the western districts in this study succeeded, they provided a blueprint that transformed historic districting nationwide. Larimer Square became a national prototype of urban revitalization, and Dana Crawford consulted with urban developer James Rouse on the restoration of Quincy Market in Boston and the construction of Harbor Place in Baltimore. Senator Warren Magnuson's role in securing urban renewal funding for the Pike Place Market set the precedent for using federal funds for preservation, and soon cities across the country petitioned Congress to fund historic preservation projects.

The conditions that allowed western city planners to use historic preservation as a development strategy related mostly to the rampant growth in western cities after World War II. Albuquerque, Denver, and Seattle all witnessed exponential population growth during the 1940s and 1950s. In Albuquerque, growth meant a dilution of the cultural and architectural traditions of the Southwest. In Denver, growth created a diminishing tax base in the central business district and decreasing importance of traditional Colorado industries such as agriculture, mining, and ranching. In Seattle, the postwar boom signaled suburban sprawl, a changing downtown landscape, and dependence of the city's economy on the vagaries of the Boeing Corporation. World War II transformed these cities from colonial economies to hubs of a global capitalist network. As actual regional differences decreased, citizens of western cities enhanced the perception of regional identity. The heritage tourist economy that spread throughout the West after World War II reinforced the need to exaggerate regional difference, since the only completely unique commodity each city had was its heritage. In each case, historic preservation activists argued for creating historic districts as a response to the changing urban conditions brought by growth, standardization, and homogenization.

It was not accidental that each district in this study became a tourist destination, or that the conventions and visitors' bureaus marketed them as such. Each district aimed to inspire consumption by marketing the city's one unique asset—its past. Visitors and residents, eager to find regional distinction, flocked to historic districts to "truly" experience each city. Yet the districts reflected the ethos of the late twentieth century more than any other time in the city's history. Each district took on an identity of its own, different from what original preservation advocates anticipated. In the end, the stories of these five districts show that identity is a created concept, based on negotiations about heritage, the economic climate, and political realities. Although preservationists tried to fix identity in brick and mortar, there was no timeless identity in any of these cities. Yet if the districts failed to re-create places as they had been in an earlier time, each district embodied, powerfully if not always successfully, an attempt to reconcile the past with the future.

Notes

Introduction

1. Jack Kerouac, *On the Road* (New York: Penguin Books, 1955), 38–39.

2. Mike Wallace, *Mickey Mouse History and Other Essays on American Memory* (Philadelphia: Temple University Press, 1996), 191–197, 200–224. See also M. Christine Boyer, *City of Collective Memory: Its Historical Imagery and Architectural Entertainments* (Cambridge, MA: MIT Press, 1998), 54.

3. William J. Murtagh, *Keeping Time: The History and Theory of Preservation in America* (New York: John Wiley and Sons, 1997), 28. See also Mitchell Schwarzer, "Myths of Permanence and Transience in the Discourse on Historic Preservation in the United States," *Journal of Architectural Education* 48 (September 1994): 2; Barbara J. Howe, "Women in Historic Preservation: The Legacy of Ann Pamela Cunningham," *Public Historian* 12 (Winter 1990): 35.

4. Schwarzer, "Myths of Permanence," 2–11.

5. Howe, "Women in Historic Preservation," 31–38. See also Norman Tyler, *Historic Preservation: An Introduction to Its History, Principles, and Practice* (New York: W. W. Norton, 2000).

6. Wallace, *Mickey Mouse History*, 181–186.

7. Schwarzer, "Myths of Permanence," 3. See also Wallace, *Mickey Mouse History*, 185–186.

8. Constance M. Greiff, "Lost America from the Atlantic to the Mississippi," in Norman Williams Jr., Edmund H. Kellogg, and Frank B. Gilbert, eds., *Readings in Historic Preservation: Why? What? How?* (New Brunswick, NJ: Center for Urban Policy Research at Rutgers University, 1983), 40.

9. Murtagh, *Keeping Time*, 51–61.

10. David A. Hamer, *History in Urban Places: The Historic Districts of the U.S.* (Columbus: Ohio State University Press, 1998), 1–3.

11. Ibid., 5, 163.

12. United States Conference of Mayors, Special Committee on Historic Preservation, *With Heritage So Rich* (New York: Random House, 1966), 46.

13. Alexander Garvin, *The American City: What Works, What Doesn't* (New York: McGraw-Hill, 2002), 56–58, 470, 476–477.

14. Murtagh, *Keeping Time*, 40–44, 51–61.

15. James A. Glass, *The Beginnings of a New National Historic Preservation Program, 1957 to 1969* (Nashville: American Association for State and Local History, 1990), 7–9.

16. Robert M. Utley, quoted in Glass, *Beginnings of a New National Historic Preservation Program*, 28.

17. Walter Muir Whitehall, in U.S. Conference of Mayors, *With Heritage So Rich*, 45.

18. Murtagh, *Keeping Time*, 64–65. See also U.S. Conference of Mayors, *With Heritage So Rich*.

19. Glass, *Beginnings of a New National Historic Preservation Program*, 29. See also *National Historic Preservation Act, U.S. Statutes at Large* 80 (1966): 915–919.

20. Congress modified the Tax Reform Act in the 1980s and reduced historic preservation benefits but still provided some incentives. Wallace, *Mickey Mouse History*, 200–224. See also Murtagh, *Keeping Time*, 74; Andrew J. Reichl, "Historic Preservation and Pro-Growth Politics in U.S. Cities," *Urban Affairs Review* 32 (March 1997): 518–519.

21. Howe, "Women in Historic Preservation," 37.

22. Wallace, *Mickey Mouse History*, 193–197; Reichl, "Historic Preservation and Pro-Growth Politics," 517.

23. Wallace, *Mickey Mouse History*, 189–191. See also Reichl, "Historic Preservation and Pro-Growth Politics," 516, 527; Murtagh, *Keeping Time*, 40–44; Richard C. Collins, Elizabeth B. Waters, and A. Bruce Dotson, *America's Downtowns: Growth, Politics, and Preservation* (Washington, DC: Preservation Press, 1991), 15–23.

24. Murtagh, *Keeping Time*, 154; Hamer, *History in Urban Places*, 174; Williams, Kellogg, and Gilbert, *Readings in Historic Preservation*, xix.

25. Hamer, *History in Urban Places*, 102–107.

26. Wallace, *Mickey Mouse History*, 193.

27. David Harvey, *The Condition of Postmodernity: An Enquiry into the Origins of Cultural Change* (Cambridge, MA: Blackwell, 1990), 69. See also Robert M. Fogelson, *Downtown: Its Rise and Fall, 1880–1950* (New Haven, CT: Yale University Press, 2001); Carl Abbott, "Five Strategies for Downtown: Policy Discourse and Planning since 1943," in Mary Corbin Sies and Christopher Silva, eds., *Planning the Twentieth-Century American City* (Baltimore: Johns Hopkins University Press, 1996), 409–412.

28. For an excellent overview on suburbanization, see Michael Schaller, Virginia Scharff, and Robert Schulzinger, *Present Tense: The United States since 1945* (Boston: Houghton Mifflin, 1996). See also Kenneth T. Jackson, *Crabgrass Frontier: The Suburbanization of the United States* (New York: Oxford University Press, 1985); Dolores Hayden, *Redesigning the American Dream: The Future of Housing, Work, and Family Life* (New York: W. W. Norton, 1984), 209–232; Elaine Tyler May, *Homeward Bound: American Families in the Cold War Era* (New York: Basic Books, 1988).

29. Harvey, *Condition of Postmodernity*, 70–75. See also Mike Davis, *City of Quartz: Excavating the Future in Los Angeles* (London: Verso, 1990); Edward Soja, *Postmodern Geographies: The Reassertion of Space in Critical Social Theory* (London: Verso, 1998), 1–9; Jane Jacobs, *The Death and Life of Great American Cities* (New York: Random House, 1961); Dolores Hayden, *The Power of Place: Urban Landscapes as Public History* (Cambridge, MA: MIT Press, 1990), 4–13; Abbott, "Five Strategies for Downtown," 412–416.

30. Joel Garreau, *Edge City: Life on the New Frontier* (New York: Random House, 1991), 3–15. See also Margaret Crawford, "The World in a Shopping Mall," in Michael Sorkin, ed., *Variations on a Theme Park: The New American City and the End of Public Space* (New York: Hill and Wang, 1992), 25–26.

31. Soja, *Postmodern Geographies*, 185–187. See also Arnold R. Hirsch, *Making the Second Ghetto: Race and Housing in Chicago, 1940–1960* (Cambridge: Cambridge University Press, 1983); Sorkin, *Variations on a Theme Park*, xii–xiii.

32. See, for example, Christine Stansell, *City of Women: Sex and Class in New York*,

1789–1860 (Urbana: University of Illinois Press, 1987); Roy Rosenzweig, *Eight Hours for What We Will: Workers and Leisure in an Industrial City, 1870–1920* (Cambridge: Cambridge University Press, 1983); Kathy Peiss, *Cheap Amusements: Working Women and Leisure in Turn-of-the-Century New York* (Philadelphia: Temple University Press, 1986); Lewis A. Erenberg, *Steppin' Out: New York Nightlife and the Transformation of American Culture, 1890–1930* (Westport, CT: Greenwood Press, 1981).

33. Timothy J. Gilfoyle, "White Cities, Linguistic Turns, and Disneylands: The New Paradigms of Urban History," published online at http://homepages.luc.edu/~tgilfoy/whitecit.htm. See also Erenberg, *Steppin' Out*, xii; John F. Kasson, *Amusing the Million: Coney Island at the Turn of the Century* (New York: Hill and Wang, 1978); John Hannigan, *Fantasy City: Pleasure and Profit in the Postmodern Metropolis* (London: Routledge Press, 1998).

34. Glass, *The Beginnings of a New National Historic Preservation Program*, 4. See also Jacobs, *Death and Life of Great American Cities*.

35. Crawford, "World in a Shopping Mall," 22–23.

36. Davis, *City of Quartz*, 221–264; Gilfoyle, "White Cities," 3.

37. E. Ann Kaplan, ed., *Postmodernism and Its Discontents* (London: Verso, 1988), 4. See also Fredric Jameson, "Postmodernism and Consumer Society," in ibid., 15, 27–29; Harvey, *Condition of Postmodernity*, 38. The dates of postmodernism vary. Kaplan claims postmodernism began in the 1960s, Jameson says it started as early as the 1950s, and Harvey pinpoints postmodernism as beginning in 1972; Anthony Giddens says that the 1990s were still late modernity (*The Consequences of Modernity* [Stanford, CA: Stanford University Press, 1990]).

38. For structural changes in the economy, see Michael A. Bernstein, "Why the Great Depression Was Great: Toward a New Understanding of the Interwar Economic Crisis in the United States," in Steve Fraser and Gary Gerstle, eds., *The Rise and Fall of the New Deal Order 1930–1980* (Princeton, NJ: Princeton University Press, 1989), 32–45. See also Soja, *Postmodern Geographies*, 98; Harvey, *Condition of Postmodernity*, 39–98.

39. Much has been written about the transition to consumer capitalism in the early twentieth century. For a sample, see William Leach, *Land of Desire: Merchants, Power, and the Rise of a New American Culture* (New York: Vintage Books, 1993); Roland Marchand, *Advertising the American Dream: Making Way for Modernity, 1920–1940* (New York: Basic Books, 1986); Richard Wightman Fox and T. J. Jackson Lears, eds., *The Culture of Consumption: Critical Essays in American History 1880–1980* (New York: Pantheon Books, 1983); Pamela Walker Laird, *Advertising Progress: American Business and the Rise of Consumer Marketing* (Baltimore: Johns Hopkins University Press, 1998); Grant McCracken, *Culture and Consumption: New Approaches to the Symbolic Character of Consumer Goods and Activities* (Bloomington: Indiana University Press, 1988), xi.

40. David Brooks, *Bobos in Paradise: The New Upper Class and How They Got There* (New York: Simon and Schuster, 2000). See also Wallace, *Mickey Mouse History*, xii; Sharon Zukin, *Loft Living: Culture and Capital in Urban Change* (New Brunswick, NJ: Rutgers University Press, 1982); Paul Groth and Todd W. Bressi, eds., *Understanding Ordinary Landscapes* (New Haven, CT: Yale University Press, 1997).

41. Harvey, *Condition of Postmodernity*, 77–82.

42. Ibid., 66, 88–92, 226–239, 284–296. See also Hannigan, *Fantasy City*, 1–4.

43. For an excellent description of this phenomenon, see Gunther Barth, *Instant Cities: Urbanization and the Rise of San Francisco and Denver* (Albuquerque: University of New Mexico Press, 1988).

44. J. B. Jackson, "The American Public Space," *Public Interest* 74 (1984): 56. See also John William Reps, *Cities in the American West: A History of Frontier Urban Planning* (Princeton, NJ: Princeton University Press, 1979), chapter 1.

45. Reps, *Cities in the American West*, 668–670. See also Earl Pomeroy, *The Pacific Slope: A History* (New York: Knopf, 1965); William Cronon, *Nature's Metropolis: Chicago and the Great West* (New York: W. W. Norton, 1991).

46. Mark S. Foster, "The Model T, the Hard Sell, and Los Angeles's Urban Growth: The Decentralization of Los Angeles in the 1920's," *Pacific Historical Review* 44 (November 1975): 459, 469–470, 481. See also Virginia Scharff, "Lighting out for the Territory: Women, Mobility, and Western Place," in Richard White and John M. Findlay, eds., *Power and Place in the North American West* (Seattle: University of Washington Press, 1999), 292–293; Bradford Luckingham, *The Urban Southwest: A Profile History of Albuquerque, El Paso, Phoenix, and Tucson* (El Paso: Texas Western Press, 1982), 95–129.

47. Gerald D. Nash, *The American West in the Twentieth Century: A Short History of an Urban Oasis* (Albuquerque: University of New Mexico Press, 1973). See also Carl Abbott, *The Metropolitan Frontier: Cities in the Modern American West* (Tucson: University of Arizona Press, 1993), 191; Raymond A. Mohl, ed., *Searching for the Sunbelt: Historical Perspectives on a Region* (Athens: University of Georgia Press, 1993).

48. There are exceptions to this model of labor relations, especially Seattle, as I will discuss. See Richard White, *It's Your Misfortune and None of My Own: A New History of the American West* (Norman: University of Oklahoma Press, 1991), 541–572. See also Richard M. Bernard and Bradley R. Rice, eds., *Sunbelt Cities: Politics and Growth since World War II* (Austin: University of Texas Press, 1983); Gilfoyle, "White Cities," 7; Soja, *Postmodern Geographies*, 1–9.

49. John M. Findlay, *Magic Lands: Western Cityscapes and American Culture after 1940* (Berkeley: University of California Press, 1992), 1–51.

50. Ibid.

51. William E. Riebsame et al., eds., *Atlas of the New West: Portrait of a Changing Region* (New York: W. W. Norton, 1997), 12. See also Jameson, "Postmodernism and Consumer Society," 17; Findlay, *Magic Lands*, 2–5.

52. Nash, *American West in the Twentieth Century*, 234–241. See also Michael P. Malone and Richard W. Etulain, *The American West: A Twentieth-Century History* (Lincoln: University of Nebraska Press, 1989), 219–265; Arthur R. Gomez, *Quest for the Golden Circle: The Four Corners and the Metropolitan West, 1945–1970* (Albuquerque: University of New Mexico Press, 1994), 156–157, 188–190.

53. David Kent Ballast, *The Denver Chronicle: From a Golden Past to a Mile-High Future* (Houston: Gulf Publishing, 1995), 127.

54. Scott Norris, ed., *Discovered Country: Tourism and Survival in the American West* (Albuquerque: Stone Ladder Press, 1994), vii–ix. See also Hal K. Rothman, *Devil's Bargains: Tourism in the Twentieth-Century American West* (Lawrence: University Press of Kansas, 1998), 1–27, 202–226; Riebsame et al., *Atlas of the New West*.

55. Anne Farrar Hyde, *An American Vision: Far Western Landscape and National Culture, 1820–1920* (New York: New York University Press, 1990). See also Katherine L. Howard and Diana F. Pardue, *Inventing the Southwest: The Fred Harvey Company and Native American Art* (Flagstaff, AZ: Northland Publishing, 1996).

56. Earl Pomeroy, *In Search of the Golden West: The Tourist in Western America* (Lincoln: University of Nebraska Press, 1957. Reprint, 1990). See also Robert G. Athearn, *The*

Mythic West in the Twentieth Century (Lawrence: University Press of Kansas, 1986), 1–9; Rothman, *Devil's Bargains,* 1–27, 202–226.

57. Athearn, *Mythic West,* 1–9, 131–159. See also Katherine Jensen and Audie Blevins, *The Last Gamble: Betting on the Future in Rocky Mountain Mining Towns* (Tucson: University of Arizona Press, 1998); Rothman, *Devil's Bargains,* 202–226; David M. Wrobel and Michael C. Steiner, eds., *Many Wests: Place, Culture, and Regional Identity* (Lawrence: University Press of Kansas, 1997), 1–8.

58. Norris, *Discovered Country,* vii–ix. See also Rothman, *Devil's Bargains*; Gomez, *Quest for the Golden Circle,* 154–157.

59. Rothman, *Devil's Bargains,* 23. See also Pomeroy, *In Search of the Golden West*; Wallace, *Mickey Mouse History,* 188–191; Reichl, "Historic Preservation and Pro-Growth Politics," 518–519.

60. Wallace, *Mickey Mouse History,* 227–231.

61. Williams, Kellogg, and Gilbert, *Readings in Historic Preservation,* 75–78.

62. David Lowenthal, *Possessed by the Past: The Heritage Crusade and the Spoils of History* (New York: Free Press, 1996), 6–24; Michael Kammen, *Mystic Chords of Memory: The Transformation of Tradition in American Culture* (New York: Vintage Books, 1991), 538. For excellent background on industrial tourism, see Dean MacCannell, *The Tourist: A New Theory of the Leisure Class* (New York: Schocken Books, 1989).

63. Roy Rosenzweig and David Thelen, *The Presence of the Past: Popular Uses of History in American Life* (New York: Columbia University Press, 1998), 20.

64. Patricia Mooney-Melvin, "Harnessing the Romance of the Past: Preservation, Tourism, and History," *Public Historian* 13 (Spring 1991): 39.

65. See, for example, Sorkin, *Variations on a Theme Park,* xiv; Harvey, *Condition of Postmodernity,* 87; Hamer, *History in Urban Places,* viii–ix; Jensen and Blevins, *The Last Gamble,* 105–131; Jameson, "Postmodernism and Consumer Society," 14–20; Lowenthal, *Possessed by the Past*; Murtagh, *Keeping Time,* 90–91.

66. See, for example, Boyer, *City of Collective Memory,* 480–481; Schwarzer, "Myths of Permanence," 9; Ada Louise Huxtable, *The Unreal America: Architecture and Illusion* (New York: New Press, 1997).

67. Rosenzweig and Thelen, *Presence of the Past,* 105.

68. See, for example, Boyer, *City of Collective Memory,* 423–424; Davis, *City of Quartz,* 221–264; J. B. Jackson, *Landscapes: Selected Writings of J. B. Jackson,* ed. by Erwin H. Zube (Amherst: University of Massachusetts Press, 1970), 79, 107–111; Hamer, *History in Urban Places,* 176; Brian J. Shaw and Roy Jones, *Contested Urban Heritage: Voices from the Periphery* (Brookfield, VT: Ashgate, 1997), 3.

69. See, for example, Sorkin, *Variations on a Theme Park,* xiv–xv; Hamer, *History in Urban Places,* 79–80; Lowenthal, *Possessed by the Past,* 89–90; Schwarzer, "Myths of Permanence," 2–3; Mike Davis, "Urban Renaissance and the Spirit of Postmodernism," in Sorkin, *Variations on a Theme Park,* 86–87; Rothman, *Devil's Bargains,* 178–179; Neil Smith, "New City, New Frontier: The Lower East Side as Wild, Wild, West," in Sorkin, *Variations on a Theme Park,* 61–93; Renato Rosaldo, "Imperialist Nostalgia," *Representations* 26 (Spring 1989): 107–122.

70. Dean MacCannell, "Tradition's Next Step," in Norris, *Discovered Country,* 161–179.

71. Clyde A. Milner II, "The View from Wisdom: Four Layers of History and Regional Identity," in William Cronon, George Miles, and Jay Gitlin, eds., *Under an Open Sky: Rethinking America's Western Past* (New York: W. W. Norton, 1992).

72. Wrobel and Steiner, *Many Wests*, 5–8. See also John Findlay, "A Fishy Proposition: Regional Identity in the Pacific Northwest," in ibid., 37–70; Riebsame et al., *Atlas of the New West*, 12; U.S. Conference of Mayors, *With Heritage So Rich*, 207–208.

73. Wrobel and Steiner, *Many Wests*, 17.

74. Hyde, *American Vision*; Jackson, *Landscapes*, 146–147; Wrobel and Steiner, *Many Wests*, 17; Stephen Leonard and Thomas J. Noel, *Denver: Mining Camp to Metropolis* (Niwot: University Press of Colorado, 1990), 407–427.

75. For excellent examples of pop culture constructions of western identity, see Robert C. Ritchie and Paul Andrew Hutton, eds., *Frontier and Region: Essays in Honor of Martin Ridge* (Albuquerque: University of New Mexico Press, 1997), 141–214. See also William H. Goetzmann and William N. Goetzmann, *The West of the Imagination* (New York: W. W. Norton, 1986), 235–350; Richard W. Etulain, *Re-Imagining the Modern American West: A Century of Fiction, History, and Art* (Tucson: University of Arizona Press, 1996), 79–80; Kerwin Klein, *Frontiers of Historical Imagination: Narrating the European Conquest of Native America, 1890–1990* (Berkeley: University of California Press, 1999), 1–12; Harold P. Simonson, *Beyond the Frontier: Writers, Western Regionalism, and a Sense of Place* (Fort Worth: Texas Christian University Press, 1989).

76. For the rural tradition in the West, see Richard White, "When Frederick Jackson Turner and Buffalo Bill Both Played Chicago in 1893," in Ritchie and Hutton, *Frontier and Region*, 201–214; Smith, *Virgin Land*. For the role of cities in western development, see Cronon, *Nature's Metropolis*; Reps, *Cities in the American West*, 667; Jackson, "The American Public Space," 64–65.

77. For more on the process of identity formation, see Findlay, *Magic Lands*, 271; Milner, "View from Wisdom," 204, 209–215; Michael M. J. Fischer, "Ethnicity and the Post-Modern Arts of Memory," in James Clifford and George B. Marcus, eds., *Writing Culture: The Poetics and Politics of Ethnography* (Berkeley: University of California Press, 1986), 196–201; George J. Sanchez, *Becoming Mexican American: Ethnicity, Culture, and Identity in Chicano Los Angeles, 1900–1945* (New York: Oxford University Press, 1993), 127; Athearn, *Mythic West*, 162–163.

78. Michael Kammen, *In the Past Lane: Historical Perspectives on American Culture* (New York: Oxford University Press, 1997), 219–220. See also Kammen, *Mystic Chords of Memory*, 3, 10, 538–546; Lowenthal, *Possessed by the Past*, 2, 127–139; Milner, "View from Wisdom," 209–215; Eric Hobsbawm and Terence Ranger, eds., *The Invention of Tradition* (Cambridge: Cambridge University Press, 1983), 12.

79. David Lowenthal, *The Past Is a Foreign Country* (Cambridge: Cambridge University Press, 1988), 41–42. See also Kammen, *Mystic Chords of Memory*, 10; Hayden, *Power of Place*.

80. Reid Karaim in "The Real Littleton," *Preservation* 53 (May/June 2001): 58.

81. Hobsbawm and Ranger, *The Invention of Tradition*, 4–5. See also Lowenthal, *Past Is a Foreign Country*, xviii.

82. Harvey, *Condition of Postmodernity*, 303; Hobsbawm and Ranger, *The Invention of Tradition*, 8–9; Hamer, *History in Urban Places*, 22–23, 133–134; Lowenthal, *Past Is a Foreign Country*, xxiv; Robert Stipe, "Why Preserve Historic Resources," in Williams, Kellogg, and Gilbert, *Readings in Historic Preservation*, 59–60.

83. Findlay, *Magic Lands*, 5. See also Hamer, *History in Urban Places*, 107–108; Kammen, *Mystic Chords of Memory*, 3–5.

84. See, for example, Schwarzer, "Myths of Permanence," 8; Hamer, *History in Urban Places*, 116; M Christine Boyer, "Cities for Sale: Merchandising History in South Street Seaport," in Sorkin, *Variations on a Theme Park*, 189–191; Wrobel and Steiner, *Many Wests*, 2–5.

85. For an excellent explanation of the social construction of subregional identity, see Wrobel and Steiner, *Many Wests*.

Chapter 1
Albuquerque, New Mexico, or Anywhere, USA? Old Town

1. The best account of Albuquerque's early history is Marc Simmons, *Albuquerque: A Narrative History* (Albuquerque: University of New Mexico Press, 1982). See also Susan DeWitt, *Historic Albuquerque Today: An Overview Survey of Historic Buildings and Districts* (Albuquerque: Historic Landmarks Survey of Albuquerque, 1978).

2. DeWitt, *Historic Albuquerque Today*, 20.

3. The fact that two settlements share the same name is confusing. Unless otherwise stipulated, "Albuquerque" refers to New Town, or the combination of New Town and Old Town, whereas "Old Town" will mean the original plaza area.

4. V. B. Price, *A City at the End of the World* (Albuquerque: University of New Mexico Press, 1992), 25.

5. Michael M. J. Fischer, "Ethnicity and the Post-Modern Arts of Memory," in James Clifford and George E. Marcus, eds., *Writing Culture: The Poetics and Politics of Ethnography* (Berkeley: University of California Press, 1986), 195–201.

6. Benny J. Andres Jr., "La Plaza Vieja (Old Town Albuquerque): The Transformation of a Hispano Village, 1880s–1950s," in Erlinda Gonzales-Berry and David R. Maciel, eds., *The Contested Homeland: A Chicano History of New Mexico* (Albuquerque: University of New Mexico Press, 2000), 243–245. See also Arthur R. Gomez, *Quest for the Golden Circle: The Four Corners and the Metropolitan West, 1945–1970* (Albuquerque: University of New Mexico Press, 1994), 150–151; Bradford Luckingham, *The Urban Southwest: A Profile History of Albuquerque, El Paso, Phoenix, and Tucson* (El Paso: Texas Western Press, 1982), 18.

7. Byron A. Johnson, *Old Town, Albuquerque, New Mexico: A Guide to Its History and Architecture* (Albuquerque: City of Albuquerque, 1980). Johnson wrote this book for the Museum of Albuquerque and includes excellent photos from the museum's collection. See also DeWitt, *Historic Albuquerque Today*, 24–25; Price, *City at the End of the World*, 53–56.

8. Luckingham, *The Urban Southwest*, 18. See also William Deverell, "Privileging the Mission over the Mexican: The Rise of Regional Identity in Southern California," in David M. Wrobel and Michael C. Steiner, eds., *Many Wests: Place, Culture, and Regional Identity* (Lawrence: University Press of Kansas, 1997), 239; Fischer, "Ethnicity and the Post-Modern Arts of Memory," 195–201.

9. Cobb Memorial Photography Collection, Center for Southwest Research, Albuquerque, NM.

10. The city's total population in 1940 was 35,449. By 1950 it had grown to 96,815, and in 1960 it stood at 201,189. For a composite of census data on Albuquerque, as well as growth projections, see University of New Mexico Bureau of Business and Economic Research, "Population Profiles of Incorporated Places and Cities in New Mexico, 1910–2015," prepared for the New Mexico Department of Highways and Transportation, 1994. See also Carl Abbott, *The Metropolitan Frontier: Cities in the Modern American West* (Tucson: University of Arizona Press, 1993), 26.

11. Raymond A. Mohl, ed., *Searching for the Sunbelt: Historical Perspectives on a Region* (Athens: University of Georgia Press, 1993), 6. See also Luckingham, *The Urban Southwest*, 76–77.

12. Luckingham, *The Urban Southwest*, 87.

13. Ibid. See also Price, *City at the End of the World*, 15–24.

14. Price, *City at the End of the World*, 17.

15. Ibid. See also DeWitt, *Historic Albuquerque Today*, 27.

16. Price, *City at the End of the World*, 17.

17. Simmons, *Albuquerque*, 369–377.

18. Ibid. See also Robert P. Hooton, interview with author, Albuquerque, NM, 15 April 1998.

19. Price, *City at the End of the World*, 16. See also Simmons, *Albuquerque*, 360–367.

20. Jack Leaman, quoted in Price, *City at the End of the World*, 7.

21. Andres, "La Plaza Vieja," 253–255. See also Sanborn Map Company, "Insurance Maps of Albuquerque, Bernalillo County, New Mexico," 1952.

22. Andres, "La Plaza Vieja," 250–260. See also Hooton interview.

23. Andres, "La Plaza Vieja," 253–254.

24. Howard N. Rabinowitz, "Growth Trends in the Albuquerque SMSA, 1940–1978," *Journal of the West* 18 (July 1979): 65–68.

25. Andres, "La Plaza Vieja," 254. See also Jim Hoffsis, telephone interview with the author, 24 March 1998.

26. Renato Rosaldo, "Imperialist Nostalgia," *Representations* 26 (Spring 1989): 107–108. See also Ann Fabian, "History for the Masses: Commercializing the Western Past," in William Cronon, George Miles, and Jay Gitlin, eds., *Under an Open Sky: Rethinking America's Western Past* (New York: W. W. Norton, 1992), 232.

27. Howard Rabinowitz, telephone interview with author, 23 March 1998. See also Simmons, *Albuquerque*, 369–377.

28. Andres, "La Plaza Vieja," 249.

29. *Albuquerque Journal*, 18 February 1948, 1.

30. *Albuquerque Journal*, 11 April 1949, 1.

31. Ibid. See also Andres, "La Plaza Vieja," 252–260.

32. G. W. Hannett was the nephew of the former governor, A. T. Hannett, who was also involved in fighting annexation. See Andres, "La Plaza Vieja," 253.

33. *Minutes of the Albuquerque City Planning Commission*, January 1949, 8, 23–29. See also *Albuquerque Journal*, 19 February 1949, 1.

34. *Journal*, 13 April 1949, 1.

35. *Planning Commission Minutes*, 1956, 1957. See also Price, *City at the End of the World*, 17.

36. Hooton interview. See also Chris Wilson, interview with author, Albuquerque, NM, 8 April 1998.

37. Ann Carson, Albuquerque Historical Society president, telephone interview with author, 10 February 1999.

38. Hooton interview.

39. Ibid. Hooton, a proponent of preserving all forms of historic architecture, restored the Victorian look of his building, which is not directly on the plaza. He was, however, in the minority, since most other preservationists wanted to protect only Pueblo and Southwestern architectural styles.

40. Ibid.

41. *Planning Commission Minutes*, 29 July 1957.

42. Ibid.

43. *Albuquerque Journal*, 11 September 1957, 15.

44. Hooton interview. The first members of the OTAC were Robert P. Hooton, William R. Leslie, Dr. Ward Alan Minge, Dr. Ralph Douglass, George Clayton Pearl, and Pete Duran. Although Hooton owned property in Old Town, he was not a resident. See *Minutes of the Old Town Architectural Review Board*, 1967, 1.

45. *Planning Commission Minutes*, 24 June 1957.

46. For more on the distinction between "history" and "heritage," see David Lowenthal, *Possessed by the Past: The Heritage Crusade and the Spoils of History* (New York: Free Press, 1996); Michael Kammen, *Mystic Chords of Memory: The Transformation of Tradition in American Culture* (New York: Vintage Books, 1991).

47. *OTARB Minutes*, 9 June 1967. Although the OTAC was formed with the historic zone in 1957, it advised the Board of Adjustments. It did not become a separate board until 1967.

48. *City Commission Minutes*, 10 September 1957.

49. Eric Hobsbawm, "Introduction," in Eric Hobsbawm and Terence Ranger, eds., *The Invention of Tradition* (Cambridge: Cambridge University Press, 1983), 4–5.

50. Andres, "La Plaza Vieja," 254–262.

51. *Hudspeth's City Directory for Albuquerque* (El Paso, TX: Hudspeth Directory Company of El Paso). Old Town was not included in Albuquerque city directories until 1940, so I consulted directories between 1940 and 1969. See also Sanborn Map Company, "Insurance Maps of Albuquerque, Bernalillo County, New Mexico." For this study I used the maps for 1891, 1908, 1924, 1931, 1952, and 1957.

52. Hobsbawm, "Introduction," *Invention of Tradition*, 6, 9.

53. Those people inventing a tradition via Old Town's architecture were following the precedent set in Santa Fe earlier in the century. Beginning with New Mexican statehood in 1912, city planners in Santa Fe had consciously stripped the city of Anglo Victorian influences in favor of Pueblo, Territorial Revival, and Spanish Colonial architectural styles. See Chris Wilson, *The Myth of Santa Fe: Creating a Modern Regional Tradition* (Albuquerque: University of New Mexico Press, 1997).

54. Ada Louise Huxtable, *The Unreal America: Architecture and Illusion* (New York: New Press, 1997), 6, 25.

55. *Planning Commission Minutes*, 8 July 1957. See also Albuquerque Landmark and Urban Conservation Ordinance, revised, 1994.

56. The exact period of Old Town's preservation is not even agreed upon by those in historic preservation. Former OTARB chair Betty Sabo claimed the architecture was true to the period before 1912, but former Landmarks and Urban Conservation Commission chair Chris Wilson, more of an authority on historic architecture, sets the date at 1875, before the arrival of the railroad. Wilson interview; see also Chris Wilson, "Artificial Stones/Precious Stones: The San Felipe Facade Controversy of 1978," paper for seminar in Art History, University of New Mexico, 1979, 10.

57. Wilson, *Myth of Santa Fe*, 112, 281.

58. Johnson, *Old Town*, 58.

59. Price, *City at the End of the World*, 53–56.

60. Hooton interview.

61. Price, *City at the End of the World*, 53–56.

62. Hooton interview.

63. Price, *City at the End of the World*, 62.

64. Ibid., 97. See also Hooton interview.

65. Price, *City at the End of the World*, 99–101.

66. Ibid., 116–118.

67. Deverell, "Privileging the Mission over the Mexican," 239–249. See also Sarah Deutsch, *No Separate Refuge: Culture, Class, and Gender on an Anglo-Hispanic Frontier in the American Southwest, 1880–1940* (New York: Oxford University Press, 1987), 190.

68. Mitchell Schwarzer, "Myths of Permanence and Transience in the Discourse on Historic Preservation in the United States," *Journal of Architectural Education* 48 (September 1994): 2–3.

69. *OTARB Minutes*, 7 January 1969.

70. Millie Santillanes, telephone interview with author, 5 May 1998. See also *Albuquerque Journal Magazine*, 30 December 1980, 4–8, 12–13; Andres, "La Plaza Vieja," 259–262.

71. Wilson, "Artificial Stones/Precious Stones."

72. Betty Sabo, interviewed by Chris Wilson, ibid., 12.

73. Ibid., 13

74. Father George Salazar, interviewed by Chris Wilson, ibid., 7.

75. Ibid.

76. Simmons, *Albuquerque*, 374–375.

77. Wilson, "Artificial Stones/Precious Stones," 12. See also Huxtable, *Unreal America*, chapter 1.

78. Hoffsis interview. See also Price, *City at the End of the World*, 55–57.

79. "Keepsake Map of Old Town, Albuquerque," Albuquerque Vertical Files, Center for Southwest Research, Albuquerque, NM.

80. "Visit Historic Old Town" pamphlet in ibid.

81. *New York Times*, 8 January 1961, T1.

82. Hoffsis interview.

83. From Old Town map and brochure, Albuquerque History Files, Drawer 1, Center for Southwest Research, Albuquerque, NM.

84. *Albuquerque Tribune*, 29 May 1980, A1. See also Santillanes interview.

85. Wrobel and Steiner, *Many Wests*, 2–4.

86. *Albuquerque Tribune*, 2 August 1990, C1.

87. Ibid., 12 August 1991, A1.

88. Hal K. Rothman, *Devil's Bargains: Tourism in the Twentieth-Century American West* (Lawrence: University Press of Kansas, 1998), 27.

89. Alexander J. Reichl, "Historic Preservation and Pro-Growth Politics in U.S. Cities," *Urban Affairs Review* 32 (March 1997): 515.

90. Hooton interview.

91. Andres, "La Plaza Vieja," 261.

92. Rosaldo, "Imperialist Nostalgia,"120.

Chapter 2
"The Most Famous Street in the West": Denver's Larimer Square

1. Dana Crawford, telephone interview with the author, 15 September 2002. See also Dan William Corson, "Dana Crawford: From Larimer Square to LoDo, Historic Preservation in Denver," MA thesis, University of Colorado at Denver, 1998.

2. For a comprehensive history of Denver, see Stephen J. Leonard and Thomas J. Noel, *Denver: Mining Camp to Metropolis* (Niwot: University Press of Colorado, 1990).

3. For a history of Larimer Street, see Thomas J. Noel, *Denver's Larimer Street: Main Street, Skid Row, Urban Renaissance* (Denver: Historic Denver, 1981).

4. Leonard and Noel, *Mining Camp to Metropolis*, 236.

5. Noel, *Denver's Larimer Street*, 21–29.

6. Donna McEncroe, *Denver Renewed: A History of the Denver Urban Renewal Authority, 1958–1986* (Denver: Denver Foundation, 1992), 102.

7. "Larimer Square Market Analysis, December 1965," in Larimer Square Associates Papers, Colorado Historical Society, Denver, CO.

8. W. A. Peterman, "Changing Commercial Patterns in Metropolitan Denver, Colorado: 1960–1970," PhD dissertation, University of Denver, 1971.

9. Dana Crawford quoted in *Christian Science Monitor*, 16 September 1975, 30.

10. Leonard and Noel, *Mining Camp to Metropolis*, 248.

11. Ibid., 240.

12. Ibid., 235–250.

13. "Larimer Square Incorporated Market Analysis, December 1965," in Larimer Square Associates Papers.

14. "Larimer Square Market Analysis, Mid-1969," in Larimer Square Associates Papers. The numbers compiled for this analysis came from the U.S. Department of Commerce, *Census of Manufacturers* and *Census of Business*.

15. Denver Planning Office, *Bulletin CAP-1: "A Demonstration Plan for Central Denver,"* Denver, CO, 1958. See also *Minutes of the Denver Planning Board*, 9 September 1963, Denver Public Library Western History and Genealogy Department, Denver, CO.

16. Denver Planning Office, *Bulleting CAP-1.*

17. Ibid.

18. Denver Urban Renewal Authority Papers, Denver Public Library Western History and Genealogy Department, Denver, CO. See also McEncroe, *Denver Renewed*, 37.

19. For more on modern city planning models, see David Harvey, *The Condition of Postmodernity: An Enquiry into the Origins of Cultural Change* (Cambridge, MA: Blackwell, 1990).

20. *Minutes of the Denver Planning Board*, Denver Urban Renewal Authority Papers, 9 September 1963.

21. Ibid., 1 July 1964.

22. Ibid., 9 August 1967. See also *Denver Post*, 4 January 1963, 19.

23. Denver Urban Renewal Authority Papers.

24. Crawford telephone interview.

25. Dana Crawford, interview with the author, Denver, CO, 29 October 2000. See also Corson, "Dana Crawford," 30–31.

26. Noel, *Denver's Larimer Street*, 38.

27. Crawford interview. See also Noel, *Denver's Larimer Street*, 38.

28. "Larimer Square Incorporated Market Analysis," December 1965. See also Corson, "Dana Crawford," 33–34.

29. Corson, "Dana Crawford," 7.

30. Ibid.

31. Investor Package Report and Annual Stockholders Minutes, 22 June 1967, Larimer Square Associates Papers. See also Corson, "Dana Crawford," 42–43.

32. Corson, "Dana Crawford," 62–63.

33. Larimer Square Associates did not buy the Replin building at 1443 Larimer until the mid-1990s. The Lafitte properties, a building and two lots, on the corner of Fourteenth and Larimer, took the corporation more than a decade to buy. See Corson, "Dana Crawford," 42–43.

34. *Denver Post*, 31 May 1965, 29.

35. Dana Crawford, *Denver Post*, 30 January 1972, 47.

36. Dana Crawford quoted in *Denver Post*, 31 May 1965, 29.

37. *Christian Science Monitor*, 16 September 1975, 30.

38. *Denver Post*, 23 May 1965, 1, 3.

39. Mayor Tom Currigan quoted in *Denver Post*, 23 May 1965, 3. See also *Daily Journal*, 25 May 1965, in Larimer Street clipping file, Denver Public Library Western History and Genealogy Department.

40. Ibid.

41. Quoted in Noel, *Denver's Larimer Street*, 32.

42. For more on heritage and identity formation, see David Lowenthal, *Possessed by the Past: The Heritage Crusade and the Spoils of History* (New York: Free Press, 1996); Michael Kammen, *Mystic Chords of Memory: The Transformation of Tradition in American Culture* (New York: Vintage Books, 1991).

43. Memo from DLPC to DURA, 22 May 1969, Denver Urban Renewal Authority Papers.

44. Dana Crawford, *Denver Post*, 30 January 1972, 47.

45. See, for example, Larimer Square map, Larimer Square Associates Papers. See also *Larimer Legend*, in Larimer Street clipping file.

46. The boxes of Larimer Square Associates Papers are filled with press releases and promotional essays that Crawford either wrote, edited, or made comments on before release. See also Corson, "Dana Crawford," 72–81.

47. "Larimer Square Incorporated Market Analysis," December 1965.

48. Undated marketing proposal, Larimer Square Associates Papers.

49. Van Arket Report, November 1969, Larimer Square Associates Papers.

50. Tourism brochure for Larimer Square, Larimer Square Files, Office of Planning and Community Development, Denver, CO.

51. *Denver Post*, 31 May 1965, 29.

52. *Rocky Mountain News*, 23 May 1965, 3.

53. Dana Crawford, quoted in ibid.

54. *Rocky Mountain News*, 25 May 1965.

55. *Denver Post* tourism section, c. 1967, Larimer Street clipping file.

56. Denver Convention and Visitor's Bureau, tourism map and brochure, Larimer Street clipping file.

57. "Investors Package 1965," in Larimer Square Associates Papers.

58. *Denver City Directory* (Denver: Gazetteer Publishing, 1965).

59. Dana Crawford, quoted in *Rocky Mountain News*, 24 November 1966, 36.

60. "Investors Package 1965," Larimer Square Associates Papers. See also *Daily Journal*, 25 May 1965, found in Larimer Street clipping file.

61. Larimer Street photo collection, Denver Public Library Western History and Genealogy Department.

62. Ordinance 739, Series of 1974, found in Larimer Square Files, Office of Planning and Community Development.

63. Larimer Street photo collection, Denver Public Library.

64. *Denver Post Empire Magazine*, 2 January 1983, 10.

65. "Skyline Urban Renewal Project Land Use Plan," in Larimer Square Associates Papers.

66. Denver Landmark Preservation Ordinance, Chapter 30 of the Revised Municipal Code. See also *Minutes of the Denver Planning Board*, 1965 and 1966.

67. *Rocky Mountain News*, 27 December 1967, 8. See also Corson, "Dana Crawford," 23–25.

68. Crawford interview. See also Corson, "Dana Crawford," 23–25.

69. Crawford interview. See also Corson, "Dana Crawford," 91.

70. *Minutes of the Denver Landmark Commission*, 21 June 1971, Larimer Square File, Office of Planning and Community Development.

71. Ibid.

72. Ibid.

73. National Register Designation Form, Larimer Square Associates Papers. See also Corson, "Dana Crawford," 118–121.

74. Owner Participation Agreement between Larimer Square Associates and Denver Urban Renewal Authority, 10 August 1971, in Larimer Square Associates Papers.

75. Map of Skyline Acquisitions, Denver Urban Renewal Authority Papers.

76. Crawford interview. See also Corson, "Dana Crawford," 6.

77. *Rocky Mountain News*, June 30, 1974, 3–4. See also *Denver Post Empire Magazine,* 2 January 1983, 4.

78. Fred Thomas, quoted in *Rocky Mountain News*, 30 June 1974, 3–4.

79. Ibid.; *Denver Post Empire Magazine*, 2 January 1983, 4.

80. "Larimer Square Incorporated Market Analysis," December 1965, Larimer Square Associates Papers.

81. Corson, "Dana Crawford," 75–76. See also *Denver City Directory*, 1969–1970; Larimer Square Associates Papers.

82. Corson, "Dana Crawford," 80–81. See also Crawford interview.

83. "Larimer Square Market Analysis, Mid-1969."

84. "Larimer Square Incorporated Market Analysis," December 1965.

85. Ibid.

86. Corson, "Dana Crawford," 122–123.

87. *Christian Science Monitor*, 16 September 1975, 30.

88. *Denver Post*, 3 June 1985, found in Larimer Street clipping file. See also Crawford interview.

89. Crawford interview. See also Corson, "Dana Crawford," 91.

90. *Rocky Mountain News*, 12 October 1982, 1, 7. See also Corson, "Dana Crawford," 108–111.

91. *Rocky Mountain News*, 13 October 1982, 1, 17. See also Corson, "Dana Crawford," 122–127.

92. *Denver Post*, 31 December 1986, 1B. See also *Rocky Mountain News*, 22 August 1986, 6; Corson, "Dana Crawford," 139–140.

93. *Rocky Mountain News*, 1 October 1993, 51A.

94. Thomas J. Noel, interview with author, Denver, CO, 3 December 1999. See also Corson, "Dana Crawford," 144–157.

95. Longwood International Survey for the Denver Metro Convention and Visitor's Bureau, 2001.

Chapter 3
Of Bums and Businessmen: Seattle's Pioneer Square

1. For histories of Seattle, see Roger Sale, *Seattle: Past to Present: An Interpretation of the History of the Foremost City in the Pacific Northwest* (Seattle: University of Washington Press, 1976); Murray Morgan, *Skid Road: An Informal Portrait of Seattle* (Seattle: University of Washington Press, 1951).

2. From the late nineteenth century until the 1950s, "Pioneer Square" referred to the triangular park where First Avenue, James Street, and Yesler Way meet. During the 1950s the park became known as "Pioneer Place," and "Pioneer Square" referred to the entire district. See Sohyun Park Lee, "From Redevelopment to Preservation: Downtown Planning in Post-War Seattle," PhD dissertation, University of Washington, 2001, 79–80.

3. National Register of Historic Places Inventory and Nomination Form, Pioneer Square–Skid Road District. Seattle, Washington, 28 January 1970. See also Jennifer Meisner, telephone interview with author, 26 September 2002.

4. Reverend Mark Matthews quoted in Alice Shorett and Murray Morgan, *The Pike Place Market: People, Politics, and Produce* (Seattle: Pacific Search Press, 1982), 113.

5. National Register of Historic Places Inventory Form, Pioneer Square–Skid Road District.

6. Lawrence Kreisman, *Historic Preservation in Seattle* (Seattle: Seattle Preservation and Development Authority, 1985), chapter 3.

7. Sale, *Seattle: Past to Present*, 181–184.

8. Ibid., 188–189, 215.

9. Between 1950 and 1967 Seattle's population experienced only a modest increase, growing from 467,591 to 557,087, whereas the population of King County as a whole increased from 844,572 in 1950 to 1,107,213 in 1960. Figures are from the U.S. Census Bureau as cited in John M. Findlay, *Magic Lands: Western Cityscapes and American Culture after 1940* (Berkeley: University of California Press, 1992), 218.

10. Lee, "From Redevelopment to Preservation," 48.

11. Sale, *Seattle: Past to Present*, 194–201.

12. Findlay, *Magic Lands*, 220; Sale, *Seattle: Past to Present*, 243.

13. Findlay, *Magic Lands*, 220–221.

14. Lee, "From Redevelopment to Preservation," 49.

15. Sally B. Woodbridge and Roger Montgomery, *A Guide to Architecture in Washington State: An Environmental Perspective* (Seattle: University of Washington Press, 1980), 120–132.

16. Sale, *Seattle: Past to Present*, 192–196.

17. Lee, "From Redevelopment to Preservation," 56–57.

18. For analysis of the Century 21 Exposition in Seattle, see Findlay, *Magic Lands*, 217–256.

19. Ibid.

20. Pike Place Market Design Report, City of Seattle, June 1974. See also Lee, "From Redevelopment to Preservation," 40–61.

21. Donald Monson, *Comprehensive Plan for Central Business District Seattle*, prepared for the City of Seattle and the Central Association of Seattle, 1963.

22. Ibid., 3–10. See also Lee, "From Redevelopment to Preservation," 60–61.

23. Correspondence between architects sponsoring the design competition, Puget Sound Regional Archives, Seattle Department of Community Development papers, Pioneer Square Historic District Manuscript Collection, Bellevue, WA. See also Victor Steinbrueck papers, University of Washington Manuscripts, Special Collections, and University Archives, Seattle; *Seattle Times Sunday Magazine*, 24 April 1960, 4–11; Lee, "From Redevelopment to Preservation," 77–82.

24. Monson, *Comprehensive Plan for Seattle*, 1963.

25. Paul W. Seibert quoted in *Seattle Times Sunday Magazine*, 24 April 1960, 4.

26. John Graham and Co., *Pioneer Square Redevelopment*, Seattle, July 1966, 34–39. See also Lee, "From Redevelopment to Preservation," 85–89.

27. Graham, *Pioneer Square Redevelopment*, 41–50.

28. Ralph Anderson, interview with author, Seattle, WA, 11 July 2001.

29. Ibid. See also Alan F. Black, "Making Historic Preservation Profitable—If You Are Willing to Wait," *Economic Benefits of Preserving Old Buildings* (Washington, DC: Preservation Press, 1976), 21–27; Lee, "From Redevelopment to Preservation," 92–94; *Seattle Times*, 30 April 1967, 20.

30. *Seattle Times*, 30 April 1967, 20, and 5 April 1970, D5. See also *Seattle City Directory* (Seattle: R. L. Polk, 1961, 1965, 1970, 1980); Anderson interview.

31. Seattle–King County Convention and Visitors Bureau, *Let Us Show You Pioneer Square* (Seattle: City of Seattle, 1976), 24. See also Bill Speidel, *Seattle Underground: In Which the Truth, the Whole Truth, and a Lot More Than the Truth Is Told about the Forgotten City Which Lies beneath Seattle's Modern Streets* (Seattle: Seattle Guide, 1968); *Seattle Post-Intelligencer Northwest Magazine*, 6 July 1975, 11.

32. *Seattle Post-Intelligencer Northwest Magazine*, 6 July 1975, 11. See also Kreisman, *Historic Preservation in Seattle*, 14.

33. Black, "Making Historic Preservation Profitable," 21–27.

34. Sohyun Park Lee, "Conflicting Elites and Changing Values: Designing Two Historic Districts in Downtown Seattle, 1958–1973," *Planning Perspectives* 16 (July 2001): 255–256.

35. Jennifer Meisner, interview with author, Seattle, WA, 14 November 2000.

36. *Seattle Post-Intelligencer*, 16 November 1969, 6. See also Kreisman, *Historic Preservation in Seattle*, 12–13.

37. Sale, *Seattle: Past to Present*, 224–227.

38. Lee, "From Redevelopment to Preservation," 85–89.

39. Ibid., 97–108. See also Lee, "Conflicting Elites and Changing Values," 257. Model Cities money ultimately funded the creation of Pioneer Place Park, on the Pioneer Square triangle, and Occidental Park along Occidental Avenue. Allied Arts of Seattle, along with Ralph Anderson and Richard White, designed Occidental Park, which used cobblestones and trees to replace a parking lot.

40. Lee, "From Redevelopment to Preservation," 89–91, 115–116.

41. Sale, *Seattle: Past to Present*, 224.

42. Ibid., 224–225.

43. Remarks by Seattle city councilman Bruce K. Chapman to the National Trust for Historic Preservation, text in councilman Michael Hildt's papers, City of Seattle Municipal Archives, Seattle, WA. See also *Seattle Post-Intelligencer*, 16 November 1969, 6; Kreisman, *Historic Preservation in Seattle*, 12–13.

44. Pioneer Square newspaper clipping file, Puget Sound Regional Archives. Both the *Seattle Times* and the *Seattle Post-Intelligencer* are filled with editorials siding with either the Central Association of Seattle or the planning commission.

45. *Seattle Post-Intelligencer*, 21 April 1970, in Pioneer Square newspaper clipping file, Puget Sound Regional Archives.

46. Sam Israel quoted in the *Seattle Sun*, 18 March 1981, 3. See also Meisner interview.

47. *Seattle Times*, 28 April 1970, C1; Lee, "Conflicting Elites and Changing Values," 256.

48. Ordinance 98852, Pioneer Square Historic District Ordinance, Puget Sound Regional Archives. See also Lee, "From Redevelopment to Preservation," 117.

49. Ordinance 102229, Hildt papers. See also Minutes of the City Planning Commission, Pioneer Square Historic District manuscript collection, Puget Sound Regional Archives.

50. Wes Uhlman, "Economics Aside," in *Economic Benefits of Preserving Old Buildings*, 6. See also John Chaney, interview with author, Seattle, WA, 4 October 1999; Sale, *Seattle: Past to Present*, 240.

51. Historic Seattle PDA Charter, Preservation and Development Authority Records, Seattle Municipal Archives. See also Chaney interview.

52. *Seattle Times*, 3 June 1970 and 6 November 1970, in Pioneer Square newspaper clipping file, Puget Sound Regional Archives.

53. Lee, "From Redevelopment to Preservation," 115–116.

54. Pioneer Square newspaper clipping file, Puget Sound Regional Archives.

55. *Seattle Times*, 4 April 1970, in Pioneer Square newspaper clipping file, Puget Sound Regional Archives.

56. Lee, "Conflicting Elites and Changing Values," 256. See also Lee, "From Redevelopment to Preservation," 6, 8–9, 62–63; *Seattle Times,* 28 July 1968, 10C.

57. For the distinction between "heritage" and "history," see David Lowenthal, *Possessed by the Past: The Heritage Crusade and the Spoils of History* (New York: Free Press, 1996); Michael Kammen, *Mystic Chords of Memory: The Transformation of Tradition in American Culture* (New York: Vintage Books, 1991).

58. Wes Uhlman, "Economics Aside," 5. See also Sale, *Seattle: Past to Present*, 195.

59. Michael Hildt, remarks to the National Trust for Historic Preservation, 20 July 1978, in Hildt papers.

60. Walt Crowley, *The Compleat Browser's Guide to Pioneer Square* (Seattle: Crowley Associates, 1981), 7.

61. Uhlman, "Economics Aside," 5.

62. *Seattle Times*, 5 April 1970, D5.

63. Ralph Anderson quoted in *Seattle Post-Intelligencer Northwest Magazine*, 7 May 1978, 4–5. See also Anderson interview.

64. For more on invented traditions, see Eric Hobsbawm and Terence Ranger, eds., *The Invention of Tradition* (Cambridge: Cambridge University Press, 1983).

65. *Seattle Post-Intelligencer*, 13 April 1980, E1.

66. "Pioneer Square Historic District Master Plan." See also *Seattle Times*, 26 March 1972, E21.

67. *Seattle Post-Intelligencer Northwest Magazine*, 6 July 1975, 11.

68. Pioneer Square Historic District Manager's files, University of Washington Manuscripts, Special Collections, and University Archives. See also Arthur M. Skolnik, "A History of Pioneer Square," in *Economic Benefits of Preserving Old Buildings*, 15; *Seattle Post-Intelligencer Northwest Magazine*, 7 May 1978, 4–5.

69. Pioneer Square Historic District Manager's files.

70. "Pioneer Square Historic District Master Plan," prepared by Makers Architectural and Design, 17 June 1974, in Pioneer Square Historic District Manager files, University of Washington Manuscripts, Special Collections, and University Archives. See also Sale, *Seattle: Past to Present*, 238–239.

71. "Pioneer Square Historic District Master Plan."

72. *Seattle Post-Intelligencer*, 8 December 1972, 11.

73. Ordinance 102229, "Landmarks Preservation Ordinance," 8 June 1973, in Hildt papers.

74. Sale, *Seattle: Past to Present*, 113–116.

75. Underground Seattle walking tour, 1992, 2001. See also Chaney interview; Meisner interview; William C. Speidel, *Sons of the Profits, Or There's No Business like Grow Business: The Seattle Story 1851–1901* (Seattle: Nettle Creek, 1967).

76. Meisner interview. See also Robert Tyler, "The I.W.W. and the West," *American Quarterly* 12 (Summer 1960): 175–187.

77. Pioneer Square Historic Preservation Ordinance, Pioneer Square Historic District Manager, Puget Sound Regional Archives. See also Lee, "From Redevelopment to Preservation," 109–110; Meisner interview.

78. Bruce Chapman, remarks to the National Trust for Historic Preservation, 5 October 1974, in Hildt papers.

79. Anderson interview.

80. Richard White quoted in *Seattle Times*, 26 January 1969, in Pioneer Square newspaper clipping file, Puget Sound Regional Archives.

81. *Seattle Times*, 25 July 1967, 14.

82. Bruce Chapman to National Trust, in Hildt papers.

83. Crowley, *Compleat Browser's Guide*, 3.

84. Speidel, quoted in *Seattle Post-Intelligencer Northwest Magazine*, 6 July 1975, 11. See also Bruce Chapman in Hildt papers.

85. *Let Us Show You Pioneer Square*, 22–25.

86. *Seattle City Directory* (Seattle: R. L. Polk, 1965).

87. Sale, *Seattle: Past to Present*, 238. See also Pioneer Square newspaper clipping file, Puget Sound Regional Archives.

88. *Seattle City Directory*, 1970.

89. Bruce Chapman to National Trust, 5 October 1974, in Hildt papers.

90. "Pioneer Square Historic District Master Plan."

91. *Seattle Post-Intelligencer Northwest Magazine*, 6 July 1975, 11–13. See also Sharon Zukin, *Loft Living: Culture and Capital in Urban Change* (New Brunswick, NJ: Rutgers University Press, 1982); David Brooks, *Bobos in Paradise: The New Upper Class and How They Got There* (New York: Simon and Schuster, 2000).

92. *Seattle Times*, 9 April 1969, 19.

93. "Pioneer Square Historic District Master Plan." See also *Seattle Times Sunday Magazine*, 30 January 1972, 4–6.

94. *Seattle Times*, 14 May 1972, A24. See also Lee, "From Redevelopment to Preservation," 96.

95. *Los Angeles Times*, 16 December 1972, in Pioneer Square newspaper clipping file, Puget Sound Regional Archives.

96. *Seattle Times*, 26 July 1985, C2.

97. *Seattle Times*, 1 February 1981, in Hildt papers; *The Weekly Wash*, 20 February 1980, in Pioneer Square newspaper clipping file, Puget Sound Regional Archives; *Los Angeles Times*, 25 November 1977, I3, 32; *Seattle Sun*, 18 March 1981, 1.

98. See, for example, *Seattle Times*, 20 February 1985, A1, A14; *Seattle Post-Intelligencer*, 13 April 1980, E1–E2. The juxtaposition of Mad Dog/Rothschild was used in so many newspaper articles that I quit making a note of it. See Pioneer Square newspaper clipping file, Puget Sound Regional Archives.

99. Demographic information comes from a survey conducted by Greenleigh and Associates in 1968, commissioned by City Council and presented in March 1969. Transcript in Steinbrueck papers. See also *Los Angeles Times*, 25 November 1977, I3, 32.

100. *Seattle Sun*, 18 March 1981, 3.

101. *Seattle Post-Intelligencer*, 13 April 1980, E1–E2.

102. Ibid., 13 September 1969, in Pioneer Square newspaper clipping file, Puget Sound Regional Archives. See also *Seattle Post-Intelligencer*, 1 February 1981, E1.

103. *Seattle Post-Intelligencer*, 27 August 1980, in Pioneer Square newspaper clipping file, Puget Sound Regional Archives; *New York Times*, 2 December 1986, in Pioneer Square newspaper clipping file, Puget Sound Regional Archives; *Seattle Times*, 20 February 1985, A1, A14.

104. Ordinance 102229, "Landmarks Preservation Ordinance," 8 June 1973, in Hildt papers. See also Meisner interview.

105. *Seattle Post-Intelligencer Northwest Magazine*, 6 July 1975, 11. See also Bruce Chapman in Hildt papers.

106. Lawson Elliott quoted in *Seattle Times*, 20 February 1985, A14.

107. *Seattle Post-Intelligencer*, 13 April 1980, E1.

108. Ibid. See also *Seattle Sun*, 18 March 1981, 1.

109. *Seattle Times*, 15 October 1978, J8.

110. *Seattle Post-Intelligencer*, 1 February 1981, E1.

111. *Weekly Wash*, 20 February 1980, and *Seattle Post-Intelligencer*, 15 April 1977, in Pioneer Square newspaper clipping file, Puget Sound Regional Archives.

112. *Weekly Wash*, 20 February 1980, in Pioneer Square newspaper clipping file, Puget Sound Regional Archives.

113. Chaney interview.

114. *Seattle Times*, 26 July 1985, C2.

115. *Ibid.*, 13 May 1984, C7; 26 July 1985, C2.

116. Murray Lamont and Associates, "Pioneer Square and Pike Place Market Case Studies," in *Lower Downtown* [Denver] *District Neighborhood Plan Newsletter*, 1995.

117. Black, "Making Historic Preservation Profitable," 21–28; Anderson interview.

Chapter 4
"An Honest Place in a Phony Time":
Pike Place Market, Seattle

1. Sohyun Park Lee, "Conflicting Elites and Changing Values: Designing Two Historic Districts in Downtown Seattle, 1958–1973," *Planning Perspectives* 16 (July 2001): 243–268.

2. This data comes from the City of Seattle's report *A Decade of Change: A Final Report on the Preservation and Redevelopment of the Pike Place Market* (Seattle: City of Seattle Department of Community Development, 1983), 47. For an excellent history of the Pike Place Market, see Alice Shorett and Murray Morgan, *The Pike Place Market: People, Politics, and Produce* (Seattle: Pacific Search Press, 1982).

3. Shorett and Morgan, *Pike Place Market*, 13–21.

4. Ibid., 45–47. See also National Register of Historic Places Inventory and Nomination Form, Pike Place Market, Seattle, Washington, 28 September 1972; City of Seattle, *Decade of Change*, 47.

5. Shorett and Morgan, *Pike Place Market*, 13–21, 23–39.

6. City of Seattle, *Decade of Change*.

7. Shorett and Morgan, *Pike Place Market,* 49.

8. Ibid., 54–65. See also City of Seattle, *Decade of Change*.

9. Community Development Services, "A Social Ecology of the Pike Place Market," 1973, in Councilman Michael Hildt's papers, City of Seattle Municipal Archives, Seattle, WA.

10. *Minutes of the City Council Hearing on Pike Plaza Redevelopment*, 1969, found in Victor Steinbrueck papers, University of Washington Manuscripts, Special Collections, and University Archives, Seattle.

11. Shorett and Morgan, *Pike Place Market*, 99–101.

12. Ibid., 103–111. See also Sohyun Park Lee, "From Redevelopment to Preservation: Downtown Planning in Post-War Seattle," PhD dissertation, University of Washington, 2001, 123–126.

13. Shorett and Morgan, *Pike Place Market*, 113–119.

14. Ibid., 121–123.

15. Pike Place Market Design Report, City of Seattle, 1974.

16. City of Seattle, *Decade of Change*, 47.

17. Demographic information comes from a survey conducted by Greenleigh and Associates, 1968, commissioned by the city council and presented in March 1969. Transcript in Steinbrueck papers. See also Lee, "From Preservation to Redevelopment," 163–164.

18. Testimony from John W. McMahon of Research Associates, at the city council hearing on Pike Plaza redevelopment, 19 March 1969. Transcript in Steinbrueck papers.

19. Ibid.

20. Testimony from citizens at city council hearing on Pike Plaza redevelopment, 24 April 1969. Transcript in Steinbrueck papers.

21. Pike Place Market Design Report. See also Lee, "From Redevelopment to Preservation," 40–61.

22. Mark Tobey quoted in Shorett and Morgan, *Pike Place Market*, 123.

23. Ben Ehrlichman quoted in ibid., 125. See also Lee, "From Redevelopment to Preservation," 133–134.

24 Lee, "From Redevelopment to Preservation," 135–138.

25. Shorett and Morgan, *Pike Place Market*, 125–126; Lee, "From Redevelopment to Preservation," 133–134, 145–146.

26. Transcripts of city council hearings on Pike Plaza redevelopment, in Steinbrueck papers.

27. Development Research Associates, "Land Utilization and Marketability Study," 1967, in Pike Place Market Collection, Seattle Municipal Archives. See also McMahon testimony, city council hearing, 19 March 1969, in Steinbrueck papers.

28. *The Weekly*, 23 September 1981, 22.

29. J. D. Braman to the city council during hearings on Pike Plaza redevelopment, 19 March 1969. Transcript of text is in Steinbrueck papers.

30. Maps of area found in Steinbrueck papers. See also report from Municipal League of Seattle to city council, 9 April 1969, text also in Steinbrueck papers.

31. Abstract history of Friends of the Market, Friends of the Market papers, University of Washington Manuscripts, Special Collections, and University Archives. See also Lee, "From Redevelopment to Preservation," 130–145.

32. Friends of the Market papers. See also Shorett and Morgan, *Pike Place Market*, 126–128; Lee, "From Redevelopment to Preservation," 130–145; Victor Steinbrueck, *Market Sketchbook* (Seattle: University of Washington Press, 1968).

33. Victor Steinbrueck quoted in *Seattle Times*, 26 November 1984, D1–D2. See also Peter Steinbrueck, interview with the author, Seattle, WA, 13 November 2000.

34. Victor Steinbrueck to city council, Pike Plaza redevelopment hearings, 21 March 1969. Transcript in Steinbrueck papers.

35. Tim Appelo, "Rescue in Seattle," *Historic Preservation* 37 (October 1985): 36.

36. Ibid. See also Shorett and Morgan, *Pike Place Market*, 126–128; Friends of the Market papers.

37. Shorett and Morgan, *Pike Place Market*, 126–128.

38. Lee, "From Redevelopment to Preservation," 142–146.

39. John Morse testimony to city council, Pike Plaza redevelopment hearings, 21 March 1969. Transcript in Steinbrueck papers.

40. Draft of the Morse/Kirk plan, 1968, in Steinbrueck papers.

41. Ibid. See also Shorett and Morgan, *Pike Place Market*, 128–131.

42. For background on gender and consumerism, see Roland Marchand, *Advertising the American Dream: Making Way for Modernity, 1920–1940* (Berkeley: University of California Press, 1985); Susan Porter Benson, *Counter Cultures: Saleswomen, Managers, and Customers in American Department Stores, 1890–1940* (Urbana: University of Illinois Press, 1986); William Leach, *Land of Desire: Merchants, Power, and the Rise of a New American Culture* (New York: Vintage Books, 1993). See also Shorett and Morgan, *Pike Place Market*, 52–93.

43. Copies of the Morse/Kirk drawings in Steinbrueck papers. See also Steinbrueck, *Market Sketchbook*.

44. Steinbrueck notes on draft of Morse/Kirk plan, in Steinbrueck papers. See also Shorett and Morgan, *Pike Place Market*, 128–131.

45. Victor Steinbrueck letter to Mayor J. D. Braman, 28 March 1968, in Steinbrueck papers.

46. *Seattle Times*, 16 March 1969, C9.

47. Mayor J. D. Braman, quoted in ibid., 4 April 1968, 33.

48. Signatures submitted at city council hearing, Pike Plaza redevelopment, 21 March 1969. Transcript in Steinbrueck papers.

49. Minutes of city council hearing, Pike Plaza redevelopment, 19 March 1969. Transcript in Steinbrueck papers.

50. Ibid., 21 March 1969. Transcript in Steinbrueck papers.

51. John Morse, testimony in city council hearing, Pike Plaza redevelopment, 21 March 1969. Transcript in Steinbrueck papers.

52. Minutes of city council hearing, Pike Plaza redevelopment, 19 March 1969. Transcript in Steinbrueck papers.

53. See, for example, Roger Sale, *Seattle, Past to Present: An Interpretation of the History of the Foremost City in the Pacific Northwest* (Seattle: University of Washington Press, 1976), 225–227.

54. Minutes of city council hearing, Pike Plaza redevelopment, 21 March 1969. Transcript in Steinbrueck papers.

55. Merle Haug, testimony in city council hearing, Pike Place redevelopment, 28 March 1969. Transcript in Steinbrueck papers.

56. Minutes of city council hearing, Pike Plaza redevelopment, 21 April 1969. Transcript in Steinbrueck papers.

57. Ibsen Nelson testimony in city council hearing, Pike Plaza redevelopment, 18 April 1969. Transcript in Steinbrueck papers.

58. Minutes of city council hearing, Pike Plaza redevelopment, 21 April 1969. Transcript in Steinbrueck papers. See also Sale, *Seattle, Past to Present*, 225–227.

59. *Seattle Post-Intelligencer*, 26 March 1969, 6.

60. Ibid., 28 April 1969, 8.

61. Seattle City Ordinance #98016, 28 August 1969.

62. Pike Plaza Urban Renewal Plan, ND 401, approved 1969. Copy found in Steinbrueck papers.

63. Press releases in Steinbrueck papers.

64. Lee, "From Preservation to Redevelopment," 149–151. See also Shorett and Morgan, *Pike Place Market*, 135–136.

65. Copy of summons, Steinbrueck papers.

66. Lee, "Conflicting Elites and Changing Values," 260–261. See also Lee, "From Preservation to Redevelopment," 158–160.

67. *Seattle Times*, 15 June 1971, clipping in Steinbrueck papers. See also Shorett and Morgan, *Pike Place Market*, 136–139.

68. Lee, "Conflicting Elites and Changing Values," 261.

69. *Seattle Post-Intelligencer Northwest Today Magazine*, 26 September 1971, 8.

70. Lee, "From Redevelopment to Preservation," 165–166.

71. *Seattle Post-Intelligencer Northwest Today Magazine*, 26 September 1971, 8–9.

72. *The Weekly*, 23 September 1981, 28–29. See also Shorett and Morgan, *Pike Place Market*, 136–137.

73. City of Seattle, *Decade of Change*, 21.

74. *Seattle Post-Intelligencer*, 21 August 1971, n.p. Clipping found in Steinbrueck papers.

75. Friends of the Market broadside quoted in *The Weekly*, 23 September 1981, 24.

76. Series of proofs for ads in both Seattle papers in Steinbrueck papers.

77. *The Weekly*, 23 September 1981. See also Pike Place Market pamphlet files, University of Washington Manuscripts, Special Collections, and University Archives.

78. *The Weekly*, 23 September 1981, 30.

79. Patrick Douglas, "Up against the System in Seattle," *Harpers Magazine* 244 (April 1972): 92–93. See also Shorett and Morgan, *Pike Place Market*, 136–139.

80. Shorett and Morgan, *Pike Place Market*, 136–139.

81. Ibid., 141.

82. City of Seattle Ordinance #100475, 1 December 1971.

83. Ibid. See also Friends of Market press release, 18 November 1971, in Steinbrueck papers; *The Weekly*, 23 September 1981, 25.

84. City of Seattle Ordinance #100475, 1 December 1971. See also Shorett and Morgan, *Pike Place Market*, 141.

85. Minutes of the city council hearings on Pike Plaza redevelopment, 19 March 1969–25 April 1969. Transcripts in Steinbrueck papers.

86. Sale, *Seattle, Past to Present*, 226–227.

87. Lee, "From Redevelopment to Preservation," 157.

88. *The Weekly*, 23 September 1981, 30.

89. Lee, "From Redevelopment to Preservation," 132–162. See also Sharon Zukin, *Loft Living: Culture and Capital in Urban Change* (New Brunswick, NJ: Rutgers University Press, 1982).

90. Minutes of city council hearing, Pike Plaza redevelopment, 19 March 1969–25 April 1969. Transcripts in Steinbrueck papers. See also Sale, *Seattle, Past to Present*, 216–252.

91. *The Weekly*, 23 September 1981, 22. See also press releases, Steinbrueck papers.

92. Irving Clark, testimony in city council hearings, Pike Plaza redevelopment, 18 April 1969. Transcript in Steinbrueck papers.

93. Friends of Market press release, 25 November 1968, in Steinbrueck papers.

94. Wolf Von Eckardt, "Unique Identity," *Seattle Times*, 3 October 1971, C1.

95. *Seattle Post-Intelligencer*, 19 May 1977, n.p. Clipping in Steinbrueck papers.

96. Deers Press Printer promotional calendar in Steinbrueck papers.

97. Sale, *Seattle, Past to Present*, 169–170.

98. Ibid., 113–116. See also Bruce K. Chapman, remarks to the National Trust for Historic Preservation, 5 October 1974, in Hildt papers.

99. Lee, "From Preservation to Redevelopment," 13.

100. Press release, 25 November 1970, Steinbrueck papers. See also John W. McMahon testimony in city council hearing, Pike Plaza redevelopment, 19 March 1969, transcript in Steinbrueck papers.

101. Notes to *Market Sketchbook*, Steinbrueck papers.

102. National Register of Historic Places Nomination and Inventory Form, Pike Place Market, 28 September 1972.

103. City of Seattle, "Pike Place Urban Renewal Plan," 1974, 48–49. See also John Turnbull, interview with author, Seattle, WA, 14 November 2000; Shorett and Morgan, *Pike Place Market*, 142.

104. City of Seattle, "Pike Place Urban Renewal Plan," 47.

105. Ibid., 48–49.

106. City of Seattle, *Decade of Change*, p. 10. See also City of Seattle, "Pike Place Urban Renewal Plan," 38–39.

107. City of Seattle, *Decade of Change*, p.11. See also Shorett and Morgan, *Pike Place Market*, 145.

108. Shorett and Morgan, *Pike Place Market*, 146–149. See also *Seattle Times*, 16 April 1972, A10.

109. Charter of Pike Place Market Preservation and Development Authority, 28 June 1973, in Preservation and Development Authority Records, Seattle Municipal Archives. See also City of Seattle, *Decade of Change*, 3–4, 21; Pike Place Market Design Report; Turnbull interview; Shorett and Morgan, *Pike Place Market*, 145–151.

110. Memo to DCD, Steinbrueck papers. See also City of Seattle, *Decade of Change*, 7; for more on this phenomenon in New York housing, see Zukin, *Loft Living*, 149–172.

111. Pike Project Chronology, Pike Place Market Collection, Seattle Municipal Archives.

112. Steinbrueck in *Seattle Post-Intelligencer*, 3 August 1978, B3.

113. "Program for Rehabilitation of the Market Core," Pike Place Market Preservation and Development Authority, 1975.

114. Ibid.

115. City of Seattle, *Decade of Change*, 12–15, 31. See also Shorett and Morgan, *Pike Place Market*, 148–150.

116. City of Seattle, *Decade of Change*, 43–44.

117. Pike Project Chronology, Pike Place Market Collection, Seattle Municipal Archives.

118. City of Seattle, *Decade of Change*, 12.

119. For more on this argument see Lee, "From Redevelopment to Preservation." See also John Hannigan, *Fantasy City: Pleasure and Profit in the Postmodern Metropolis* (London: Routledge, 1998), 129–150.

120. George Rolfe quoted in City of Seattle, *Decade of Change*, 24.

121. Turnbull interview.

122. City of Seattle, *Decade of Change*, 51–61. See also Marlys Ericsson, interview with author, Seattle, WA, 15 November 2000.

123. For more on invented traditions, see Eric Hobsbawm and Terence Ranger, eds., *The Invention of Tradition* (Cambridge: Cambridge University Press, 1983).

124. City of Seattle, *Decade of Change*, 47.

125. Ibid.

126. Turnbull interview.

127. James Mason, director of the Pike Place Urban Renewal Project, quoted in City of Seattle, *Decade of Change*, 6. See also City of Seattle, "Pike Place Urban Renewal Plan," 38.

128. Tom Quackenbush, Seattle Department of Community Development, interview with author, Seattle, WA, 4 October 1999.

129. This is still true today with one exception—Starbucks. When the guidelines were written, Starbucks had only one store, in the Pike Place Market. Because it is the original store, Starbucks remains, but it can only sell coffee and coffee-related merchandise, such as mugs. The store cannot sell pastries, games, or compact discs. See Quackenbush interview.

130. Preservation and Development Authority, "Program for Rehabilitation of the Market Core," 1975, in Steinbrueck papers.

131. City of Seattle, *Decade of Change*, 27.

132. City of Seattle, "Pike Place Urban Renewal Plan," 50–57.

133. For background on the transition of a "market" from a physical location to an abstract concept, see Jean Christophe Agnew, *Worlds Apart: The Market and the Theater in Anglo-American Thought, 1550–1750* (Cambridge: Cambridge University Press, 1986).

134. David Wright quoted in City of Seattle, *Decade of Change*, 29.

135. Quackenbush interview.

136. Hildt Amendment, in Hildt papers.

137. John Pastier, "Uncommon Market," *Historic Preservation* 48 (January/February 1996): 103.

138. City of Seattle, *Decade of Change*, 68.

139. *Seattle City Directory*, R. L. Polk and Co., 1938–1980.

140. Steinbrueck interview.

141. City of Seattle, *Decade of Change*, 47–48.

142. Ibid., 73.

143. Turnbull interview.

144. City of Seattle, *Decade of Change*, 65–66.

145. Pastier, "Uncommon Market," 52. See also Steinbrueck interview.

146. Ibid., 103. See also Hal Rothman, *Devil's Bargains: Tourism in the Twentieth Century West* (Lawrence: University Press of Kansas, 1998).

147. Dean MacCannell, *The Tourist: A New Theory of the Leisure Class* (New York: Schocken Books, 1989); Marchand, *Advertising the American Dream*; Leach, *Land of Desire*; Martyn J. Lee, *Consumer Culture Reborn: The Cultural Politics of Consumption* (London: Routledge, 1993).

Chapter 5
If You Preserve It, They Will Come:
Lower Downtown, Denver

1. Barbara Gibson, *The Lower Downtown Historic District* (Denver: Historic Denver, 1995), 6–7. See also National Register of Historic Places Nomination Form, Lower Downtown Historic District, 22 December 1988; Denver Streets Photo Collection, Colorado Historical Society, Denver.

2. *Denver City Directory* (Denver: Gazetteer Publishing, 1890, 1936).

3. National Register Nomination Form.

4. Gibson, *Lower Downtown*, 6–7.

5. Stephen J. Leonard and Thomas J. Noel, *Denver: Mining Camp to Metropolis* (Niwot: University Press of Colorado, 1990), 102–189.

6. Ibid., 446–458. See also Gibson, *Lower Downtown*, 6–7; Denver Streets Photo Collection; *Denver City Directory*, 1956.

7. Architectural drawing found in Denver Streets Photo Collection.

8. Denver Planning Office, *Bulletin CAP–6: Lower Downtown Denver: Expressway and Adjacent Redevelopment Areas*, 1958. See also Denver Planning Office, *Bulletin CAP–1: A Demonstration Plan for Central Denver*, 1958.

9. Dan William Corson, "Dana Crawford: From Larimer Square to LoDo, Historic Preservation in Denver," master's thesis, University of Colorado at Denver, 1998, 148. See also Jennifer Moulton, interview with author, Denver, CO, 14 September 2000; *Denver Post Empire Magazine*, 12 July 1981, 16.

10. Zoning ordinance quoted in *Denver Post*, 12 July 1981, 16. See also William Saslow, interview with author, Denver, CO, 2 July 2002.

11. Article in *Seventeenth Street West*, 15 October 1980, in Denver Downtown Urban Renewal Clipping File, Colorado Historical Society, Denver.

12. *Denver Post Empire Magazine*, 12 July 1981, 11. See also Saslow interview.

13. Ibid., 11–12, 16. See also Saslow interview; Corson, "Dana Crawford," 148.

14. *Denver Post Empire Magazine*, 12 July 1981, 16.

15. Corson, "Dana Crawford," 153–154.

16. *Rocky Mountain News*, 4 July 1993, 23A. See also Saslow interview.

17. TDRs were commonly used as a way to promote historic preservation nationally. See Richard Moe and Carter Wilkie, *Changing Places: Rebuilding Community in the Age of Sprawl* (New York: Henry Holt, 1997), 184–185. See also "Economic Impact of Historic District Designation," 1990, in Lower Downtown District File, Office of Planning and Community Development, Denver, CO; Lisa Purdy, interview with author, Denver, CO, 3 July 2002.

18. Corson, "Dana Crawford," 151. See also Purdy interview.

19. Purdy interview. See also *Denver Post*, 13 December 1995, in Historic Denver Clipping File, Denver Public Library Western History and Genealogy Department, Denver, CO.

20. Moe and Wilkie, *Changing Places*, 185–186.

21. Leonard and Noel, *Mining Camp to Metropolis*, 404–405.

22. Downtown Denver Partnership, Inc., and the Denver Planning Office, "Downtown Area Plan: A Plan for the Future of Downtown Denver," 1986, i. See also Bill Hornby, *Denver Post*, 11 January 1987, 9G.

23. Purdy interview.

24. Lane Ittleson, letter to Historic Denver members, LoDo Clipping File, Denver Public Library.

25. Purdy interview.

26. *Rocky Mountain News*, 23 February 1986, 38.

27. "Downtown Area Plan," 38–72. See also Purdy interview.

28. "Downtown Area Plan," 46–50. See also Sharon Zukin, *Loft Living: Culture and Capital in Urban Change* (New Brunswick, NJ: Rutgers University Press, 1982).

29. "Downtown Area Plan," 46. See also Purdy interview; Moe and Wilkie, *Changing Places*, 185–186.

30. "Downtown Area Plan."

31. Purdy interview. See also Hornby, *Denver Post*, 28 February 1988, 4F.

32. Peter H. Dominick Jr., *Rocky Mountain Journal* 29, 37 (31 May 1978), in Larimer Square Associates papers, Colorado Historical Society.

33. Federico Peña quoted in Moe and Wilkie, *Changing Places*, 189.

34. Sam Maddox, *Denver Magazine*, June 1981, 32–36, in Denver Downtown Urban Renewal Clipping File, Colorado Historical Society.

35. Richard C. D. Flemming quoted by Maddox, *Denver Magazine*.

36. Hornby, *Denver Post*, 11 January 1987, 9G.

37. Moe and Wilkie, *Changing Places*, 198.

38. Moulton interview.

39. Purdy quoted in Moe and Wilkie, *Changing Places*, 185.

40. Bill Mosher, quoted in Moe and Wilkie, *Changing Places*, 199.

41. Downtown Denver Partnership, Inc., "Lower Downtown Urban Design Project," 1987, 4.

42. Tom Gougeon, quoted in Moe and Wilkie, *Changing Places*, 188.

43. Peña, quoted in ibid., 189.

44. Purdy interview; Moulton interview; Kathleen Brooker, interview with the author, Denver, CO, 14 February 2001; Moe and Wilkie, *Changing Places*, 184–187.

45. "Downtown Area Plan," 46–48.

46. "Lower Downtown Urban Design Project," in Lower Downtown Historic District File, Office of Planning and Community Development, Denver, CO, 4.

47. *Denver Post*, 11 January 1987, 9G; 29 February 1988, 7B; 17 March 1988, 7B.

48. Maddox, *Denver Magazine*, 32–36.

49. For more on invented traditions, see Eric Hobsbawm and Terence Ranger, eds., *The Invention of Tradition* (Cambridge: Cambridge University Press, 1983).

50. Bill Mosher, quoted in Moe and Wilkie, *Changing Places*, 199.

51. "Downtown Area Plan," 48.

52. Ibid., 48.

53. "Lower Downtown Urban Design Project," 17.

54. Memo from DLPC to city council, 8 December 1987, in Lower Downtown Historic District file, Office of Planning and Community Development.

55. Lower Downtown Historic District Ordinance, in Lower Downtown Historic District file, Office of Planning and Community Development.

56. "Downtown Area Plan," 48.

57. Saslow interview; Purdy interview; Moulton interview. See also Hornby, *Denver Post*, 28 February 1988, 4F; Moe and Wilkie, *Changing Places*, 186–187; Brooker interview.

58. Moe and Wilkie, *Changing Places*, 186. See also Corson, "Dana Crawford," 150–151.

59. *New York Times*, 26 June 1988, in Larimer Square Associates papers, Colorado Historical Society.

60. Leonard and Noel, *Mining Camp to Metropolis*, 425.

61. Saslow interview. See also Barbara Norgren, interview with author, Denver, CO, 2 February 2001; Moe and Wilkie, *Changing Places*, 186; Leonard and Noel, *Mining Camp to Metropolis*, 407–427.

62. Thomas J. Noel, *Denver Landmarks and Historic Districts: A Pictorial Guide* (Niwot: University Press of Colorado, 1996), 117–118.

63. Purdy interview.

64. Ibid.

65. Moe and Wilkie, *Changing Places*, 187–188. See also Moulton interview.

66. *Denver Post*, 2 March 1988, 3. See also Saslow interview; Purdy interview; Barbara Gibson, interview with author, Denver, CO, 22 July 2001.

67. Purdy interview; Saslow interview.

68. Minutes of a joint meeting of the Denver Landmarks Preservation Commission and the Denver Planning Commission, 14 October 1987, in Lower Downtown Historic District File, Office of Planning and Community Development.

69. *Denver Post*, 2 March 1988, 3.

70. Purdy interview. See also Brooker interview; Moe and Wilkie, *Changing Places*, 189; Gibson interview.

71. Moe and Wilkie, *Changing Places*, 190. See also "Lower Downtown Urban Design Project," 5–17; Moulton interview.

72. "Lower Downtown Urban Design Project," 6–17.

73. Moe and Wilkie, *Changing Places*, 189. See also Moulton interview; Brooker interview.

74. Purdy interview. See also Moe and Wilkie, *Changing Places*, 192.

75. Moe and Wilkie, *Changing Places*, 192. See also Thomas J. Noel, interview with author, Denver, CO, 3 December 1999.

76. "Block by Block: Reclaiming Neighborhoods by Design," video, American Architectural Foundation, 2001. See also Hornby, *Denver Post*, 28 February 1988, 4F.

77. Corson, "Dana Crawford," 151–152.

78. *Denver Post*, 6 June 1988, 1A, 6A.

79. Purdy interview. See also Moe and Wilkie, *Changing Places*, 189–190.

80. "Block by Block" video. See also Moe and Wilkie, *Changing Places*, 189–190.

81. Moe and Wilkie, *Changing Places*, 189–190. See also Corson, "Dana Crawford," 151–155; Dana Crawford, interview with author, Denver, CO, 29 October 2000.

82. Moe and Wilkie, *Changing Places*, 193. See also Purdy interview.

83. *Denver Post Empire Magazine*, 12 July 1981, 17.

84. "Downtown Area Plan," 47. See also Moulton interview.

85. Zukin, *Loft Living*, 2–6. See also David Brooks, *Bobos in Paradise: The New Upper Class and How They Got There* (New York: Simon and Schuster, 2000); *Rocky Mountain News*, 17 August 1997, 6G.

86. *Rocky Mountain News,* 17 August 1997, 6G–7G.

87. The Pacific Mercantile at 19th and Lawrence streets near LoDo is an Asian grocery store that functions as a convenience store for LoDo residents; however, most drive to King Soopers or Safeway, each over 2 miles away.

88. *Denver Post*, 18 September 1999, 1C. See also Gibson interview.

89. Purdy interview. See also *LoDo News*, April 1996, 1, 26; Brooker interview; Moe and Wilkie, *Changing Places*, 190–191.

90. *LoDo News*, April 1996, 1, 26.

91. Purdy interview; Brooker interview; Gibson interview; Noel interview; Saslow interview.

92. *Denver Post*, 2 March 1998, 2A.

93. Moe and Wilkie, *Changing Places*, 193. See also Brooker interview.

94. Dick Kreck, *Denver Post*, 2 March 1998, 2A.

95. Ibid.

96. *Denver Post*, 4 February 1996, 7B.

97. Ibid., 4 August 1996, 1A; *Rocky Mountain News*, 18 July 1996, 3B.

98. *Denver Post*, 4 August 1996, 12A.

99. Ibid., 22 May 1996, 1C.

100. Ibid., 21 November 1998, 1C; 5 March 2000, 33A. See also Moe and Wilkie, *Changing Places*, 198.

101. Longwood International Survey for the Denver Metro Convention and Visitor's Bureau, 1997–2001.

Bibliography

Books and Articles

Abbott, Carl. *The Metropolitan Frontier: Cities in the Modern American West*. Tucson: University of Arizona Press, 1993.

Agnew, Jean Christophe. *Worlds Apart: The Market and the Theater in Anglo-American Thought, 1550–1750*. Cambridge: Cambridge University Press, 1986.

Andres, Benny J., Jr. "La Plaza Vieja (Old Town Albuquerque): The Transformation of a Hispano Village, 1880s–1950s." In Erlinda Gonzales-Berry and David R. Maciel, eds., *The Contested Homeland: A Chicano History of New Mexico*. Albuquerque: University of New Mexico Press, 2000.

Appelo, Tim. "Rescue in Seattle." *Historic Preservation* 37 (October 1985): 34–39.

Athearn, Robert G. *The Mythic West in the Twentieth Century*. Lawrence: University Press of Kansas, 1986.

Baer, William C. "When Old Buildings Ripen for Historic Preservation: A Predictive Approach to Planning." *American Planning Association Journal* 6 (Winter 1995): 82–98.

Ballast, David Kent. *The Denver Chronicle: From a Golden Past to a Mile-High Future*. Houston: Gulf Publishing, 1995.

Banham, Reyner. *Los Angeles: The Architecture of Four Ecologies*. New York: Harper and Row, 1971.

Barth, Gunther. *Instant Cities: Urbanization and the Rise of San Francisco and Denver*. Albuquerque: University of New Mexico Press, 1988.

Barthel, Diane. "Nostalgia for America's Village Past: Stated Symbolic Communities." *International Journal of Politics, Culture, and Society* 4, 1 (1990): 79–93.

Benson, Susan Porter. *Counter Cultures: Saleswomen, Managers, and Customers in American Department Stores, 1890–1940*. Urbana: University of Illinois Press, 1986.

Bernard, Richard M., and Bradley R. Rice, eds. *Sunbelt Cities: Politics and Growth since World War II*. Austin: University of Texas Press, 1983.

Berner, Richard C. *Seattle 1900–1920: From Boomtown, Urban Turbulence, to Restoration*. Seattle in the 20th Century, 1. Seattle: Charles Press, 1991.

———. *Seattle 1921–1940: From Boom to Bust*. Seattle in the 20th Century, 2. Seattle: Charles Press, 1992.

———. *Seattle Transformed: World War II to the Cold War*. Seattle in the 20th Century, 3. Seattle: Charles Press, 1999.

Biel, Steve, ed. *American Disasters*. New York: New York University Press, 2001.

Bluestone, Daniel. *Constructing Chicago*. New Haven, CT: Yale University Press, 1991.

Boorstin, Daniel J. *The Americans: The Democratic Experience*. New York: Vintage Books, 1973.

Boyer, M. Christine. *The City of Collective Memory: Its Historical Imagery and Architectural Entertainments*. Cambridge, MA: MIT Press, 1998.

Bridges, Amy. *Morning Glories: Municipal Reform in the Southwest*. Princeton, NJ: Princeton University Press, 1997.

Brooks, David. *Bobos in Paradise: The New Upper Class and How They Got There*. New York: Simon and Schuster, 2000.

Bumpus, Greg. "Analogous Cities and Tiny Towns: A Postmodern Geography of Colorado." *University of Colorado at Denver Historical Studies Journal* 10 (Spring 1993): 1–21.

Byrkit, James W. "Land, Sky, and People: The Southwest Defined." *Journal of the Southwest* 34 (Winter 1992): 256–387.

Cline, William Erich. *Historic Preservation Literature, 1969–1977*. Monticello, IL: Council of Planning Librarians, 1978.

Cocks, Catherine. *Doing the Town: The Rise of Urban Tourism in the United States, 1850–1915*. Berkeley: University of California Press, 2001.

Collins, Richard C., Elizabeth B. Waters, and A. Bruce Dotson. *America's Downtowns: Growth, Politics, and Preservation*. Washington, DC: Preservation Press, 1991.

Cott, Nancy F. *The Bonds of Womanhood: "Woman's Sphere" in New England, 1780–1835*. New Haven, CT: Yale University Press, 1977.

Cronon, William. *Nature's Metropolis: Chicago and the Great West*. New York: W. W. Norton, 1991.

———. *Uncommon Ground: Toward Reinventing Nature*. New York: W. W. Norton, 1995.

Cronon, William, George Miles, and Jay Gitlin, eds. *Under an Open Sky: Rethinking America's Western Past*. New York: W. W. Norton, 1992.

Cross, Gary. *Time and Money: The Making of Consumer Culture*. London: Routledge, 1993.

Crowley, Walt. *The Compleat Browser's Guide to Pioneer Square*. Seattle: Crowley Associates, 1981.

Crumb, Lawrence N. *Historic Preservation in the Pacific Northwest: A Bibliography of Sources, 1947–1978*. Chicago: CPL Bibliographies, 1979.

Cullingworth, Barry. "Historic Preservation in the U.S.A." *Built Environment* 23 (1997): 137–143.

Davis, Mike. *City of Quartz: Excavating the Future in Los Angeles*. London: Verso, 1990.

Delafons, John. *Politics and Preservation: A Policy History of the Built Heritage, 1882–1996*. London: E. and F. N. Spon, 1997.

Deutsch, Sarah. *No Separate Refuge: Culture, Class, and Gender on an Anglo-Hispanic Frontier in the American Southwest, 1880–1940*. New York: Oxford University Press, 1987.

DeWitt, Susan. *Historic Albuquerque Today: An Overview Survey of Historic Buildings and Districts*. Albuquerque: Historic Landmarks Survey of Albuquerque, 1978.

Donaldson, Scott. *The Suburban Myth*. Lincoln, NE: iUniverse, 1996.

Douglas, Patrick. "Up against the System in Seattle." *Harpers Magazine* 244 (April 1972): 90–94.

Economic Benefits of Preserving Old Buildings. Washington, DC: Preservation Press, 1976.

Erenberg, Lewis A. *Steppin' Out: New York Nightlife and the Transformation of American Culture, 1890–1930*. Westport, CT: Greenwood Press, 1981.

Etulain, Richard W. *Re-Imagining the Modern American West: A Century of Fiction, History, and Art*. Tucson: University of Arizona Press, 1996.

Ewen, Stuart. *All-Consuming Images: The Politics of Style in Contemporary Culture*. New York: Basic Books, 1988.

Farber, David, ed. *The Sixties: From Memory to History*. Chapel Hill: University of North Carolina Press, 1994.

Findlay, John M. *Magic Lands: Western Cityscapes and American Culture after 1940*. Berkeley: University of California Press, 1992.

Fischer, Michael M. J. "Ethnicity and the Post-Modern Arts of Memory." In James Clifford and George E. Marcus, eds., *Writing Culture: The Poetics and Politics of Ethnography*. Berkeley: University of California Press, 1986.

Fogelson, Robert M. *Downtown: Its Rise and Fall, 1880–1950*. New Haven, CT: Yale University Press, 2001.

Foster, Dick. "Lower Downtown Mecca for Investors." *Denver Magazine* 12 (June 1982): 20–27, 88–89.

Foster, Mark S. *From Streetcar to Superhighway: American City Planners and Urban Transportation, 1900–1940*. Philadelphia: Temple University Press, 1981.

———. "The Model T, the Hard Sell, and Los Angeles' Urban Growth: The Decentralization of Los Angeles in the 1920's." *Pacific Historical Review* 44 (November 1975): 459–484.

Fox, Richard Wightman, and T. J. Jackson Lears, eds. *The Culture of Consumption: Critical Essays in American History, 1880–1980*. New York: Pantheon Books, 1983.

Francaviglia, Richard V. *Main Street Revisited: Time, Space, and Image Building in Small-Town America*. Iowa City: University of Iowa Press, 1996.

Fraser, Steve, and Gary Gerstle. *The Rise and Fall of the New Deal Order, 1930–1980*. Princeton, NJ: Princeton University Press, 1989.

Garreau, Joel. *Edge City: Life on the New Frontier*. New York: Random House, 1991.

Garvin, Alexander. *The American City: What Works, What Doesn't*. New York: McGraw Hill, 2002.

Gibson, Barbara. *The Lower Downtown Historic District*. Denver: Historic Denver, 1995.

Giddens, Anthony. *The Consequences of Modernity*. Stanford, CA: Stanford University Press, 1990.

———. *A Contemporary Critique of Historical Materialism*. Stanford, CA: Stanford University Press, 1995.

Gilfoyle, Timothy J. "White Cities, Linguistic Turns, and Disneylands: The New Paradigms of Urban History." http://homepages.luc.edu/~tgilfoy/whitecit/htm.

Glass, James A. *The Beginnings of a New National Historic Preservation Program, 1957–1966*. Nashville: American Association for State and Local History, 1990.

Goetzmann, William H., and William N. Goetzmann. *The West of the Imagination*. New York: W. W. Norton, 1986.

Gomez, Arthur R. *Quest for the Golden Circle: The Four Corners and the Metropolitan West, 1945–1970*. Albuquerque: University of New Mexico Press, 1994.

Groth, Paul, and Todd W. Bressi, eds. *Understanding Ordinary Landscapes*. New Haven, CT: Yale University Press, 1997.

Gusky, Diane. *A History of the Beginnings of Zoning in Albuquerque*. Albuquerque: Society of the Built Environment, 1982.

Hamer, David A. *History in Urban Places: The Historic Districts of the U.S.* Columbus: Ohio State University Press, 1998.

Hannigan, John. *Fantasy City: Pleasure and Profit in the Postmodern Metropolis*. London: Routledge, 1998.

Harlan, David. *The Degradation of American History*. Chicago: University of Chicago Press, 1997.

Harvey, David. *The Condition of Postmodernity: An Enquiry into the Origins of Cultural Change*. Cambridge, MA: Blackwell, 1990.

Hayden, Dolores. *The Power of Place: Urban Landscapes as Public History*. Cambridge, MA: MIT Press, 1997.

———. *Redesigning the American Dream: The Future of Housing, Work, and Family Life*. New York: W. W. Norton, 1984.

Hirsch, Arnold R. *Making the Second Ghetto: Race and Housing in Chicago, 1940–1960*. Cambridge: Cambridge University Press, 1983.

Hobsbawm, Eric, and Terence Ranger, eds. *The Invention of Tradition*. Cambridge: Cambridge University Press, 1983.

Horowitz, Daniel. *The Morality of Spending: Attitudes toward the Consumer Society in America, 1875–1940*. Baltimore: Johns Hopkins University Press, 1985.

Horowitz, Roger, and Arwen Mohun, eds. *His and Hers: Gender, Consumption, and Technology*. Charlottesville: University Press of Virginia, 1998.

Hosmer, Charles B. *Presence of the Past: A History of the Preservation Movement before Williamsburg*. New York: Putnam, 1965.

———. *Preservation Comes of Age: From Williamsburg to the National Trust, 1926–1949*. Charlottesville: University Press of Virginia, 1981.

Howard, Katherine L., and Diana F. Pardue. *Inventing the Southwest: The Fred Harvey Company and Native American Art*. Flagstaff, AZ: Northland Publishing Company, 1996.

Howe, Barbara J. "Women in Historic Preservation: The Legacy of Ann Pamela Cunningham." *Public Historian* 12 (Winter 1990): 31–61.

Huxtable, Ada Louise. *The Unreal America: Architecture and Illusion*. New York: New Press, 1997.

Hyde, Anne Farrar. *An American Vision: Far Western Landscape and National Culture, 1880–1920*. New York: New York University Press, 1990.

———. "Nothing New under the Sun: Continuities in the West." *Pacific Historical Review* 67 (August 1998): 393–400.

Jackle, John. *The Tourist: Travel in 20th-Century North America*. Lincoln: University of Nebraska Press, 1985.

Jackson, J. B. "The American Public Space." *Public Interest* 74 (1984): 52–65.

———. *Landscapes: Selected Writings of J. B. Jackson*. Edited by Ervin H. Zube. Amherst: University of Massachusetts Press, 1970.

Jackson, Kenneth T. *Crabgrass Frontier: The Suburbanization of the United States*. New York: Oxford University Press, 1985.

Jacobs, Jane. *The Death and Life of Great American Cities*. New York: Random House, 1961.

Jameson, Fredric. *Postmodernism; Or, The Cultural Logic of Late Capitalism*. Durham, NC: Duke University Press, 1991.

Jensen, Katherine, and Audie Blevins. *The Last Gamble: Betting on the Future in Rocky Mountain Mining Towns*. Tucson: University of Arizona Press, 1998.

Johnson, Byron A. *Old Town, Albuquerque, New Mexico: A Guide to Its History and Architecture*. Albuquerque: City of Albuquerque, 1980.

Kammen, Michael. *In the Past Lane: Historical Perspectives on American Culture*. New York: Oxford University Press, 1997.

———. *Mystic Chords of Memory: The Transformation of Tradition in American Culture*. New York: Vintage Books, 1991.

Kaplan, E. Ann, ed. *Postmodernism and Its Discontents*. London: Verso, 1988.

Kasson, John F. *Amusing the Million: Coney Island at the Turn of the Century*. New York: Hill and Wang, 1978.

Klein, Kerwin. *Frontiers of Historical Imagination: Narrating the European Conquest of Native America, 1890–1990*. Berkeley: University of California Press, 1999.

Kreisman, Lawrence. *Historic Preservation in Seattle*. Seattle: Seattle Preservation and Development Authority, 1985.

Kuhn, Thomas S. *The Structure of Scientific Revolutions*. Chicago: University of Chicago Press, 1970.

Laird, Pamela Walker. *Advertising Progress: American Business and the Rise of Consumer Marketing*. Baltimore: Johns Hopkins University Press, 1998.

Leach, William. *Land of Desire: Merchants, Power, and the Rise of a New American Culture*. New York: Vintage Books, 1993.

Lears, T. J. Jackson. *Fables of Abundance: A Cultural History of Advertising in America*. New York: Basic Books, 1994.

———. *No Place of Grace: Antimodernism and the Transformation of American Culture, 1880–1920*. New York: Pantheon, 1981.

Lee, Martyn J. *Consumer Culture Reborn: The Cultural Politics of Consumption*. London: Routledge, 1993.

Lee, Sohyun Park. "Conflicting Elites and Changing Values: Designing Two Historic Districts in Downtown Seattle, 1958–1973." *Planning Perspectives* 16 (July 2001): 243–268.

Leonard, Stephen J., and Thomas J. Noel. *Denver: Mining Camp to Metropolis*. Niwot: University Press of Colorado, 1990.

Linenthal, Edward T., and Tom Engelhardt. *History Wars: The Enola Gay and Other Battles for the American Past*. New York: Henry Holt, 1996.

Lowenthal, David. *The Past Is a Foreign Country*. Cambridge: Cambridge University Press, 1988.

———. *Possessed by the Past: The Heritage Crusade and the Spoils of History*. New York: Free Press, 1996.

Luckingham, Bradford. *The Urban Southwest: A Profile History of Albuquerque, El Paso, Phoenix, and Tucson*. El Paso: Texas Western Press, 1982.

MacCannell, Dean. *The Tourist: A New Theory of the Leisure Class*. New York: Schocken Books, 1989.

Malone, Michael P., and Richard W. Etulain. *The American West: A Twentieth-Century History*. Lincoln: University of Nebraska Press, 1989.

Marchand, Roland. *Advertising the American Dream: Making Way for Modernity, 1920–1940*. Berkeley: University of California Press, 1985.

May, Elaine Tyler. *Homeward Bound: American Families in the Cold War Era*. New York: Basic Books, 1988.

McCracken, Grant. *Culture and Consumption: New Approaches to the Symbolic Character of Consumer Goods and Activities*. Bloomington: Indiana University Press, 1988.

McEncroe, Donna. *Denver Renewed: A History of the Denver Urban Renewal Authority, 1958–1986*. Denver: Denver Foundation, 1992.

McKay, Ian. "History and the Tourist Gaze: The Politics of Commemoration in Nova Scotia, 1935–1964." *Acadiensis* 22 (Spring 1993): 103–138.

Miller, Ross. *American Apocalypse: The Great Fire and the Myth of Chicago*. Chicago: University of Chicago Press, 1990.

Moe, Richard, and Carter Wilkie. *Changing Places: Rebuilding Community in the Age of Sprawl.* New York: Henry Holt, 1997.

Mohl, Raymond A., ed. *Searching for the Sunbelt: Historical Perspectives on a Region.* Athens: University of Georgia Press, 1993.

Mooney-Melvin, Patricia. "Harnessing the Romance of the Past: Preservation, Tourism, and History." *Public Historian* 13 (Spring 1991): 35–47.

Morgan, Murray. *Skid Road: An Informal Portrait of Seattle.* Seattle: University of Washington Press, 1951.

Morley, Judy Mattivi. "Albuquerque, New Mexico, or Anywhere, USA? Historic Preservation and the Construction of Civic Identity." *New Mexico Historical Review* 74 (April 1999): 155–178.

Mumford, Lewis. *The City in History: Its Origins, Its Transformations, and Its Prospects.* New York: Harcourt, Brace, and World, 1961.

Murtagh, William J. *Keeping Time: The History and Theory of Preservation in America.* New York: John Wiley and Sons, 1997.

Nash, Gerald D. *The American West in the Twentieth Century: A Short History of an Urban Oasis.* Albuquerque: University of New Mexico Press, 1973.

Noel, Thomas J. *Buildings of Colorado.* Buildings of the United States, no. 5. New York: Oxford University Press, 1997.

———. *Denver Landmarks and Historic Districts: A Pictorial Guide.* Niwot: University of Colorado Press, 1996.

———. *Denver's Larimer Street: Main Street, Skid Row, and Urban Renaissance.* Denver: Historic Denver, 1981.

Norris, Scott, ed. *Discovered Country: Tourism and Survival in the American West.* Albuquerque: Stone Ladder Press, 1994.

Nuryanti, Wiendu. "Heritage and Postmodern Tourism." *Annals of Tourism Research* 23 (Summer 1996): 249–260.

Page, Max, and Randall Mason. *Giving Preservation a History: Histories of Historic Preservation in the United States.* New York: Routledge, 2004.

Pastier, John. "Uncommon Market." *Historic Preservation* 48 (January/February 1996): 50–55, 99, 102–103.

Peiss, Kathy. *Cheap Amusements: Working Women and Leisure in Turn-of-the-Century New York.* Philadelphia: Temple University Press, 1986.

Price, V. B. *A City at the End of the World.* Albuquerque: University of New Mexico Press, 1992.

Pomeroy, Earl. *In Search of the Golden West: The Tourist in Western America.* Lincoln: University of Nebraska Press, 1957. Reprint, 1990.

———. *The Pacific Slope: A History.* New York: Knopf, 1965.

Rabinowitz, Howard N. "Growth Trends in the Albuquerque SMSA, 1940–1978." *Journal of the West* 18 (July 1979): 62–74.

Reichl, Alexander J. "Historic Preservation and Pro-Growth Politics in U.S. Cities." *Urban Affairs Review* 32 (March 1997): 513–535.

Renovating Decaying Urban Areas: An Analysis of Seattle's Pioneer Square Historical District. Seattle: Institute for Economic Research at the University of Washington, 1974.

Reps, John William. *Cities of the American West: A History of Frontier Urban Planning.* Princeton, NJ: Princeton University Press, 1979.

Riebsame, William E., Hannah Gosneil, David Theobald, James J. Robb, Paul Breding, Chris Hansen, and Keith Rokoske, eds. *Atlas of the New West: Portrait of a Changing Region.* New York: W. W. Norton, 1997.

Ritchie, Robert C., and Paul Andrew Hutton. *Frontier and Region: Essays in Honor of Martin Ridge.* Albuquerque: University of New Mexico Press, 1997.

Rosaldo, Renato. "Imperialist Nostalgia." *Representations* 26 (Spring 1989): 107–122.

Rosenberg, Rosalind. *Beyond Separate Spheres: Intellectual Roots of Modern Feminism.* New Haven, CT: Yale University Press, 1982.

Rosenzweig, Roy. *Eight Hours for What We Will: Workers and Leisure in an Industrial City, 1870–1920.* Cambridge: Cambridge University Press, 1990.

Rosenzweig, Roy, and David Thelen. *The Presence of the Past: Popular Uses of History in American Life.* New York: Columbia University Press, 1998.

Rothman, Hal K. *Devil's Bargains: Tourism in the Twentieth-Century American West.* Lawrence: University Press of Kansas, 1998.

Sale, Roger. *Seattle, Past to Present: An Interpretation of the History of the Foremost City in the Pacific Northwest.* Seattle: University of Washington Press, 1976.

"The San Felipe de Neri Affair." *New Mexico Architecture* 8 (May-June 1966): 8–17.

Sanchez, George J. *Becoming Mexican American: Ethnicity, Culture, and Identity in Chicano Los Angeles, 1900–1945.* New York: Oxford University Press, 1993.

Schaller, Michael, Virginia Scharff, and Robert Schulzinger. *Present Tense: The United States since 1945.* Boston: Houghton Mifflin, 1996.

Scharff, Virginia. "Appropriate Technology." *Perspecta 29: The Yale Architectural Journal.* Edited by William Deresiewicz, Garrett Finney, Sam Kirby, and Clay Miller. Cambridge, MA: MIT Press, 1998.

———. "Honey, I Shrunk the West." *Pacific Historical Review* 67 (August 1998): 409–420.

———. *Taking the Wheel: Women and the Coming of the Motor Age.* Albuquerque: University of New Mexico Press, 1992.

Schwarzer, Mitchell. "Myths of Permanence and Transience in the Discourse on Historic Preservation in the United States." *Journal of Architectural Education* 48 (September 1994): 2–11.

Sharpe, William, and Leonard Wallock. "Bold New City or Built-up 'Burb? Redefining Contemporary Suburbia." *American Quarterly* 46 (March 1994): 1–30.

Shaw, Brian J., and Roy Jones. *Contested Urban Heritage: Voices from the Periphery.* Brookfield, VT: Ashgate, 1997.

Shorett, Alice, and Murray Morgan. *The Pike Place Market: People, Politics, and Produce.* Seattle: Pacific Search Press, 1982.

Sies, Mary Corbin, and Christopher Silver, eds. *Planning the Twentieth-Century American City.* Baltimore: Johns Hopkins University Press, 1996.

Simmons, Marc. *Albuquerque: A Narrative History.* Albuquerque: University of New Mexico Press, 1982.

Simonson, Harold P. *Beyond the Frontier: Writers, Western Regionalism, and a Sense of Place.* Fort Worth: Texas Christian University Press, 1989.

Sklar, Kathryn Kish. *Catharine Beecher: A Study in American Domesticity.* New Haven, CT: Yale University Press, 1973.

Slotkin, Richard. *Gunfighter Nation: The Myth of the Frontier in Twentieth-Century America.* New York: Atheneum, 1992.

Smith, Duane. *Rocky Mountain Mining Camps: The Urban Frontier*. Bloomington: Indiana University Press, 1967.

Smith, Henry Nash. *Virgin Land: The American West as Symbol and Myth*. Cambridge, MA: Harvard University Press, 1950.

The Smithsonian Guide to Historic America. New York: Stewart, Tabori, and Chang, 1989.

Soja, Edward W. *Postmodern Geographies: The Reassertion of Space in Critical Social Theory*. London: Verso, 1989.

Sorkin, Michael, ed. *Variations on a Theme Park: The New American City and the End of Public Space*. New York: Hill and Wang, 1992.

Speidel, Bill. *Seattle Underground: In Which the Truth, the Whole Truth, and a Lot More Than the Truth Is Told about the Forgotten City Which Lies Beneath Seattle's Modern Streets*. Seattle: Seattle Guide, 1968.

Speidel, William C. *Sons of the Profits; Or, There's No Business Like Grow Business: The Seattle Story 1851–1901*. Seattle: Nettle Creek Publishing, 1967.

Stansell, Christine. *City of Women: Sex and Class in New York, 1789–1860*. Urbana: University of Illinois Press, 1987.

Steinbrueck, Victor. *Market Sketchbook*. Seattle: University of Washington Press, 1968.

Stipe, Robert E., and Antoinette J. Lee. *The American Mosaic: Preserving a Nation's Heritage*. Detroit: Wayne State University Press, 1997.

Tilly, Charles. "What Good Is Urban History?" *Journal of Urban History* 22 (September 1996): 702–719.

Tunnard, Christopher, and Henry Hope Reed. *American Skyline: From Log Cabin to Skyscraper—How the American City Is Shaped by, and Shapes, American Life*. Boston: Houghton Mifflin, 1953.

Turner, Frederick Jackson. *History, Frontier, and Section*. Albuquerque: University of New Mexico Press, 1993.

Tyler, Norman. *Historic Preservation: An Introduction to Its History, Principles, and Practice*. New York: W. W. Norton, 2000.

Tyler, Robert. "The I.W.W. and the West." *American Quarterly* 12 (Summer 1960): 175–187.

United States Conference of Mayors. Special Committee on Historic Preservation. *With Heritage So Rich*. New York: Random House, 1966.

Wade, Richard C. *The Urban Frontier: The Rise of Western Cities, 1790–1830*. Urbana: University of Illinois Press, 1959.

Wallace, Mike. *Mickey Mouse History and Other Essays on American Memory*. Philadelphia: Temple University Press, 1996.

Warner, Sam Bass, Jr. *Streetcar Suburbs: The Process of Growth in Boston (1870–1900)*. Cambridge, MA: Harvard University Press, 1962.

Weigle, Marta, and Barbara Babcock, eds. *The Great Southwest of the Fred Harvey Company and the Santa Fe Railroad*. Phoenix: Heard Museum, 1996.

White, Richard. *It's Your Misfortune and None of My Own: A New History of the American West*. Norman: University of Oklahoma Press, 1991.

White, Richard, and John M. Findlay, eds. *Power and Place in the North American West*. Seattle: University of Washington Press, 1999.

Wiebe, Robert H. *The Search for Order, 1877–1920*. New York: Hill and Wang, 1967.

Williams, Norman, Jr., Edmund H. Kellogg, and Frank B. Gilbert. *Readings in Historic Preservation: Why? What? How?* New Brunswick, NJ: Center for Urban Policy Research at Rutgers University, 1983.

Wilson, Chris. *The Myth of Santa Fe: Creating a Modern Regional Tradition*. Albuquerque: University of New Mexico Press, 1997.

Woodbridge, Sally B., and Roger Montgomery. *A Guide to Architecture in Washington State: An Environmental Perspective*. Seattle: University of Washington Press, 1980.

Wrobel, David M. "The View from Philadelphia." *Pacific Historical Review* 67 (August 1998): 383–392.

Wrobel, David M., and Michael C. Steiner, eds. *Many Wests: Place, Culture, and Regional Identity*. Lawrence: University Press of Kansas, 1997.

Wycoff, William. "Inside the New West: A View from Suburban Montana." *Pacific Historical Review* 67 (August 1998): 401–408.

Yaeger, Michael. *An Insider's Tour of the Pike Place Public Market*. Seattle: Studio Solstone, 1992.

Zukin, Sharon. *Loft Living: Culture and Capital in Urban Change*. New Brunswick, NJ: Rutgers University Press, 1982.

Newspapers

Albuquerque Journal
Albuquerque Tribune
Christian Science Monitor
Denver Business Journal
Denver Post
Los Angeles Times
New York Times
Rocky Mountain News
Seattle Post-Intelligencer
Seattle Sun
Seattle Times

Archival Sources

Center for Southwest Research. University of New Mexico. Albuquerque, New Mexico.
   Albuquerque History Files. Drawers 1 and 2.
   The Cobb Memorial Photography Collection.
   Southwest Travel Literature. MSS 115. Boxes 1 and 4.

City of Seattle Municipal Archives. City Clerk's Office. Seattle, Washington.
   Michael Hildt Papers. Collection # 4636–02. Boxes 1, 3, and 7.
   Pike Place Market Files. Collection # 1628–01. Boxes 131, 132, and 190.
   Pike Place Market Preservation and Development Authority Records. Collection # 1802–D3.
   Pioneer Square Files. Collection # 1802–B7. Box 1.

Colorado Historical Society. Stephen H. Hart Library. Denver, Colorado.
   Blake Street Photo Collection.
   Denver Downtown Urban Renewal clipping file.

Denver Streets Photo Collection.

Larimer Square Associates Collection. Manuscript file #1741.

Larimer Street Photo Collection.

Market Street Photo Collection.

Denver City Directory. Denver: Gazetteer Publishing, 1950–1985.

Denver Urban Renewal Authority. Manuscript Collection. Denver Public Library, Western History Department. Denver, Colorado.

Hudspeth's City Directory for Albuquerque. El Paso, TX: Hudspeth Directory Company of El Paso, 1940–1969.

Kroll's Atlas of Seattle, 1920.

Larimer Square clipping file. Denver Public Library, Western History and Genealogy Department. Denver, Colorado.

Larimer Street Photo Collection. Denver Public Library, Western History and Genealogy Department. Denver, Colorado.

Office of Planning and Community Development. Denver, Colorado.

Larimer Square Historic District File.

Lower Downtown Historic District File.

Puget Sound Regional Archives. Bellevue, Washington.

Pioneer Square clipping file.

Seattle Department of Community Development Directors Files. Manuscript file #1600–03.

Seattle Department of Community Development Pioneer Square Historic District Files. Manuscript file # 1613–01.

Sanborn Map Company. "Insurance Map of Albuquerque, Bernalillo County, New Mexico." 1891, 1898, 1908, 1924, 1952, 1957. New York: Sanborn Map Company.

Seattle City Directory. Seattle: R. L. Polk, 1938–1990.

University of Washington Manuscripts, Special Collections, and University Archives. Seattle.

James Braman Files. Seattle Community Development Department. Manuscript file #1297.

Curtis and Miller Photo Collection.

Friends of the Market Papers. Manuscript file #1985. Boxes 1, 2, 6, and 7.

Hamilton Photo Collection.

Pike Place Market Pamphlet Files.

Pioneer Square District Study Photo Collection.

Pioneer Square Pamphlet Files.

Seattle Building Department Pioneer Square Historic District Manager Papers. Manuscript file #3507.

Victor Steinbrueck Papers. Manuscript file #3252, 3252–2. Boxes 1, 2, 5, 6, and 7.

Government Documents

Albuquerque Landmarks and Urban Conservation Ordinance. Section 14–12–1 of the Revised Ordinances of Albuquerque. 1994.

Carper, Robert. *A Plan for Historic Preservation in Denver*. Prepared by the Denver Planning Office, City and County of Denver, Colorado, assisted by the Denver Landmark

Preservation Commission, Historic Denver, Inc. Denver: Denver Planning Office, 1974.

City of Seattle. *A Decade of Change: A Final Report on the Preservation and Redevelopment of the Pike Place Market*. Seattle: City of Seattle Department of Community Development, 1983.

Denver Landmark Preservation Ordinance. City and County of Denver. Chapter 30 of the Revised Municipal Code, 1967. Revised 1994.

Denver Planning Office. *Bulletin CAP-1: "A Demonstration Plan for Central Denver."* Denver, 1958.

———. *Bulletin CAP-6: "Lower Downtown Denver: Expressway and Adjacent Redevelopment Areas."* Denver, 1958.

Downtown Area Plan: A Plan for the Future of Downtown Denver. Denver Planning Office and Denver Partnership, 1986.

Graham, John, and Co. *Pioneer Square Redevelopment*. Seattle, 1966.

Historic Districts in Baltimore City. Baltimore City Commission on Historical and Architectural Planning, 2000.

Historical and Architectural Preservation Laws of Baltimore City. Mayor and City Council of Baltimore, 2000.

Lower Downtown Urban Design Project. Downtown Denver Partnership, 1987.

Minutes of the Albuquerque City Planning Commission, 1947–1960.

Minutes of the City Commission of Albuquerque 48, 1948.

Minutes of the Denver City Council, 1964–1995.

Minutes of the Denver Landmark Commission, 1965–1990.

Minutes of the Landmark and Urban Conservation Commission. Albuquerque, 1976–1992.

Minutes of the Old Town Architectural Review Board. Albuquerque, 1969–1977.

Minutes of the Pike Place Historical Commission. Seattle, 1971–1998.

Minutes of the Pioneer Square Preservation Board. Seattle, 1975–1998.

Monson, Donald. *Comprehensive Plan for Central Business District Seattle*. Prepared for the City of Seattle and Central Association of Seattle, 1963.

Moy, Peter. *Completion of the Pike Place Urban Renewal Plan and the Financial Condition of the Pike Place Market PDA: A Survey Report to the Seattle City Council*. Seattle: Pike Place Market PDA, 1980.

National Historic Preservation Act. U.S. Statutes at Large 80 (1966): 915–919.

New Mexico Cultural Properties Act, 1978.

New Mexico State Planning Office. *Historic Preservation: A Plan for New Mexico.* 1971.

———. The *Historic Preservation Program for New Mexico* 1. 1973.

Philadelphia Historical Commission. *The Philadelphia Register of Historic Places.* 2000.

Pike Place Market Design Report. City of Seattle Department of Community Development, June 1974.

Pike Place Market Historical District. City of Seattle. Chapter 25.24 of the Municipal Code.

Pike Place Market Urban Renewal Plan. City of Seattle Department of Community Development, January 1974.

Pioneer Square Historic District Bulletin. Seattle: Department of Commercial Development, n.d.

Seattle Department of Community Development. *Let Us Show You Pioneer Square,* 1976.

Seattle Landmark Preservation Ordinance. City of Seattle. Chapter 25.12 of the Municipal Code, 1998.

Seattle Land Use Code. Pioneer Square Preservation District. City of Seattle. Chapter 23.66 of the Land Use Code.

U.S. Bureau of the Census. Characteristics of the Population of New Mexico, 1940–1960. Washington, DC: Government Printing Office.

University of New Mexico Bureau of Business and Economic Research. "Population Profiles of Incorporated Places and Cities in New Mexico, 1910–2015." Prepared for the New Mexico Department of Highways and Transportation, August 1994.

Theses, Dissertations, and Unpublished Material

Bundy, Mary Priscilla. "Historic Preservation: A Case Study of the Pike Place Market." Master's thesis, University of Washington, 1977.

Corson, Dan William. "Dana Crawford: From Larimer Square to LoDo, Historic Preservation in Denver." Master's thesis, University of·Colorado at Denver, 1998.

Dubrow, Gail Lee. "Preserving Her Heritage: American Landmarks of Women's History." PhD dissertation, University of California at Los Angeles, 1991.

Eden, Susanna. "Huning's Highland Addition to the City of Albuquerque: A Description and Analysis of Architectural and Neighborhood Development with Recommendations for Preservation." Master's thesis, University of New Mexico, 1979.

Lee, Sohyun Park. "From Redevelopment to Preservation: Downtown Planning in Post-War Seattle." PhD dissertation, University of Washington, 2001.

Peterman, W. A. "Changing Commercial Patterns in Metropolitan Denver, Colorado: 1960–1970." PhD dissertation, University of Denver, 1971.

Rabinowitz, Howard. Untitled manuscript. 1996.

Thrush, Coll-Peter. "The Crossing-over Place: Native American Histories and Urban American Visions of Seattle's Pioneer Square Historic District." In Kevin R. McNamara, ed., The Ethnic Landscape. New York: Rutgers University Press, forthcoming.

Wilson, Chris. "Artificial Stones/Precious Stones: The San Felipe Façade Controversy of 1978." Paper for Seminar in Art History, University of New Mexico, 1979.

Interviews

Anderson, Ralph. Interview with author, Seattle, 11 July 2001.

Brooker, Kathleen. Interview with author, Denver, 14 February 2001.

Carson, Ann. Telephone interview with author, 10 February 1999.

Chaney, John. Interview with author, Seattle, 4 October 1999.

Crawford, Dana. Interview with author, Denver, 29 October 2000.

———. Telephone interview with author, 15 September 2002.

Erickson, Marlys. Interview with author, Seattle, 15 November 2000.

Galbraith, Cathy. Telephone interview with the author, 12 April 2004.

Gibson, Barbara. Interview with author, Denver, 22 July 2001.

Hoffsis, Jim. Telephone interview with author, 24 March 1998.

———. Interview with author, Albuquerque, 28 November 2000.

Hooton, Robert P. Interview with author, Albuquerque, 15 April 1998.

Lutino, Cielo. E-mail interview with the author, 13 April 2004.
Meisner, Jennifer. Interview with author, Seattle, 14 November 2000.
————. Telephone interview with author, 27 September 2002.
Moulton, Jennifer. Interview with author, Denver, 14 September 2000.
Noel, Thomas J. Interview with author, Denver, 3 December 1999.
Norgren, Barbara. Interview with author, Denver, 2 February 2001.
Purdy, Lisa. Interview with author, Denver, 3 July 2002.
Quackenbush, Tom. Interview with author, Seattle, 4 October 1999.
Rabinowitz, Howard. Telephone interview with author, 23 March 1998.
Romero, Robert. Interview with author, Albuquerque, 28 November 2000.
Saslow, William. Interview with author, Denver, 2 July 2002.
Steinbrueck, Peter. Interview with author, Seattle, 13 November 2000.
Tanner, Renee. Telephone interview with author, 10 July 2001.
Turnbull, John. Interview with author, Seattle, 14 November 2000.
White, Edward D., Jr. Interview with author, Denver, 13 July 2001.
Wilson, Chris. Interview with author, Albuquerque, 8 April 1998.

Tourist Literature

Downtown Seattle Walking Tours. Seattle: City of Seattle, 1985.
Ghirardelli Square: One Place in a City's History. San Francisco: 2 M&G Marketing and
    Ghirardelli Square, 1994.
Let Us Show You Pioneer Square. Seattle: Seattle-King County Conventions and Visitors
    Bureau, 1976.
Longwood International Survey for the Denver Metro Convention and Visitors Bureau,
    1997–2001.
Pioneer Square and Kingdome Tourmap, 1978. Spokane: Tourmap, 1978.

Planning and Development Documents

Lower Downtown Neighborhood Plan. Denver, 2000.
Lower Downtown Neighborhood Plan Newsletter and Case Studies. Denver, 1995.
Pioneer Square Neighborhood Plan. Seattle, 1998.

Videotape

"Block by Block: Reclaiming Neighborhoods by Design." American Architectural Founda-
    tion, 2001.

Index